Paper and the British Empire

Paper and the British Empire examines the evolution of the paper industry within British organisational frameworks and highlights the role of the Empire as a market and business-making area in a world of shrinking commerce and rising trade barriers.

Drawing on a valuable range of primary sources, this book covers the period 1861–1960 and examines events from the establishment of free trade backed by the gold standard to Britain's membership of the European Free Trade Association. In the field of the paper industry, the speed and intensity of the industrialisation process around the globe have been shaped by a wide variety of variables, including the surrounding institutional framework; entrepreneurial and organisational strategies; the cost and accessibility of transport; and the availability of capital, knowledge, energy resources, and technology. The supply of papermaking raw materials has also been key and has historically been the most important determinant for geographical location and dominance. The research in this work focuses on the roles played by such variants, on the one hand, and demand characteristics on the other. In particular, it considers developments connected to a quest for Empire-grown raw materials in order to tackle the problem of the lack of indigenous raw materials and the resulting dependence on Scandinavian wood pulp imports.

This text is of considerable interest to advanced students and researchers in economic history, business history, and the paper industry, and will also be useful to organisations working within the pulp and paper industries.

Timo Särkkä is a Docent in Economic History at the University of Jyväskylä, Finland, Department of History and Ethnology. He specialises in global economic history with an emphasis on economic imperialism.

Routledge Explorations in Economic History

Edited by **Lars Magnusson**, *Uppsala University, Sweden*

The Economic Development of Europe's Regions
A Quantitative History Since 1900
Edited by Nikolaus Wolf and Joan Ramón Rosés

Family Firms and Merchant Capitalism in Early Modern Europe
The Business, Bankruptcy and Resilience of the Höchstetters of Augsburg
Thomas Max Safley

An Economic History of Famine Resilience
Edited by Jessica Dijkman and Bas van Leeuwen

Modern Advertising and the Market
The US Advertising Industry from the 19th Century to the Present
Zoe Sherman

A Global History of Money
Akinobu Kuroda

An Economic History of Regional Industrialization
Edited by Bas van Leeuwen, Robin C. M. Philips and Erik Buyst

The Political Economy of International Commodity Cartels
An Economic History of the European Timber Trade in the 1930s
Elina Kuorelahti

Paper and the British Empire
The Quest for Imperial Raw Materials, 1861–1960
Timo Särkkä

For more information about this series, please visit www.routledge.com/series/SE0347

Paper and the British Empire
The Quest for Imperial Raw Materials, 1861–1960

Timo Särkkä

LONDON AND NEW YORK

First published 2021
by Routledge
2 Park Square, Milton Park, Abingdon, Oxon OX14 4RN

and by Routledge
52 Vanderbilt Avenue, New York, NY 10017

Routledge is an imprint of the Taylor & Francis Group, an informa business

© 2021 Timo Särkkä

The right of Timo Särkkä to be identified as author of this work has been asserted by him in accordance with sections 77 and 78 of the Copyright, Designs and Patents Act 1988.

All rights reserved. No part of this book may be reprinted or reproduced or utilised in any form or by any electronic, mechanical, or other means, now known or hereafter invented, including photocopying and recording, or in any information storage or retrieval system, without permission in writing from the publishers.

Trademark notice: Product or corporate names may be trademarks or registered trademarks, and are used only for identification and explanation without intent to infringe.

British Library Cataloguing-in-Publication Data
A catalogue record for this book is available from the British Library

Library of Congress Cataloging-in-Publication Data
A catalog record has been requested for this book

ISBN: 978-0-367-34156-5 (hbk)
ISBN: 978-0-429-32418-5 (ebk)

Typeset in Bembo
by codeMantra

Contents

List of figures		vii
List of tables		ix
Preface		xi
Acknowledgements		xiii
1	Introduction	1
2	The political economy of raw materials in the global paper industry 1861–1960	14
3	The esparto grass trade	35
4	The pursuit of wood pulp	53
5	Bamboo for papermaking	73
6	The paper trade and the British Empire	106
7	A retrospective view of the British paper industry	128
8	Conclusions	152
	Index	161

Figures

5.1	Business Structure of the Bamboo Paper Company	85
7.1	Labour Productivity (tons per employee) in the Census of Production Years 1907, 1912, 1924, 1935, 1948, and 1951	141

Tables

2.1	Pulping Processes and Their Characteristics 1861–1960	29
2.2	Technical Suitability of Raw Materials for Various Papers 1861–1960	30
4.1	Raw Material Imports 1913–1959 (1,000 tons and %)	58
4.2	Imports and Exports of Paper and Board 1913–1959 (tons and %)	60
4.3	Imports of Paper and Board by Country in 1949 and 1959 (tons and %)	67
5.1	Annual Rated Capacity of Bamboo Pulp and Paper Mills in India 1957 (tons)	93
6.1	Paper and Board Imports into India 1899–1910 (Tons and %)	112
7.1	Total Output of Paper and Board 1907–1951 (Tons and %)	139
7.2	Number of Establishments 1924–1951	139
7.3	Size of Establishments by Employment 1935–1951	140
7.4	Distribution of Mills and Employment by Standard Region 1948 and 1951	140
7.5	Number of Persons Employed in the Paper Trade 1907–1951	141

Preface

This research monograph originates from a paper 'The British Paper Trade and Empire: The Quest for Imperial Raw Materials, c. 1850 to c. 1950' read at the 43rd Annual Conference of the Economic and Business History Society organised at the University of Jyväskylä on 1 June 2018. It was followed by an intensive research period, during which research materials from the following archives and libraries in the UK, Finland, and Canada were consulted: The National Archives, Kew; the Library, Art & Archives Royal Botanic Gardens, Kew; the London Metropolitan Archives; The British Library of Political and Economic Science, London; the Guildhall Library, London; The British Newspapers Archive, London; The British Library, London; the Central Archives of United Paper Mills, Valkeakoski; the Central Archives for Finnish Business Records, Mikkeli; the J.N. Desmarais Library, Laurentian University, Sudbury, Ontario; the Robarts Library, University of Toronto; the McGill University Library, Montréal, Quebec.

Much of the research was conducted during a visiting researcher period at the Faculty of Economics, Kyoto Sangyo University (1 March–7 May 2020). There were several aims in this research period: to prepare the book manuscript, to strengthen research cooperation with the research collaborators, to further the research of the author and the international collaborators both individually and collectively, to add a more international and critical element to the national research systems, and to provide new insights for the research. I hope that all of these aims will be realised through the quality of this study.

The research results were read at the 87th Global History Seminar, the Graduate School of Letters, Osaka University, on 24 April 2020.

The research was supported by the Academy of Finland (Grant Number 334541). The author wishes to thank the abovementioned archives and libraries, the hosting institutions, the funding body, and the publisher for the faith displayed in his work.

Timo Särkkä
Kyoto

Acknowledgements

The author wishes to thank Springer Nature for their permission to reproduce the following copyright material: Särkkä, T. (2018) 'The Quest for Raw Materials in the British Paper Trade: The Development of the Bamboo Pulp and Paper Industry in British India up to 1939'. In T. Särkkä, M. Gutiérrez-Poch & M. Kuhlberg, eds, *Technological Transformation in the Global Pulp and Paper Industry 1800–2018: Comparative Perspectives*. World Forests 23. Springer, Dordrecht, 237–259 and Särkkä, T. (2012) 'The British Paper Industry, 1800–2000'. In J.-A. Lamberg, J. Ojala, M. Peltoniemi & T. Särkkä, eds, *The Evolution of Global Paper Industry 1800–2050: A Comparative Analysis*. World Forests 17. Springer, Dordrecht, 167–190. These investigations analysed the past 200 years of technological transformation in the global pulp and paper industry from longitudinal and global perspectives. The research results revealed several obvious reasons for the need of an in-depth study of the political economy of raw materials in the context of the British Empire. These reasons will be discussed in the subsequent pages.

1 Introduction

In the field of the paper industry, the speed and intensity of the industrialisation process around the globe have been shaped by a wide variety of variables, including the surrounding institutional framework; entrepreneurial and organisational strategies; the cost and accessibility of transport; the availability of capital, knowledge, energy resources, and technology, and, in particular, the constant supply of papermaking raw materials, which has historically been the most important determinant for geographical location and dominance. In previous studies, historians have been able to explain how these variables have all played a role – to different degrees – in determining which countries have been able to dominate the industry and how they did so (Lamberg et al. 2012; Särkkä et al. 2018).

Technological development and market demand characteristics have played the key role in the success of the industry. Sometimes dominance was achieved because the industry aggressively embraced the latest technological innovations (Bergquist & Söderholm 2018) and at other times because the opposite was true (Kuhlberg 2018). Typically, a lack of indigenous raw materials and the resulting lack of financial support for research and development work in the field of cellulose chemistry were enormous impediments to the paper industry (Dadswell 2018; Roche 2018; Särkkä 2018). Then again, even a bountiful supply of raw materials has not always guaranteed long-term growth, for the reason that the institutional framework into which the new technology is applied is a crucial consideration that affects the process of industrialisation (Gutiérrez-Poch 2018; Nykänen 2018).

By taking a longitudinal perspective on these dynamics, *Paper and the British Empire* examines the evolution of the paper industry within British organisational frameworks and highlights the role of the Empire as a market and business-making area in a world of shrinking commerce and rising trade barriers. The research focuses on the roles played by the availability of technology, knowledge, and capital, on the one hand, and demand characteristics on the other, and, in particular, considers developments connected to a quest for Empire-grown raw materials to tackle the problems of the lack of indigenous raw materials and the resulting dependence on wood pulp imports.

2 *Introduction*

This is the setting for *Paper and the British Empire*, which uses in-depth and rich historical descriptions to illustrate the often troubled road the paper industry travelled from the establishment of a free trade system backed by the gold standard in 1861 to the British entry into the European Free Trade Association in 1960. The research takes its inspiration from the changes in the British paper industry's structure since the beginning of the 1960s and looks back at its performance while it was a leader in world markets in contrast to times when its leading role was challenged by various competitors. It is motivated by the realisation that analysing the evolution of the paper industry by using longitudinal and global history approaches is a very revealing way of illustrating the often troubled road the British paper manufacturing has travelled in the past, and of exposing the complexities the paper industry is still facing today.

The research premise, aims, and objectives

The most significant paradigmatic objective of the investigation is to renew, readjust, and even restructure the contemporary study of the British paper industry making use of hitherto less consulted primary sources. With respect to the British paper industry, there is a notable lack of systematic research. In contrast to the detailed examination of the pre-1861 history by Coleman (1958) and Spicer (1907), modern paper industry historians have studied subsequent developments less. The turbulent interwar years are particularly understudied. The most comprehensive investigations of papermaking in the British Isles are those by Shorter (1971) and Hills (1988). Magee (1997a, 1997b) covers the years from 1860 to 1914, and Owen (2000) includes a chapter on the paper industry within a framework of a broader post-Second World War analysis of British manufacturing industries. Existing studies on various paper mills and papermakers tend to lack consistency of method in investigating the history of the paper industry. However, they do provide powerful insights into the lives of the manufacturers behind the development of the industry. The business histories of Bowater (Reader 1981) and Reed (Sykes 1981) may be mentioned as illustrative examples. The lack of earlier research invites in-depth study of the British paper industry.

The second objective is to introduce new ways of reading primary sources. In his seminal study *Industry and Empire* (1968 [1999]), Eric Hobsbawn famously asserted that Britain's relative decline as a leading technological innovator (he was witnessing this process in the 1960s) was due to its early and sustained involvement as a leading international industrial power. To understand why the Industrial Revolution and many of the technological innovations attendant upon it took place in Britain and not another country, Hobsbawn claimed that we must focus on the world economy of which Britain was a part. In other words, he was referring to the 'advanced' areas of (mainly) Western Europe and North America and their relations with the colonial or semi-colonial dependent economies. More recently, an increasingly global perspective in business history has emerged. It advocates the study of the behaviour of firms over extended periods of time and an understanding of the global framework, composed of markets, institutions, and organisations, in which this behaviour occurs (e.g. McNeill 1990; Pomeranz 2000; O'Brien 2006). With this case method, it is hoped information will be provided that will add to our understanding of the British paper industry's history and possibly extend or clarify the history of the paper industry as a whole.

Finally, our objective is to present new perspectives on interpretation to strengthen the points being made. Research to date has firmly advocated firm-specific or country-specific history, while the role of the Empire as a market and a business-making area has been largely neglected. The British paper industry was historically deficient in terms of the industry's traditional fibre resources, and it was initially forced to satisfy its domestic demand for pulp through imports. This shortcoming was an impediment to the growth of the industry. Since the mid-nineteenth century, industry and papermakers cooperated to overcome their fibre challenge by using various strategies. The most notable of these was the introduction of esparto grass to the British paper industry. Nonetheless, the demand for raw materials was in no way satisfactorily met. The First World War was both a short-term curse and a long-term blessing for many pulp and paper makers, and the conflict certainly highlights how necessity is truly the mother of invention. This investigation underscores how the shortage of pulp in the UK was the impetus behind its producers searching for alternative supplies of raw materials, and how their quest led them to the Empire and its enormous stock of fibrous raw materials. This was the precursor to a colonial policy that sought first to foster the development of the native pulp and paper industry in the dominions and colonies, and to later efforts by both local and British firms to develop the technology to process these fibrous resources into marketable paper products.

Research questions

Britain was the first country in the world to possess the capital, enterprise, and skill necessary to develop its industrial capacity in the field of mechanical papermaking. This process began when experiments were undertaken with papermaking technology at Frogmore Mill, on the River Gade, near Hemel Hempstead in Hertfordshire, and the adjoining Two Waters Mill, where the first Fourdrinier papermaking machines were installed in 1803 and 1804 (Mokyr 1990).

Immensely strong cotton and flax fibres in the form of rags from cotton and linen fabrics formed the principal and almost sole source of fibre in British mills from the eighteenth century, when large quantities of Indian fibres started to be imported into Britain. The use of rags as the primary papermaking material started to show symptoms of saturation in early-Victorian Britain – the first 'journalising' society in the world (i.e. the mass media has been interpreted as the ideological environment of the early-Victorian

4   *Introduction*

society) (Shattock and Wolff 1982, xiv; Willinsky 1994, 118). The extension of education and literature, and the increased literacy and heightened social consciousness directly increased demand for paper.

Furthermore, the mechanisation of the industry indirectly gave people and institutions more reason to need paper. During the first part of the nineteenth century, British paper mills and printing presses were undergoing technical and organisational changes that made them capable of producing a much higher output than they had ever done before. Technological developments from 1801 to 1817 connected to the invention of the steam-powered printing press allowed for the mass production of penny and halfpenny newspapers, journals, magazines, reviews, and cheap editions of books; they thus came within the reach of the very poorest members of society. By the mid-nineteenth century, mechanisation had become widespread in the British paper industry, which by 1848 had 407 papermaking machines at work (Munsell 1876, 115; Coleman 1958, 179–183).

The stimulus given by this early mechanisation revolutionised the whole process of paper manufacturing, and with the introduction of the free trade principle in October 1861, the world of mechanised papermaking was established in Britain. The reasons behind this early British industrial success were related to the improvements in technology. In addition, the manufacturers in Britain were operating with other significant advantages on their side, including a supply of cheap and accessible coal and craftsmanship within a relatively orderly society that had an efficient transport system (Mokyr 1990). The productivity of the industry, however, was relatively low, not least because of a raw material shortage that threatened to cripple the industry's development. By the mid-nineteenth century, the demand for paper had become so great that there was a permanent famine in cotton and linen rags. The more economical methods of manufacture and larger output to meet larger demand led to the quest for a new raw material.

As it transpired, it was esparto, which constitutes two perennial grasses both endemic to the Western Mediterranean, that first offered a solution to the raw material shortage in Britain. Since its introduction to the British paper trade in the 1850s, esparto formed the mainstay for supplying the British raw material markets. The competitive advantage of esparto, being a wild grass, lay in the simplicity of the harvesting process, which basically required merely pulling by hand. Instead of converting esparto into 'half-stuff' for export, only the drying and baling were carried out in Southern Spain and North Africa, keeping the cost of raw material low. Another explanation for the affordability of esparto as a papermaking material was the very liberal terms on which concessions were granted by the French Government to develop the alfa trade, as well as relatively low transport costs. Despite its being an excellent papermaking material and available at low cost, it was difficult to assure the continuity of esparto supply at a constant price. By the late 1880s, esparto was getting both scarce and dear for British papermakers. Supplies from Spain had been almost exhausted, as they were too in North Africa.

Furthermore, there were fears of protective customs duties in North Africa because of French interference there.

As the supply of esparto started to wane, wood pulp began its steady rise to prominence in the British raw material markets. Mechanical wood pulp's first obvious advantage was in being the cheapest to produce because it was manufactured in locations where the very large amount of waterpower required for grinding wood cost little apart from the cost of harnessing waterfalls (e.g. in Norway and Newfoundland). The transport costs were also relatively low, because pulp was dried and baled before being transported. After the mid-1870s, chemical pulping units were built adjoining wood-grinding plants, and gradually these two products, dry mechanical and chemical wood pulp, replaced esparto, straw, and rags as the primary raw material in the British markets. Finally, the First World War revealed Britain's vulnerability in terms of the supply of raw materials, which led to a quest for Empire-grown raw materials to tackle the problems of the lack of indigenous raw materials and the resulting dependence on foreign imports.

The outlook of the global paper industry changed dramatically in the course of the twentieth century. Britain was surpassed by its much more competitive rivals in countries like Canada, Sweden, and Finland, who – endowed with hydroelectric power for energy, coniferous softwoods as a raw material, and an efficient transport networks of lakes, rivers, and canals, as well as ports for ocean-going vessels – became major players in the field of papermaking. By 1960, the British paper market had entered a period of stagnation with sharply decreasing demand, which resulted in a wave of mergers and acquisitions as well as closures of mills. As a result of falling demand, declining prices, and the relative scarcity of cheap raw material, together with high energy and labour costs, British paper markets became the least attractive geographical area for the paper industry. The first new paper machine to be built in Britain in more than 30 years was in 1995, when the Finnish machine shop Valmet delivered a new machine to the Aylesford Paper Mills, near Maidstone in Kent, which at the end of the 1950s was Europe's largest papermaking site. A reorganisation of the global paper industry has occurred since the beginning of the new millennium. An increasing demand for papers of all kinds in quickly developing economies like China has moved the centre of activities away from the established economic heartlands, and pressure on profit margins has forced the closure of mills all over Europe and North America. Such a dramatic reorganisation of the industry is reminiscent of the dark days of the British paper industry but also poses an important research question: what we can learn from the history of the British paper industry in hindsight?

Secondly, it will be asked how the constant supply of papermaking raw materials and lack of them have played a role in determining which countries have been able to dominate the industry and also how they did so. In 1959, Canada and Scandinavian countries collectively (Sweden, Finland, and Norway) each had a 36.3% share of the total British imports of paper, thereby

6 *Introduction*

controlling almost three-quarters of the British paper imports in total (Särkkä 2012). Almost all of the exports were handled by cartel-like formal sales organisations such as the Finnish Pulp and Paper Association, whose aim was to set prices at a profitable level (Heikkinen 2000; Jensen-Eriksen 2008; Jensen-Eriksen & Ojala 2015). Backed by natural advantages, Finnish producers used price policy – relatively cheap paper, relatively dear pulp – to further their dominance in the British markets. To the best of our knowledge, there is a notable lack of systematic research on the paper trade in the context of the Nordic threat. The lack of earlier research invites in-depth study of primary sources dealing market regulation in the UK market.

Finally, the study will investigate how the combinations of the inputs of investments and of knowledge and technology have determined which raw materials have prevailed globally. This research will particularly concern bamboo – the fastest growing plant on earth. Bamboo can be considered as an ideal papermaking raw material. Under favourable conditions of climate and soil, the plant produces a heavy crop with minimal care and cost. In terms of quality, bamboo possesses a high-quality fibre, capable of withstanding considerable wear and tear, and therefore, the plant is especially suitable for printing papers.

Bamboo's suitability as a papermaking material for mechanical paper manufacturing had been under consideration since 1875, when the first serious attempt to utilise it as a regular source of supply for pulp was initiated at the Ford Paper Mills on the River Wear, at South Hylton, Sunderland, England. However, it took 25 years before this experimental work led to the first serious attempts to use bamboo for mechanical papermaking and nearly 50 years before the first mill using bamboo as primary raw material entered into production in India (Särkkä 2018). Despite being an excellent papermaking material as well as plentifully available and easily cultivable in the Tropics, the use of bamboo as a papermaking raw material has remained sporadic and marginal. Our hypothesis is that the main reason for this can be found from the path-dependent nature of the paper industry. Paper manufacturing is a highly capital-intensive industry, which is characterised by rather inflexible combinations of inputs of investments, knowledge, and technology, and breaking the 'path' demands both capital and innovativeness, as this investigation illustrates.

Materials and methods

The investigation will follow the economic and business historical tradition of in-depth and rich historical accounts based on primary (mainly archival) sources. It will employ, for instance, records of various government bodies, trade, and production returns as well as company archives. The research material is divided into the following (a–g) categories:

a The Imperial Institute. The Records of the Tropical Products Institute and its predecessor, the Imperial Institute at the National Archives, Kew,

Introduction 7

relating to scientific investigations and enquiries undertaken by the Plant and Animal Products Department, are the main set of sources for analysing the paper industry in the context of the British Empire.

b   Company Archives. Archives of many businesses with City of London connections are held at the London Metropolitan Archives. Relevant collections for the present purposes include, for instance, the Records of the Bamboo Paper Company at the London Metropolitan Archives, the first London-based company, to carry on the business of manufacturing and dealing in pulp from bamboo.

c   The British Paper Makers' Association. The papermakers' weekly trade journal *The World's Paper Trade Review* serves to illustrate industrialists' concerns in the UK. Trade journals of some of the most important foreign papers, paperboards, and raw materials trading countries provide material for further comparison.

d   Scandinavian sales organisations. Records for studying various aspects of market regulations in the UK can be found in the Central Archives of United Paper Mills. Relevant collections for present purposes include, for instance, the Records of the Finnish Pulp and Paper Association (Finnpap). They also provide insights into the operations of cartel-like sales organisations (e.g. Scankraft; Scanticon) in the UK market.

e   Production returns. The Census is the most important source of business statistics. It was originally designed to meet a specific policy need regarding trade tariffs, but soon became the definitive source of statistics on the structure of the industry and its contribution to the economy. The Census of Production Act was passed in 1906, and the Final Report on the Census of Production of the United Kingdom furnishes a basis for an analysis of production returns from 1907 onwards.

f   Trade returns. The most valuable trade returns include Accounts Relating to Trade and Navigation of the United Kingdom, which focuses on import–export trade. Trade and navigation records of some of the most important colonial and foreign papers, paperboards, and raw materials trading countries provide material for further comparison.

g   Business family histories. The existing archival sources on papermakers provide powerful insights into the lives of the manufacturers behind the development of the industry. The Papers of Thomas Routledge, an English papermaker who devoted his attention to Economic Botany, at the Library, Art & Archives Royal Botanic Gardens, Kew, provide convincing evidence of the amount of research devoted in bygone years to the subject now under consideration.

The research methods to be applied in the research have been chosen with regard to their suitability for the material available for the topic. The subject matter included in British economic and business history has ranged from big business to family firms, from technology and innovation to corporate governance, and from entrepreneurship to the roles of the state (Jones &

8   *Introduction*

Zeitlin 2007). At first, business historical study strongly advocated firm-specific histories but it was not until Chandler (1962, 1977, 1990) that the use of firm-specific histories expanded to develop theoretical frameworks of relevance to the corporate economy. Chandler's work prompted the development of a comparative approach to business history and showed that business history can provide a powerful insight into the evolution of capitalism, thus advancing the use of business history methods as part of a broader analysis of economic history. In the UK context, for example, Hannah (1976) has investigated how the relationship between government and business explained the growing industrial concentration in Britain during the interwar years. Elbaum and Lazonick (1986) showed how particular industries in the British economy such as the textile and iron and steel industries have influenced national economic performance. Recently, methodological issues have become a subject of lively debate among economic and business historians (Eloranta et al. 2010; De Jong et al. 2012; Mollan 2018) and new approaches in business history have emerged, such as interaction between historians and management and strategy research, empirical research and cliometrics, to name a few. The historical context for studying business behaviour has retained its prominence, however, because the nature of economic and business history research requires in-depth investigation based on primary sources (Friedman & Jones 2011; De Jong et al. 2012; Popp 2015).

Chapter synopses

There are seven chapters that follow. Chapter 2 introduces the theoretical premise of this book. Paper and board (i.e. the often multi-layered stiffer variety of paper) are manufactured from filament products obtained by mechanically or chemically separating plant fibres from each other. In papermaking, the liberated fibres are brought together again on the paper machine, where they interact with each other in the presence of chemicals charged to the liquid stock. As paper consists of plant fibres, distributed in their natural form throughout the plant kingdom, it partakes not only of the chemical nature of the fibre, but also of its physical nature as well. The properties of paper depend on the colour, length, diameter, flexibility, and strength of the fibres used, and that is why papermakers have historically tended to devote serious attention to the selection of the best available raw material for the finished paper. While the knowledge of the properties of the fibre is based on research done in the field of cellulose chemistry, it also stems from changes in product market demand, investments, knowledge, technology, the surrounding institutional environment, and organisational solutions. The interplay between these variables – collectively termed the political economy of raw materials – is discussed in this chapter.

Chapter 3 discusses the esparto grass trade. The introduction of esparto grass for papermaking in 1861 by Thomas Routledge offered the first viable solution to the raw material shortage in Britain. Despite being an excellent

Introduction 9

papermaking material and plentifully available in places in North Africa, it was difficult to assure the continuity of esparto supply at a constant price. By the late 1880s, esparto was getting both scarce and dear for the British papermakers. Supplies from Spain had been almost exhausted, as they were too in North Africa. Furthermore, there were fears of protective customs duties in North Africa because of French interference there. The First World War revealed the difficulty in obtaining esparto and Britain's vulnerability in terms of the supply of raw materials, and led to the developments connected to a quest for Empire-grown raw materials to tackle the problems of the lack of indigenous raw materials and the resulting dependence on foreign imports.

Chapter 4 considers the introduction of wood pulp to the British paper industry. Wood emerged as the predominant source of fibre in the late 1880s, when international breakthroughs in the production of chemical wood pulp had made the product available for British manufacturers. Wood pulp began its steady rise to prominence in Britain initially at the expense of esparto but then later at the expense of both esparto and rags. In the absence of readily available domestic wood resources, British manufacturers quickly availed themselves of Scandinavian timber, and there were several reasons for this development. These included its close proximity, the suitability of the product for newsprint, and the low cost of the product compared to other available raw materials. The British companies' dependency on wood pulp allowed Scandinavian cartel-like sales organisations to make various types of price agreements and market sharing arrangements regarding the UK markets. This chapter maintains that the lack of indigenous raw materials and the resulting lack of financial support for research and development work in the field of cellulose chemistry were enormous impediments to the British paper industry. This adverse situation reflected negatively in the level of investment in new plant and machinery as well as in the profit margins of British paper companies.

Chapter 5 concerns the development of the bamboo pulp and paper industry in India from its early beginnings up to 1960. Bamboo – the fastest growing plant on earth – can be considered as an ideal raw material for papermaking. Under favourable conditions of climate and soil, the plant produces a heavy crop with minimal care and cost. In terms of quality, the bamboo stem possesses a high-quality fibre, capable of withstanding considerable wear and tear, and therefore, the plant is especially suitable for paper manufactured for printing. In Britain, the likelihood of a pulp famine and the consequent increase in the price of esparto were among the factors that first raised interest in the possibility of making commercial volumes of pulp from bamboo. Despite being an excellent papermaking material as well as plentifully available and easily cultivable in the Tropics, the use of bamboo as a papermaking raw material has remained sporadic and marginal. India, which is the setting for this chapter, is the only country in the world where bamboo has been used on a large scale for papermaking.

10 *Introduction*

Chapter 6 investigates business formulas adopted by London-based firms engaged in overseas raw material business. The usual method adopted by a London-based firm engaged in overseas raw material business was to court investment, primarily from British individuals but also from imperial sources. After this initial establishment period, it was usual to leave technical and production matters in the hands of local managers who ran operations in the host countries with the help of engineering firms and raw material suppliers. The board exercised complete financial control with the support of the corporate secretary and the financial and marketing services provided by commercial and financial City firms. This chapter reveals that an analysis of London-based companies engaged in overseas natural resources business can contribute to our understanding of the ambiguous relationship between the interests of the Empire and those of the City in the field of papermaking.

Chapter 7 focuses on the history of the British paper industry and the environment in which it has operated from the birth of mechanised papermaking in the first years of the nineteenth century to the changing market dynamics and consumer behaviour of the last years of the twentieth century. This chapter shows how the nature, the scale, and the distribution of papermaking changed in Britain over a period of about 200 years. Britain was the first country in the world to enter into the field of the paper manufacturing industry. It is a matter of particular significance to analyse with hindsight the consequences of coming first in a line of business. With this case method, it is hoped to provide information which will add to our understanding of British paper manufacturing history, and possibly extend or clarify our understanding of the history of the paper manufacturing industry as a whole.

Chapter 8 summarises the theoretical framework presented and discusses the key empirical findings of the case studies analysed. The pulp and paper industry has developed from being considered one of the greatest polluters of the twentieth century to an industry that is essential for the transition towards a more sustainable bio-based economy. In the Scandinavian countries, the pulp and paper industry already constitutes the biggest single industrial producer and user of renewable energy; there are big hopes that the industry will take the lead in clean-tech innovation in terms of new products and the second generation of biofuels. This trend is global, and most paper and pulp companies are working in this direction. As we move towards a world of greater diversity and balance with the natural cycles of various raw materials, it is important to ask what we can learn for the future from the history of the paper industry. While the research results will add to our historical understanding of the use of various vegetable fibrous raw materials in papermaking, they have the potential to extend or clarify the use of vegetable fibrous raw materials as part of a broader sustainable bio-based economy as a whole. Furthermore, it is hoped new insights will be provided for research institutions, business organisations, and policymakers dealing with questions related to renewable natural resources, especially in developing countries.

References

Bergquist, A.-K. & Söderholm, K. (2018) 'The Greening of the Pulp and Paper Industry: Sweden in Comparative Perspective'. In T. Särkkä, M. Gutiérrez-Poch & M. Kuhlberg, eds, *Technological Transformation in the Global Pulp and Paper Industry 1800–2018: Comparative Perspectives*. World Forests 23. Springer, Dordrecht, 65–90.

Chandler, A. D. (1962) *Strategy and Structure. Chapters in the History of the Industrial Enterprise*. Massachusetts Institute of Technology, Cambridge.

Chandler, A. D. (1977) *The Visible Hand: The Managerial Revolution in American Business*. Harvard University Press, Cambridge, MA.

Chandler, A. D. (1990) *Scale and Scope: The Dynamics of Industrial Capitalism*. Belknap Press of Harvard University Press, Cambridge, MA.

Coleman, D. C. (1958) *The British Paper Industry, 1495–1860*. Clarendon Press, Oxford.

Dadswell, G. (2018) 'Making Paper in Australia: Developing the Technology to Create a National Industry, 1818–1928'. In T. Särkkä, M. Gutiérrez-Poch & M. Kuhlberg, eds, *Technological Transformation in the Global Pulp and Paper Industry 1800–2018: Comparative Perspectives*. World Forests 23. Springer, Dordrecht, 217–236.

Elbaum, B. & Lazonick, W. (1986) *The Decline of the British Economy*. Oxford University Press, Oxford.

Eloranta, J., Ojala, J. & Valtonen, H. (2010) 'Are Business Historians Qualitatively Illiterate?' *Management & Organisation History*, 5, 1, 79–107.

Friedman, W. E. & Jones, G. (2011) 'Business History: Time for Debate'. *Business History Review*, 85, 1–8.

Gutiérrez-Poch, M. (2018) 'The Endless Sheet: Technology Transfer and the Papermaking Industry in Spain, 1800–1936'. In T. Särkkä, M. Gutiérrez-Poch & M. Kuhlberg, eds, *Technological Transformation in the Global Pulp and Paper Industry 1800–2018: Comparative Perspectives*. World Forests 23. Springer, Dordrecht, 161–188.

Hannah, L. (1976) *The Rise of the Corporate Economy*. Methuen, London.

Heikkinen S. (2000) *Paper for the World: The Finnish Paper Mills' Association – Finnpap, 1918–1966*. Otava, Helsinki.

Hills, R. L. (1988) *Papermaking in Britain 1488–1988. A Short History*. Athlone Press, London.

Hobsbawn, E. (1968 [1999]) *Industry and Empire*. Penguin, London.

Jensen-Eriksen, N. (2008) 'A Stab in the Back? The British Government, the Paper Industry and the Nordic Threat, 1956–72'. *Contemporary British History*, 22, 1, 1–21.

Jensen-Eriksen, N. & Ojala, J. (2015) 'Tackling Market Failure or Building a Cartel? Creation of an Investment Regulation System in Finnish Forest Industries'. *Enterprise & Society*, 16, 3, 521–555.

Jones, G. & Zeitlin, J., eds (2007) *The Oxford Handbook of Business History*. Oxford University Press, Oxford.

De Jong, A., Higgins, D. & van Driel, H. (2012) 'New Business History? An Invitation to Discuss'. A paper read at the 16th European Business History Conference, Paris, 1 September 2012.

Kuhlberg, M. (2018) 'Natural Potential, Artificial Restraint: The Dryden Paper Company and the Fetters on Adopting Technological Innovation in a Canadian Pulp and Paper Sector, 1900–1950'. In T. Särkkä, M. Gutiérrez-Poch &

12 *Introduction*

M. Kuhlberg, eds, *Technological Transformation in the Global Pulp and Paper Industry 1800–2018: Comparative Perspectives*. World Forests 23. Springer, Dordrecht, 133–160.

Lamberg, J.-A., Ojala, J., Peltoniemi, M. & Särkkä, T. (2012) 'Research on Evolution and the Global History of Pulp and Paper Industry: An Introduction'. In J.-A. Lamberg, J. Ojala, M. Peltoniemi & T. Särkkä, eds, *The Evolution of Global Paper Industry 1800–2050: A Comparative Analysis*. World Forests 17. Springer, Dordrecht, 1–18.

Magee, G. B. (1997a) 'Technological Divergence in a Continuous Flow Production Industry: American and British Paper Making in the Late Victorian and Edwardian Era'. *Business History*, 39, 1, 21–46.

Magee, G. (1997b) *Productivity and Performance in the Paper Industry. Labour, Capital, and Technology in Britain and America, 1860–1914*. Cambridge Studies in Modern Economic History 4. Cambridge University Press, Cambridge.

McNeill, W. (1990) 'The Rise of the West after Twenty-Five Years'. *Journal of World History*, 1, 1–21.

Mokyr, J. (1990) *The Lever of Riches. Technological Creativity and Economic Progress*. Oxford University Press, Oxford.

Mollan, S. (2018) 'The Free-Standing Company: A "Zombie" Theory of International Business History?' *Journal of Management History*, 24, 2, 156–173.

Munsell, J. (1876) *Chronology of the Origin and Progress of Paper and Paper-Making*, 5th ed. J. Munsell, Albany.

Nykänen, P. (2018) 'Research and Development in the Finnish Wood Processing and Paper Industry, c. 1850–1990'. In T. Särkkä, M. Gutiérrez-Poch & M. Kuhlberg, eds, *Technological Transformation in the Global Pulp and Paper Industry 1800–2018: Comparative Perspectives*. World Forests 23. Springer, Dordrecht, 35–64.

O'Brien, P. (2006) 'Historiographical Traditions and Modern Imperatives for the Restoration of Global History'. *Journal of Global History*, 1, 3–39.

Owen, G. (2000) *From Empire to Europe. The Decline and Revival of British Industry since the Second World War*. HarperCollins, London.

Pomeranz, K. (2000) *The Great Divergence: China, Europe, and the Making of the Modern World Economy*. Princeton University Press, Princeton, NJ.

Popp, A. (2015) 'Editor's Introduction'. *Enterprise & Society*, 16, 1, 1–4.

Reader, W. J. (1981) *Bowater. A History*. Cambridge University Press, Cambridge.

Roche, M. (2018) 'Technology Transfer and Local Innovation: Pulp and Paper Manufacturing in New Zealand, c.1860 to c.1960'. In T. Särkkä, M. Gutiérrez-Poch & M. Kuhlberg, eds, *Technological Transformation in the Global Pulp and Paper Industry 1800–2018: Comparative Perspectives*. World Forests 23. Springer, Dordrecht, 189–216.

Särkkä, T. (2012) 'The British Paper Industry, 1800–2000'. In J.-A. Lamberg, J. Ojala, M. Peltoniemi & T. Särkkä, eds, *The Evolution of Global Paper Industry 1800–2050: A Comparative Analysis*. World Forests 17. Springer, Dordrecht, 167–190.

Särkkä, T. (2018) 'The Quest for Raw Materials in the British Paper Trade: The Development of the Bamboo Pulp and Paper Industry in British India up to 1939'. In T. Särkkä, M. Gutiérrez-Poch & M. Kuhlberg, eds, *Technological Transformation in the Global Pulp and Paper Industry 1800–2018: Comparative Perspectives*. World Forests 23. Springer, Dordrecht, 237–259.

Särkkä, T., Gutiérrez-Poch, M. & Kuhlberg, M. (2018) 'Technological Transformation in the Global Pulp and Paper Industry: Introduction'. In T. Särkkä, M.

Gutiérrez-Poch & M. Kuhlberg, eds, *Technological Transformation in the Global Pulp and Paper Industry 1800–2018*. World Forests 23. Springer, Dordrecht, 1–10.

Shattock, J. & Wolff, M. (1982) 'Introduction'. In J. Shattock & M. Wolff, eds, *The Victorian Periodical Press: Samplings and Soundings*. Leicester University Press, Leicester; Toronto University Press, Toronto, xiii–xx.

Shorter, A. H. (1971) *Paper Making in the British Isles. An Historical and Geographical Study*. David & Charles, Newton Abbot.

Spicer, D. A. (1907) *The Paper Trade. A Descriptive and Historical Survey of the Paper Trade from the Commencement of the Nineteenth Century*. Methuen, London.

Sykes, P. (1981) *Albert E. Reed and the Creation of a Paper Business 1860–1960*. X.525/5617, unpublished manuscript. The British Library, London.

Willinsky, J. (1994) *Empire of Words: The Reign of the OED*. Princeton University Press, Princeton, NJ.

2 The political economy of raw materials in the global paper industry 1861–1960

Paper and board (i.e. the often multi-layered thicker variety of paper having a substance of more than 220 grams per square metre) are manufactured from filament products obtained by mechanically or chemically separating plant fibres from each other. The processes that are used to convert fibrous feedstocks into a mass of liberated fibres by dissolving the components (mainly lignin) that bind the cellulosic fibres together are collectively called 'pulping'. Chemically known as $(C_6H_{10}O_5)_n$, cellulose is the fibrous part of the plant, from which the paper is made, while lignin is the substance that holds the cellulose fibres together. The purpose of pulping is to separate the fibres from lignin – i.e. delignification – and render the fibres suitable for papermaking. These conversions can be accomplished either by overcoming the binding between the fibres and lignin forces by means of mechanical grinding (Sundholm 1999, 17) or by means of chemicals in which the ligneous substances acting as binders between the fibres are dissolved in a cooking liquor (Gullichsen 2000, 14), or by combining these two types of treatment (Alén 2018, 19). According to the processes used, the resulting products are called 'mechanical pulp' or 'chemical pulp'.

Paper is a less homogenous commodity than pulp. The very numerous different paper qualities vary greatly in their technical requirements and are dependent on their intended end-use. For the present purposes, paper has been divided into four main categories in accordance with FAO statistics: (1) newsprint, (2) printing and writing papers, (3) other papers (e.g. wrapping papers), and (4) boards. The first two categories constitute the so-called cultural papers (i.e. newsprint, printing and writing papers). They were increasingly needed as illiteracy was reduced, education extended, and mass media became important. The demand for the 'industrial papers' (i.e. wrapping papers and boards), on the other hand, increased because of the rise of the consumer society in general. Much of the increase, which took place during and since the Second World War, was in the consumption of wrapping papers, which came to replace other packaging materials such as wood, tin, iron, and glass (FAO 1954, 75). Significantly, however, for most of the research period investigated in this study, by far the most dominant uses of paper were for newsprint, printing, or writing. Naturally, then, the fundamentals that have

The political economy of raw materials 15

defined technology transfer until very recently have mainly been connected to communication in one way or another.

A standard definition of paper is 'the deposit from an aqueous solution of vegetable fibres' (Bullock 1933, 5). As paper consists of vegetable fibres, distributed in their natural form throughout the plant kingdom, it partakes not only of the chemical nature of the fibre, but also of its physical nature as well. The properties of paper depend on the colour, length, diameter, flexibility, and strength of the fibres used (Alén 2007, 18, 20), which is why papermakers have historically tended to devote serious attention to the selection of the best available raw material for the finished paper. While knowledge of the properties of the fibre is based on research done in the field of cellulose chemistry, its acquisition is also a function of changes in product market demand; availability of capital, knowledge, and technology; the surrounding institutional environment; and organisational solutions (Särkkä et al. 2018, 3). The interplay between these variables – collectively termed the political economy of raw materials – is discussed in the subsequent pages.

What follows is an endeavour to introduce the theoretical premise of pulp manufacture and mechanical papermaking from a historical perspective in four sections. The first section summarises the main elements in the progress of papermaking technologies from their places of origin in the East to the West. The second section discusses the introduction of mechanical and chemical pulping processes, and the third section discusses the world's fibrous raw material resources. The final section presents some comments on the technical suitability of raw materials for various grades of paper.

Papermaking technology transfers from the East to the West

The physical form of cellulosic fibre (collectively called 'paper') was first introduced in China over 2,000 years ago to replace the use of the thin wooden tablets (i.e. flat pieces of wood) on which records were written with brush and *sumi*, an ink composed principally of soot and binders. The precise origin of paper is obscured by time and has remained under speculation including up to today, and the processes and materials used are largely unknown by science (Maddox 1922; Blum 1934; Norris 1952; Sutermeister 1962[1954]; Heller 1978; Weber 2007; Müller 2014; Kurlansky 2017). By the fifth century AD, when papermaking was already a fully developed craft, Chinese papermakers had mastered the preparation of pulp from agricultural residues (i.e. by-products of agricultural operations), the bark of the paper mulberry tree, various natural-growing grasses, bamboo, and rags from hemp fabrics by using the lime process (Herring 1855, x, 22–23, 31–33).

In principle, delignification of the material with caustic lime meant simply soaking the material in lime solution but the process varied according to the fibres used (Dodge 1897, 10). In the case of bamboo, the process began by stripping the stems (the culms) of their leaves and shoots and

16   *The political economy of raw materials*

binding them into bundles, which were then soaked in water in order to remove the green skin or the bark from the stems. The debarked stems were split longitudinally and soaked back in water under stones with layers of lime. Bamboo was allowed to soak in the lime solution for several months until it was partially disintegrated. In place of lime, wood ash (lye) was sometimes used to break down the material. Finally, the material was cleansed with clean water to remove any caustic traces and beaten into pulp by hand or by using water- or buffalo power. This process rendered the fibre suitable for forming into sheets of paper by using a hand-mould made from bamboo (Hunter 1947, 215–216; Müller 2014, 3). The lime process could be still found in use in places in East Asia as late as the 1950s, mainly in small-scale operations for the production of pulp from cereal straws and grasses. In the modern lime process, the retted fibres were separated mechanically in a beater. Another modern variation of the lime process involved cooking the raw material at an elevated temperature and under pressure in a rotary digester (FAO 1954, 72).

The transition period from wooden tablets to paper was long and with variations according to the locality. From China, the art of papermaking spread to the Korean Peninsula and then in 610 to Japan, where wooden tablets known as *mokkan* were still widely used as an alternative to more expensive paper during the Nara period (710–94). Rare specimens of *mokkan* have been excavated from the grounds of the Heijō Palace in Nara, the ancient capital of Japan, where government officials used large quantities of wooden tablets in their everyday work (Nara Palace Site Museum 2017). In Japan, paper gained prominence as a writing and printing medium during the subsequent Heian period (794–1184), with the establishment of Heian-kyō (Kyoto) as the nation's capital and the advent of a highly developed paper culture for cultural and industrial purposes (see, for instance, Perkins 1940).

The Japanese papermakers used phloem fibres from the bark of the paper mulberry (*Broussonetia papyrifera*) known as *kōzo* and white mulberry tree (*Morus alba*) together with a deciduous shrub (*Wikstroemia canescens*) known as *ganpi* or *kaminoki* (meaning literally paper tree) and the Oriental paperbush or giant leaf paper plant (*Edgeworthia papyrifera*) known as *mitsumata* to make *washi*, Japanese paper. The *washi*-making process is described as follows in Jihei Kunisaki's (1948 [1798]) *A Handy Guide to Papermaking (Kamisuki Chohoki)*, the oldest book in the Japanese language devoted to papermaking. To make a sheet of *washi* from *kōzo*, branches were first steamed to loosen the outer bark. The stronger inner bark was soaked in cold stream in order to be rinsed by the flow of water, cleaned, and boiled with alkali (*sōda*) to break down the fibres. The boiled fibres were then pounded into pulp with a wooden stick (*bai*) and mixed with mucilage (*neri*) in large wooden vats (*sukibune*). *Neri*, which was extracted from a malvaceous (i.e. belonging to a family of *Malvaceae*, or the mallows) Tororo-aoi plant (*Abelmoschus manihot*), caused the fibres to be evenly dispersed in water and also increased the strength of the paper. The resulting liquid was poured into a square sieve-like papermaking mould (*sugeta*) in order to form a sheet of paper. Once the desired thickness

The political economy of raw materials   17

was attained and the fibres settled in the suspension, the screen was removed from the frame, and the wet paper was peeled off the screen. The sheets were stacked, dehydrated by weighing down the stacks of the sheets, stretched out on wooden boards one by one, and finally dried in the sun.

The manufacture of machine-made western paper, *yoshi*, was introduced to Japan during the Meiji period (1868–1912), but *washi*-making persisted and coexisted together with *yoshi* industry. Remarkably, the *washi*-making technique has remained nearly unchanged since ancient times until today. The persistence of the *washi*-making tradition is due to Japan's long economic isolation, relative geographical isolation, abundant indigenous raw material resources, and large domestic markets as well as rich and varied uses of paper (Kurosawa & Hashino 2012; Kurosawa & Hashino 2017), which are all included in the fundamentals of the political economy of raw materials in the global pulp and paper industry.

The domestication of important papermaking plants such as cotton, hemp, and flax and their use for fabrics were other important milestones in the history of papermaking. In the Arab papermaking tradition, papermakers have historically tended to prefer recycled fibres over virgin fibres because the former had undergone the process of semi-manufacture, and thus, this material could very easily and cost-effectively be reduced by simple mechanical means to a mass of fine fibres which interlace and form a continuous, even-textured web. For instance, a flax thread, from which linen is woven, is but an aggregation of bundles of bast fibres (i.e. plant fibre collected from the phloem, the 'inner bark', sometimes called 'skin' or bast surrounding the stem) purified and cleansed of all extraneous matter and simply twisted together (Dodge 1897, 10).

The semi-tropical fibre-yielding plants such as hemp, flax, cotton, jute, and rhea used in East Asia for papermaking did not grow in the arid climate of Central Asia, and local papermakers apparently discovered (or rediscovered through the Chinese) that paper could be made from rags of cotton, linen, and hemp fabrics. Arab papermakers consequently learned to make paper from both phloem fibres and rags. In medieval Islamic times, fabrics were more often linen or hemp than cotton, as the plant flourished in only a few regions in the Arab Empire. With the Arabs, the secrets of the fibre migrated to North Africa and then to al-Andalus, gradually replacing papyrus and parchment, the two writing mediums that had been used in the Mediterranean region for millennia (Bloom 2017, 52–58). The immensely strong fibres in the form of rags from fabrics and technological innovations connected with printing technology ensured, since the late fifteenth century, the establishment of paper mills and printing presses, first in the Old World, and then following European colonisation, in the New World (Särkkä et al. 2018, 4).

In papermaking, the preparation of the raw material is the first process of making paper. The rags were first sorted, cleaned, and cut into pieces and then steeped in water for a period of six weeks in order to be fermented before they were ready to be beaten into pulp. In medieval times, rags had

18   *The political economy of raw materials*

been pulped by using water-powered stamping mills. At the beginning of the 1680s, an improvement on the stamps was developed by the Dutch in the form of a Hollander beating engine (i.e. 'Hollander'), the rotating metal bars of which reduced the rags to pulp far more efficiently. The pulp of rags, thoroughly churned and chopped as finely as possible by the beaterman, was run into a vat, where the papermaker, or the vatman, scooped up some of the liquid – otherwise known as 'stuff', a suspension of 98–99% warm water and 1–2% of fibres – onto a rectangular mould of wire mesh. By means of agitating the mould, the vatman ensured that the fibres were distributed evenly onto the mesh, while the coucher turned the made sheet of paper out onto a felt (see, for instance, Cormack 1933, 19–20, 24; Papermaking 1968, 31–48).

The same principles and terminology of handmade papermaking endured into mechanical practice. The paper machine represented a straightforward mechanisation of what was formerly done by hand. In principle, it performed an exactly similar sequence of actions to handmade papermaking, only faster. The main separating factor was that in the mechanised making of paper, the papermaking process was continuous instead of dividing into separate processes. In an early nineteenth-century Fourdrinier paper machine, the machine wire was an endless band of wire gauze of 65–80 meshes to the inch, depending on the type of paper being made. As soon as the 'stuff' was delivered to the wire, water began to drain through into the wire pit, where it was collected and reused at the beaters. A sideways shaking motion was generated on the machine wire, and suction was applied to the paper on the wire. At the end of the machine wire, the paper was transferred to a wet felt and passed through a large press to remove more water (Green 1963, 46, 48; Clapperton 1967). The subsequent changes accompanying mechanisation came through the modification of traditional methods, rather than altering them completely. The beaters, wires, moulds, and vats themselves were modified, to improve quantities and qualities and at the same time to enable finer control over the product to be obtained.

The more economical methods of manufacture and exponentially greater output to meet larger demand led to the quest for new raw materials. In the 1860s and 1870s, two separate developments took place: the introduction of new processing treatments to some of the old papermaking materials (i.e. rags, straws, grasses, and bamboo) and the introduction of a range of new technologies connected with the utilisation of coniferous wood fibres, the use of which prevailed (Cross 1916, 35–37; Särkkä et al. 2018, 5).

The introduction of mechanical and chemical pulping processes

Until the mid-nineteenth century, paper had been almost exclusively manufactured from non-wood feedstocks, but within a matter of just 20 years or so, the old raw materials were ousted in the Western papermaking by the successful application of processes permitting the mechanical and chemical pulping of wood. At first, the raw material basis for the paper manufacture was immeasurably expanded with the introduction of the groundwood process in the 1840s and 1850s. The technology is attributed to three German inventors, F. G. Keller, Heinrich Voelter, and Johan Matthäus Voith, who presented the principles of a grinder suitable for a large-scale production of groundwood pulp (Alén 2018, 22). The groundwood process fell into the following phases. The logs of wood were first debarked and cut into small pieces, and then pounded into fibre by a grinding machine. Next, water was added to the fibre and the resulting pulp was cleaned by pressing it through sieves. Then, the pulp was graded into equal lengths of fibre, thickened, and fed into a machine that spread it into an even layer. The excess water was removed by means of a high-pressure press. Finally, the layer of pulp was cut into sheets, which were pressed into bales with a hydraulic baling press and dried in a dehydrating machine (The Finnish Sawmilling, Pulp and Paper Industries 1936). By this means, the wood was mechanically reduced into a product, known in the industry as 'dry mechanical pulp', consisting of more or less separated fibres and fibre bundles of high yield (90% or over).

The invention of delignification of wood fibres from wood by using alkaline solvent, commonly known as caustic soda (i.e. sodium hydroxide, chemically known as NaOH), is attributed to Hugh Burgess and Charles Watt, two British cellulose experts, who experimented with various fibrous materials at Frogmore Mill in the early 1850s. The soda process involved digesting the raw material in an aqueous solution of caustic soda at an elevated temperature and under pressure. The commercial utilisation of Burgess' and Watt's experiments, initially made with chipped wood raw material, was patented in 1851, but in the absence of large indigenous wood resources in Britain, there was little investment forthcoming for the development of a pulping process based on wood. Three years later, in 1854, Burgess took out a patent in the USA, where the first mill utilising the soda process began its operations near Philadelphia in 1855 (The Paper Trail 2013).

Although this was the starting point of what became the chemical pulp industry, the soda process was not the technical or economical answer for wood pulp for the yield of cellulose was only about 30% on the dry weight of the material and the strength of the pulp was poor (Cross & Bevan 1907, 140–142). In place of wood, British papermakers widely applied the soda process for sundry locally available recycled fibres such as rags from fabrics. Being essentially pure cellulose, rags could be treated in a very weak alkaline solution by cooking them for a relatively short period of time at little or no pressure, thereby greatly reducing the need for chemicals and energy, so keeping the cost of treatment low. In the 1850s, Thomas Routledge, an English papermaker, devised the soda process for esparto (Chap. 3) and in the 1870s for bamboo (Chap. 5), which eventually led to a wide dissemination of the soda process throughout the British Empire (Chap. 6).

Anselme Payen, a French botanist, laid the foundations for another line of cooking of wood with sulphuric acid. At the turn of the 1830s and 1840s,

20   *The political economy of raw materials*

Payen managed to isolate cellulose and lignin from a residue which he had obtained by breaking down various vegetable plants in nitric acid solvent. The commercial adaption of the method to wood is known as the sulphite process, which is credited to Benjamin Chew Tilghman, an American chemist who patented the process in the USA and Britain in 1867. The sulphite process involved cooking wood chips at an elevated temperature and under pressure in a rotary digester, in a rotating cylinder, and in an immersion of aqueous calcium hydrogen sulphite and sulphur dioxide (Alén 2018, 24). The process was subsequently perfected by the Swedish chemist Carl Ekman, enabling the establishment of the world's first sulphite pulp mill in Bergvik, Sweden, in 1874. By 1900, the sulphite process had become the dominant chemical pulping method for wood in other forest-rich countries such as Finland, the USA, and Canada (Järvinen et al. 2012; Kuhlberg 2012; Toivanen 2012).

The main uses of the pulps manufactured with the sulphite process were wrapping and bag papers; newsprint (15–20% of the total fibre furnish); and all kinds of books, printing, and fine papers. One of the advantages of the process was that the unbleached pulps from the suitable softwood species had a relatively light colour and thus they were easy to bleach to high brightness. The main disadvantage of the process was that the acidic immersion stained the pulp, which consequently tended over time to tarnish papers made from the sulphite wood pulp to a yellowish brown colour. Apart from the colour instability, another disadvantage of the sulphite process was the steam pollution effect, which caused high sulphur dioxide gas emissions (FAO 1954, 72; Bergquist & Söderholm 2018).

Another chemical pulping process – the sulphate process – was originally so termed because sodium sulphate (salt cake) was used as a make-up chemical (FAO 1954, 71). The process is credited to the American Asahel Knowlton Eaton, who patented it in 1870. Based on the same idea, German Carl Ferdinand Dahl, working in Danzig, devised the process for softwood species in 1884, which was the decisive impetus towards the rise of the modern sulphate pulp industry. The sulphate process produced a dark coloured strong pulp which made a very strong paper known as 'kraft' (Species of Wood Used in Various Processes in Making Paper Pulp 20 March 1937; Alén 2018, 20–23). Initially, the applicability of the process was restricted outside major conurbations due to the extremely disagreeable odours caused by the organic sulphur compounds (Cross & Bevan 1907, 141). Over time, the problem of steam pollution was partly solved by the evaporation and burning of the calcium base waste liquor. By burning the waste liquor, chemicals and steam used for digestion could be recovered, which meant also a saving in processing chemicals and fuel (FAO 1954, 72).

The advancement of the sulphate process outside Continental Northern Europe was delayed by the high capital cost of constructing the recovery plant and the dark colour of the unbleached pulp, which called for chlorine bleaching when light-coloured papers were manufactured. A spectacular

The political economy of raw materials   21

increase in the world's sulphate mill capacity took place in the 1930s, mainly because of the successful design and application of modern recovery units and the multi-stage bleaching processes. In the 1930s, many of the world's soda mills were converted to sulphate mills simply by adding small amounts of sulphur to cooking liquor. In this way, these soda mills started to operate in principle with the same digesting chemicals as the sulphate mills, but in slightly different proportions. Many mills, however, switched to using other sodium and sulphur compounds so the name 'sulphate mill' was no longer fully descriptive (FAO 1954, 71).

The combined pulping processes are characterised by a combination of chemical and mechanical actions on the fibre structure of the raw material. They came into use after the Second World War, when pulp manufacturers developed a range of new processes with the object of increasing the yields by the chemical processes and broadening the raw material field for the production of mechanical pulp. The use of the new combined processes was still very limited in 1950, when about 35% of the world production of pulp was made by mechanical processes, 63% by chemical processes (35% of which being by the sulphate process alone), and only about 2% by combined processes. The most widely used combined process was the chemi-groundwood process, which consisted of impregnating logs of temperate broadleaved species with neutral sulphite liquor and mildly digesting the logs prior to grinding. The resulting pulp was darker in colour than spruce groundwood but three to four times stronger (Species of Wood Used in Various Processes in Making Paper Pulp 20 March 1937; FAO 1954, 70, 73).

The world's fibrous raw material resources

Cellulosic fibrous feedstock for papermaking is harvested from virgin forests, secondary forests, and industrial forest plantations, or recovered by mechanical and chemical means from various refuse materials (e.g. rags from fabrics and waste paper). Vegetable fibrous materials for papermaking – whether indigenous or exotic – are collectively termed raw materials as opposed to refuse materials (i.e. recovered fibres). Sundry miscellaneous waste materials were the basic materials in Western paper manufacturing until the mid-nineteenth century. Although rags were used on a very limited scale after the 1860s in comparison with the raw materials, they were by no means unimportant, since their long fibres improved the necessary strength characteristics of the pulps. Cotton, jute, and hemp have extremely long fibres, usually counted in centimetres instead of millimetres, and that is why papers manufactured from rags were known for their high tear resistance. Rag pulps were used primarily for the production of fine writing papers, to which they give extra durability and permanence as well improved appearance (Cross & Bevan 1907, 2–3; Weatherill 1974, 20). Rag pulps were also used to manufacture certain grades of strong wrapping papers (e.g. manilas). Other paper qualities made almost exclusively from rags included banknote papers and cigarette

22 *The political economy of raw materials*

papers, the former being made from rags and the latter from raw hemp, flax, or ramie fibres (FAO 1954, 65).

Another important group of refuse material for making paper is paper itself, i.e. the quantities of recycled paper, which are recovered and returned to the pulp mills. The amount of waste paper that may be used in the manufacture of new products is limited by technical (quality) reasons and by its availability (waste paper recovery rate) (FAO 1961, 52, 2018, 11; for more details, see Bajpai 2014). Thus, for instance, the amount of waste paper which could be incorporated in newsprint and high-strength wrapping paper was very limited, while certain qualities of industrial papers could be produced almost entirely from waste (e.g. cardboard, corrugating board, and building papers) (FAO 1954, 65). Another disadvantage of waste paper is that the boards are softer than those made from virgin fibres and therefore unsuitable for high-speed box erecting machines. Furthermore, historically, there has been a degree of prejudice against using waste-based board in the packaging of some foodstuffs. As to the collection of waste paper, the quantities available depend on the paper consumption level, the density and distribution of the population, and the efficiency of the waste paper collecting organisation. Consequently, the overall percentage of waste which could be used for the manufacture of new products varies considerably from region to region and was generally higher in developed than in the less developed regions of the world (FAO 1961, 52–53).

Wood has been the predominant source for cellulosic fibrous feedstocks since the 1860s. Today, the typical wood species for papermaking are coniferous softwoods – such as pine (*Pinus spp.*), spruce (*Picea spp.*), fir (*Abies spp.*), hemlock (*Tsuga spp.*), and larch (*Larix spp.*) – and deciduous hardwoods, especially eucalypts. By the mid-1950s, forest trees provided about 95% of all raw materials used for paper (FAO 1954, 54), while non-wood materials constituted much of the rest – a ratio of the world's total fibre furnish that has been more or less constant until today. In 2018, the world's total fibre furnish amounted to 421 million tons, of which forest trees constituted about 90% (FAO 2018, 9). In developing countries, however, roughly 60% of the total fibre furnish is derived from perennial plants belonging to the family *Poaceae* (i.e. cereal straws, grasses, and bamboo) (Bajpai 2012, 7).

In general, most of the coniferous tree species occur naturally in regions enjoying a cool temperate climate. Hence, the bulk of coniferous forest is located in the Boreal forest, otherwise known as the Taiga, a broad belt encircling the earth below the treeless tundra of the Northern Hemisphere. Because of their northerly position, most of the forests in the coniferous belt have only a slow natural growth. Most favourably situated conifer forests, for example, those in the Southern States of the USA and on the Pacific Coast in North America, have a considerably higher rate of growth. Moreover, higher yields could be obtained from secondary forests, where intensive forest management, which involves the use of tree planting, bush clearing, and thinning

The political economy of raw materials 23

methods as well as the use of fertilisers, aims to increase the rate of growth (Hiley 1930, 203–210; FAO 1954, 55).

The Boreal forest offers a number of benefits with respect to logging. The varieties of timber are few in number, consisting mainly of woods of coniferous species and some deciduous broadleaved species (Hölzl & Oosthoek 2018). Much of Scandinavia was covered in coniferous forests, and primarily two species – Norway spruce (*Picea abies*) and Scots pine (*Pinus sylvestris L.*) – were being harvested. The uniformity of this raw material permitted pulp manufacturers and papermakers to obtain a regular product, and because logging operations were occurring on a very large scale, standard products could be made available in international markets at very low rates. Temperate broadleaved species such as birch, poplar, and aspen have been mentioned as a source of pulpwood since the early twentieth century. The fact that they are usually lacking in strength qualities and have a shorter fibre length did not seriously hamper making use of them for a wide range of papers, since an admixture of conifer pulp can make up for this shortcoming. In the early 1950s, it was found that sulphate pulps from temperate broadleaved woods such as birch and aspen have strength characteristics approaching and in some cases exceeding those of coniferous sulphite pulps. The successful pulping of temperate non-conifers prepared the way for utilising the tropical and sub-tropical broadleaved species (FAO 1954, 55).

Initially, high-density tropical and subtropical hardwoods were not considered suitable for either mechanical pulp (because the damage to the fibres was too heavy and the fibre length of the pulp consequently too short) or chemical pulp (because the dark colour of some of the hardwood species was objectionable because of the prohibitive cost of bleaching). However, over time, technological transformation showed that some of these disadvantages could be partly overcome. The first tropical and subtropical hardwood species to be commercially pulped were eucalypts, which were introduced to paper manufacture in Australia in the 1920s (Jeffreys 1965, 240; Dadswell 2018).

The practical difficulties of logging virgin stands of tropical and subtropical woods were greater because species suitable for pulping usually occurred in very mixed stands and varied in size and density. This factor prompted the use of forest plantations for pulpwood production. An early example of using planted eucalyptus for pulpwood is the Caima Pulp Company at Aveiro, Portugal, which started to use planted *Eucalyptus globulus* in the 1920s (Branco & Neves 2018, 116–117). However, the primary purpose of the first tree plantations was not papermaking but the need for charcoal and timber for firing locomotives and the construction of railway crosstie sleepers and numerous other purposes (Lima-Toivanen 2012, 264). For instance in South Africa, where experimental planting of fast-growing eucalypt species started in 1880, the aim of the plantation work was to provide pitprops for the booming Witwatersrand gold mining industry, which developed along the lines of deep-level mining (FAO 1954, 63). In some places, environmental

24 *The political economy of raw materials*

reasons (e.g. the need to provide wind barriers) might have been the dominant considerations at first.

In the 1950s, many countries which lacked adequate natural stands of timber – some with important pulp and paper industries, others desirous of creating such industries – were turning to plantations to augment their natural resources. Besides eucalypts, industrial plantations of other suitable wood species were established, in particular certain varieties of pine, *Pinus patula* in South Africa (King 1965, 235–236), *Pinus radiata* in New Zealand (Roche 2018), and paraná pine (*Araucaria angustifolia*) in Brazil (FAO 1954, 63). It was only after large-scale plantations of the fast-growing eucalypt species were established for pulpwood in many parts of the world that the global pulp and paper industry developed along the borders of industrial forest plantations. The development of eucalyptus forest plantations in Brazil is a case in point (Lima-Toivanen 2012). There were many negative effects attached to a policy of industrial plantations. Clearly, they invaded the soil needed by agriculture. Moreover, the dangers of monoculture were by no means fully understood at the time. For example, in India, industrial eucalyptus plantations increased the bamboo forests' susceptibility to disease and, in the long run, caused soil exhaustion (Savur 2003, I, 22–28). On the other hand, man–made forests may have provided the answer to some of the problems which had arisen from exploiting virgin rain forests. For instance, some South American tropical hardwood species, such as cetico (*Cecropia sp.*) and parasolier (*Musanga cecropioides*), which grew in pure stands on river banks in the Amazon basin, were also found suitable but logging and transport costs were prohibitive for commercial operations without heavy tariff protection (Analysis and Projections of Economic Development 1959, 206).

The first research on the use of tropical hardwoods in Equatorial Africa for pulp and papermaking commenced at the beginning of the twentieth century and was undertaken by several countries. Investigations at the French papermaking school (École Française de Papeterie of Grenoble) can be mentioned here as an illustrative example. These studies, like those undertaken by the Belgians, sometimes generated promising results, but did not lead to the establishment of the pulp and paper industry in the tropical or subtropical regions of the world. At the onset of the Second World War, the French Government recognised the importance that tropical forests can play in the papermaking industry. In 1944, it entrusted the setting up a pilot plant to a public establishment specially created for this purpose, the Régie Industrielle de la Cellulose Coloniale, which was operating under the authority of the French Overseas Territories Department (Ministère de la France d'Outre-Mer). Opened in April 1952 on the banks of the Ebrié lagoon, at Bimbresso, near Abidjan, on the Ivory Coast, French West Africa, this pilot plant was the first of its kind on the African Continent. It manufactured kraft paper using the soda–sulphur process with imported chemicals from mixed tropical hardwood species of primary species and old secondary ones, sourced from the forest of Anguédédou (an area of 8,400 hectares). The successful operation of

The political economy of raw materials   25

the pilot mill at Bimbresso proved that the sulphate process was even suitable for mixed tropical hardwood species (Peteri 1952, 43–50).

Bamboo, which belongs to the grass family, occurs in abundance throughout the Tropics and, if conditions are favourable, also in the subtropical areas of the world. The only country where bamboo has been used as a primary raw material for pulp is India, which at the end of the research period consumed more than 300,000 tons of bamboo as a raw material a year, representing over 60% of the country's requirements of fibrous raw materials. Bamboo reaches maturity in two or three years and thus constitutes a quickly renewing source of fibrous raw material. The yield was usually high, and the fibre characteristics of bamboo are excellent for papermaking purposes, especially for printing and writing papers. The paper made from bamboo pulp has an excellent tear resistance as the fibre length equals, and in some cases exceeds, that of conifers (FAO 1954, 63; for further details, see Chap. 5).

Grasses were important raw materials in certain countries lacking forests or other suitable raw materials. Esparto grasses (*Stipa tenacissima; Lygeum spartum*) from Spain and North Africa were imported to British mills as raw material for paper from the late 1850s. At the end of the research period, over 300,000 tons of esparto grass was exported annually, mainly to Britain, for the production of high-class book or printing papers (for further details, see Chap. 3). Sabai (*Eulaliopsis binata*) was the primary raw material in the Indian paper mills up to the 1930s and remained the second most important raw material up to the end of the 1950s (for further details, see Chap. 6). Although the prices of grasses (esparto and sabai) rose sharply after the Second World War, partly due to increased extraction costs, the use of grasses tended to increase because of their special fibre characteristics and lower consumption of processing chemicals. Several other grasses and reeds, which generally occurred in marshy lands, on lakeshores, and along riverbanks, were found suitable for paper, but economic considerations often hindered large-scale operations (FAO 1954, 64).

The largest resources of the annual crop fibres for pulp and paper were wheat and rye straw as well as sugarcane bagasse. Although their fibre length is shorter than that of conifers, bamboos, and most grasses, technology transfer made it possible to produce a wide variety of paper products from these agricultural residues, partly in blends with small amounts of longer fibres (FAO 1954, 64; for further details, see Chap. 3). Sugarcane bagasse is the fibrous residue obtained from the sugar cane mills after crushing the cane and extracting the sugar with water in a leaching operation. The bagasse, which has an average fibre length of 1.5–2 mm (i.e. longer than that of most broadleaved wood species and straw), contains, besides about 45–50% water, roughly 30% (on the dry weight) of a non-fibrous matter called the pith, which had a detrimental effect on the pulp quality. The pith increased the consumption of processing chemicals and regularly prevented the successful utilisation of bagasse for pulp and paper. The largest users of bagasse for pulp manufacture were some Latin American and Caribbean countries as well as India, where, too,

26 *The political economy of raw materials*

however, sugarcane bagasse remained only a supplementary material forming 2–3% of the total basic raw material at the end of the research period (FAO 1954, 64; for further details, see Chap. 5).

Technical suitability of raw materials for various papers

Because the pulps produced by various processes from the different fibres vary greatly in their papermaking qualities, the account we have just given would be incomplete without a discussion of the technical suitability of different fibres for various paper products.

The wood species suitable for the mechanical grinding process are limited in number and constitute mainly certain coniferous species. Thus, spruce, fir, and hemlock remained the principal materials for mechanical pulp for newsprint. Pine was considered unsuitable for either mechanical or sulphite pulp on account of its resin content. However, in the 1930s, certain varieties of pine such as *Pinus radiata* and *Pinus patula* were increasingly used as well, and among the hardwood species, poplar and eucalyptus were already proving their value in the manufacture of newsprint. Temperate broadleaved species were considered less desirable for mechanical grinding because groundwood pulp made from broadleaved species required a higher admixture percentage of chemical pulp because of their shorter fibre length, increasing the cost of finished product. However, some species, notably poplar and aspen, were used in Italy as well as in France, the UK, the USA, and Canada for newsprint and printing papers (FAO 1954, 70).

The main disadvantage of the mechanical process is that a large percentage of the fibres are damaged and reduced in length in the course of the grinding process. Thus, the tear strength of papers produced from mechanical groundwood pulp was less than that of papers produced from the same raw material by the chemical processes. Conversely, in the chemical pulping, the yield of pulp from the raw material was found to be much lower (depending on the raw material and the chemical process used, it typically varied between 45 and 50% for unbleached pulp qualities) than what was obtained by using the mechanical grinding action. The chemical separation of fibres proved to be less destructive to the fibres, however, than mechanical action, and papers made from chemical pulps therefore had better tear resistance than those manufactured by solely mechanical means. Furthermore, the removal of the ligneous substances during the chemical process improved the colour stability of the pulp, which made chemical pulps more versatile (FAO 1964, 101, 104; Alén 2018, 18–19).

The sulphate process was generally preferred for coniferous wood species since it gave higher yields and had better strength characteristics as well as a wider range of pulp qualities (Alén 2018, 19–20). Arising from these factors, the use of unbleached sulphite pulp in newsprint, fine writing, book, and printing papers was gradually replaced by the use of semi-bleached sulphate pulp, especially after the 1930s. While the number of mills using the sulphite process declined after the Second World War, the old sulphite process was not completely taken over by the sulphate process. By substituting the calcium base with sodium, magnesium, or ammonium, it was possible to use raw materials that previously did not lend themselves to sulphite pulping (FAO 1954, 72). In the 1920s, it was demonstrated that by substituting the calcium base with magnesium, it was possible to pulp bamboo with the sulphite process (for further details, see Chap. 5). Another benefit of the sulphite process was that it was considered the most suitable chemical process for dissolving pulps used primarily for the manufacture of non-paper products such as viscose, otherwise known as rayon, the artificial silk, which was patented by the English chemists Charles Frederick Cross, Edward John Bevan, and Clayton Beadle in 1894 (Álen 2018, 18). Progress was slow at first. In 1930, the world's output of viscose was just 200,000 tons. Following the application of new industrial applications in the 1930s, the production of various synthetic cellulosic fibres had already risen by 1948 to close to 2 million tons, which represented 15–20% of the world's annual fibre supply at the time (Forestry and Forest Products 1948, 55). In principle, however, the sulphate process was the most generally applicable pulping process that could be used for pulping practically all kinds of fibrous raw materials.

The largest world production of bleached pulp from annual plant fibres was obtained from the use of the caustic soda-chlorine process, i.e. the 'Pomilio' cellulose process, which was owned by the Sindicato Cellulosa Pomilio of Naples and so named after its Italian inventor, Dr. Umberto Pomilio. This process was suitable for a wide variety of cereal straws, sugarcane bagasse, and other agricultural residues, and, therefore, was particularly suitable in countries deficient in virgin coniferous wood resources. Primary delignification of the raw material was achieved by treatment with weak caustic soda solution followed, in the case of finer grades, by a chlorination and alkali extraction stage. The unbleached semi-manufactured pulp could be used in all types of boards and, in blends with coniferous groundwood, for newsprint and cheap varieties of printing and writing papers. The bleached qualities were used for high-grade printing, writing, and glassine papers, but usually in admixture with long-fibred pulps (Salvatore 1942, 12–19; FAO 1954, 72). Besides the Italian and French pulp and paper industries, which were the main users of the process, by 1939 the Pomilio process had been installed for the creation of a pulp and paper industry in Argentina (Rosario), Chile (Santiago), Uruguay (Montevideo), and South Africa (Springs near Johannesburg) (Pomilio Corporation Limited to Imperial Institute 24 January 1939).

Mechanical pulp was usually the cheapest grade of wood pulp as the groundwood process did not require the use of processing chemicals or steam for digestion and it was manufactured in locations where the very large amount of waterpower required for grinding wood cost little apart from the cost of harnessing waterfalls. The cheap hydroelectric energy contributed directly to a lower cost of the finished product. In terms of quality, mechanical pulp was unsuited to the manufacture of better qualities of paper, as sunlight

28   The political economy of raw materials

caused it to fade and change its colour. Due to mechanical pulp's relatively low price, the product is perfect for the manufacture of newsprint, which is more exacting in its raw material requirements than most other kinds of paper and board for technical and economic reasons. Because newsprint is a service commodity – what the consumer usually buys is news, as newsprint was originally called, and not paper as such – its object is fulfilled, generally speaking, once the news is consumed. Since these papers have a short life, the paper on which they are printed does not need to possess either purity or permanence, nor does it have to be of high quality. But above all, newsprint has to be cheap. Moreover, certain basic technical qualities are necessary: newsprint must be capable of absorbing ink rapidly, it must possess bulk and opacity, and it must have sufficient strength for high-speed paper machines. Initially, these requirements could be most economically achieved by using a high-yield mechanical pulp, with an admixture of 15–25% unbleached sulphite pulp, which gave the end-product necessary strength qualities to enable a high-speed printing process (FAO 1954, 82; 1964, 60).

Newsprint production was usually, though not invariably, integrated with pulp manufacture. The reasons for this were both technical and economic. Wet mechanical pulp did not store well, and therefore, the excessive water, which could be accounted for as much as 50% of the weight of the pulp, was removed by means of a high-pressure press. The main disadvantage of dry mechanical pulp was that it is more costly due to the necessary preparatory manipulation than wet pulp, and occasioned loss in strength when dried. In the integrated operations, these disadvantages could be overcome because pulp could be used in its wet state (FAO 1954, 82). While in a Scandinavian or Canadian integrated pulp and paper mill the wet 'half-stuff' went directly to the paper machine, in a British paper mill, the mechanical pulp was imported in the form of sheets of pulp to the docks, handled and transported to the mill, and reconstituted back to wet 'half-stuff' in a beater until it could be used.

Those countries adequately endowed with supplies of coniferous softwood species and enjoying a sufficiently ample market in close proximity were the most successful in their newsprint projects. The extraordinary growth of the Canadian pulp and paper industry in the first part of the twentieth century is a case in point (Kuhlberg 2012, 107–116, 2015). Both technical and economic reasons favoured economics of scale in newsprint manufacture. Nevertheless, many smaller newsprint mills did operate successfully in spite of these technical and economic hindrances. It is also notable that the very large British newsprint industry operated primarily on imported mechanical pulp. In general, however, non-integrated newsprint mills were viable only if they enjoyed special advantages, which could be either natural (e.g. a large domestic market or an accessible export market for newsprint; exceptionally cheap indigenous raw material) or artificial (e.g. tariff protection) (FAO 1954, 82).

In very few major industrial commodities was the geographical imbalance between production and demand so markedly pronounced as in newsprint.

The political economy of raw materials 29

The size of the market, therefore, was of paramount importance when establishing newsprint mills was being considered. In 1952, fewer than 20 countries had a newsprint consumption large enough to support a modern newsprint mill of a 75,000-ton capacity, which was regarded as the economic minimum at the time. Nearly two-thirds of the world's newsprint was produced in Canada and Scandinavia, Canada's share alone being just over half. A further 19% was produced in Britain, 10% in the USA, and most of the remaining 5% in Continental Europe. Outside these regions, only Japan and the Soviet Union manufactured newsprint on any significant scale. Four largest producers – Canada, Finland, Norway, and Sweden – exported most of their production. Total world imports in 1952 amounted to 5.8 million tons; of this total, 4.6 million tons went to the USA and just over 250,000 tons to Britain. Only Argentina, Australia, and Brazil imported as much as 100,000 tons. Factors that arose in both the supply and demand sides accounted for the fact that the production of newsprint was more heavily concentrated than that of any other major category of paper and board (FAO 1954, 82–83; Kuhlberg 2012, 2015).

Conclusions

The foregoing discussion is summarised in Tables 2.1 and 2.2, which list the most important pulping processes used during the research period, describe their characteristic features, and indicate the raw materials suitable to each. The tables show that many of the pulps which could be derived from non-traditional fibres – grasses, bamboo, straw, bagasse, and tropical and subtropical broadleaved species – called for admixture of long-fibred pulps if a wide range of end-products was to be obtained. Therefore, in most instances, the need to import long-fibred coniferous mechanical pulp for blending remained – a fact that tended to keep the deficient regions of the world dependent on overseas supplies of either wood pulp or paper.

Table 2.1 Pulping Processes and Their Characteristics 1861–1960

Process	Characteristics	Raw material
Mechanical		
Groundwood	Mechanical defibration by grindstones	Spruce, fir, hemlock, some varieties of pines, poplar, aspen, eucalyptus as well as low-density broadleaved species
Chemical		
Lime process	Digestion with lime	Agricultural residues
Soda process	Digestion with caustic soda	Grasses, bamboo, straw, and some deciduous woods

(Continued)

30   *The political economy of raw materials*

Process	Characteristics	Raw material
Sulphite process	Digestion with an acid liquor containing calcium, sodium, magnesium, or ammonium bisulphite and sulphuric acid	Spruce, fir and hemlock, some deciduous woods such as birch, aspen and eucalyptus, bamboo (certain spp. only)
Sulphate and soda-sulphur processes	Digestion with a mixture of caustic soda and sodium sulphite	Practically all kinds of raw materials
Caustic soda-chlorine (Pomilio) process	Delignification by caustic soda followed by chlorination and alkali extraction	Agricultural residues and bagasse
Combined		
Chemi-groundwood	Mild digestion of logs prior to conventional grinding	Broadleaved species

Sources: Species of Wood Used in Various Processes in Making Paper Pulp 20 March 1937; FAO (1954); Särkkä et al. (2018); Lamberg et al. (2012b).

Table 2.2 Technical Suitability of Raw Materials for Various Papers 1861–1960

Raw material	*Newsprint, printing and writing papers*	*All other papers and boards*
Conifers	For mechanical pulp fraction (some pine species preferable); for chemical pulp fraction (all species)	Suitable for all grades of paper
Broadleaved woods		
Temperate species	For mechanical pulp fraction only; long-fibred pulps necessary for chemical pulp fraction	Limited suitability
Eucalypts	Certain species suitable for mechanical pulp fraction; long-fibred pulps necessary for chemical pulp fraction	Suitable in large percentage for all papers but for high strength, admixture with long-fibred pulps necessary
Bamboo	Suitable for chemical pulp fraction only	Suitable for most papers but blending with coniferous pulps necessary for some wrapping papers
Grasses	Suitable for chemical pulp fraction only	Suitable for fine papers and some wrapping papers
Straws and bagasse	Suitable for chemical pulp fraction only	Suitable for most paper qualities but requires blending with long-fibred pulps for high-strength requirements

Sources: Species of Wood Used in Various Processes in Making Paper Pulp 20 March 1937; FAO (1954); Särkkä et al. (2018); Lamberg et al. (2012a).

References

Alén, R. (2007) 'Introduction to Papermaking'. In R. Alén, ed, *Papermaking Chemistry*. 2nd ed. Finnish Paper Engineers' Association, Helsinki, 16–26.

Alén, R. (2018) 'Manufacturing Cellulosic Fibres for Making Paper: A Historical Perspective'. In T. Särkkä, M. Gutiérrez-Poch & M. Kuhlberg, eds, *Technological Transformation in the Global Pulp and Paper Industry 1800–2018: Comparative Perspectives*. World Forests 23. Springer, Dordrecht, 13–34.

Analysis and Projections of Economic Development (1959) VI. The Industrial Development of Peru. UN, The Department of Economic and Social Affairs, Mexico.

Bajpai, P. (2012) *Biotechnology for Pulp and Paper Processing*. Springer, New York.

Bajpai, P. (2014) *Recycling and Deinking of Recovered Paper*. Elsevier, London and Waltham, MA.

Bergquist, A.-K. & Söderholm, K. (2018) 'The Greening of the Pulp and Paper Industry: Sweden in Comparative Perspective'. In T. Särkkä, M. Gutiérrez-Poch & M. Kuhlberg, eds, *Technological Transformation in the Global Pulp and Paper Industry 1800–2018: Comparative Perspectives*. World Forests 23. Springer, Dordrecht, 65–90.

Bloom, J. M. (2017) 'Papermaking: The Historical Diffusion of an Ancient Technique'. In J. Heike, P. Meusburger & M. Heffernan, eds, *Mobilities of Knowledge*. Knowledge and Space 10. Springer, Cham, 51–66.

Blum, A. (1934) *On the Origin of Paper*. Transl. from the French by Harry Miller Lydenberg, R. R. Bowker Company, New York.

Branco, A. & Neves, P. (2018) 'From Backward to Modern: The Adoption of Technology by the Pulp Industry in Portugal, 1891–2015'. In T. Särkkä, M. Gutiérrez-Poch & M. Kuhlberg, eds, *Technological Transformation in the Global Pulp and Paper Industry 1800–2018: Comparative Perspectives*. World Forests 23. Springer, Dordrecht, 111–132.

Bullock, W. B. (1933) *The Romance of Paper*. The Gorham Press, Boston, MA.

Clapperton, R. H. (1967) *The Paper-Making Machine: Its Invention, Evolution and Development*, Pergamon, Oxford.

Cormack, A. A. (1933) *Our Ancient and Honourable Craft. Being an Account of the Rise and Development of Paper-Making in Scotland, and at Culter, Aberdeenshire, in Particular*. Reprinted from *The Paper Market*. Loxley Bros, London.

Cross, C. F. (1916) 'Wood Pulps for Paper-Making'. *Nature*, 97, 2419, 35–37.

Cross, C. F. & Bevan, E. J. (1907) *A Text-Book of Paper-Making*. 3rd ed. E. & F. N. Spon, London; Spon & Chamberlain, New York.

Dadswell, G. (2018) 'Making Paper in Australia: Developing the Technology to Create a National Industry, 1818–1928'. In T. Särkkä, M. Gutiérrez-Poch & M. Kuhlberg, eds, *Technological Transformation in the Global Pulp and Paper Industry 1800–2018: Comparative Perspectives*. World Forests 23. Springer, Dordrecht, 217–236.

Dodge, C. R. (1897) *A Descriptive Catalogue of Useful Fibre Plants of the World*. Report No. 9. U.S. Department of Agriculture. Fiber Investigations. Government Printing Office, Washington, DC.

FAO. (1954) *Wood Pulp and Paper Resources and Prospects*. A survey prepared by the Food and Agriculture Organization in co-operation with the secretariats of the United Nations Educational, Scientific and Cultural Organization (UNESCO); the Economic Commission for Europe (ECE); and the Economic Commission for Latin America (ECLA). AO, New York.

FAO. (1961) *World Demand for Paper to 1975: A Study of Regional Trends*. FAO, Rome.

32 The political economy of raw materials

FAO. (1964) *European Timber Tends and Prospects. A New Appraisal 1950–1975.* FAO, New York.

FAO. (2018) *Global Forest Products. Facts and Figures 2018.* Available at http://www.fao.org/3/ca7415en/ca7415en.pdf. Accessed 15 July 2020.

The Finnish Sawmilling, Pulp and Paper Industries (1936) Central Association of Finnish Wood-Working Industries, Helsinki.

Forestry and Forest Products World Situation 1937–1946 (1948) Stockholms Bokindustri Aktiebolag, Stockholm.

Green, T. (1963) *Yates Duxbury & Sons, Papermakers of Bury 1863–1963.* Newman Neame, London.

Gullichsen, J. (2000) 'Introduction'. In J. Gullichsen & C.-J. Fogelholm, eds, *Chemical Pulping. Paper-Making Science and Technology.* Book 6A. Finnish Paper Engineers' Association; TAPPI, Helsinki, 14–16.

Heller, J. (1978) *Paper-Making.* Watson-Guptill Publications, New York.

Herring, R. (1855) *Paper & Paper Making, Ancient and Modern.* Longman, Brown, Green, and Longmans, London.

Hiley, W. E. (1930) *The Economics of Forestry.* Oxford Manuals of Forestry. The Clarendon Press, Oxford.

Hölzl, R. & Oosthoek, K. J. (2018) 'Introduction: State Forestry in Northern Europe'. In K. J. Oosthoek & R. Hölzl, eds, *Managing Northern Europe's Forests. Histories from the Age of Improvement to the Age of Ecology.* The Environment History: International Perspectives 12. Berghahn, New York and Oxford, 1–13.

Hunter, D. (1947) *Papermaking. The History & Technique of an Ancient Tradition.* 2nd ed. Alfred A. Knopf, New York.

Järvinen, J., Ojala, J., Melander, A. & Lamberg, J.-A. (2012) 'The Evolution of Pulp and Paper Industries in Finland, Sweden and Norway 1800–2005'. In J.-A. Lamberg, J. Ojala, M. Peltoniemi & T. Särkkä, eds, *The Evolution of Global Paper Industry 1800–2050: A Comparative Analysis.* World Forests 17. Springer, Dordrecht, 19–48.

Jeffreys, R. B. (1965) 'Pulp and Paper Making from Eucalyptus in Australia'. In *Pulp and Paper Prospects in Latin America.* Report on the Latin American Meeting of the Experts of the Pulp and Paper Industry. Second part: Working papers submitted to the Meeting. FAO, United Nations, 240–248.

King, N. L. (1965) 'South African Experience in Planting of Exotic Species'. In *Pulp and Paper Prospects in Latin America.* Report on the Latin American Meeting of the Experts of the Pulp and Paper Industry. Second part: Workin papers submitted to the Meeting. FAO, United Nations, 235–238.

Kuhlberg, M. (2012) 'An Accomplished History, An Uncertain Future: Canada's Pulp and Paper Industry since the Early 1800s'. In J.-A. Lamberg, J. Ojala, M. Peltoniemi & T. Särkkä, eds, *The Evolution of Global Paper Industry 1800–2050: A Comparative Analysis.* World Forests 17. Springer, Dordrecht, 101–134.

Kuhlberg, M. (2015) *In the Power of the Government: The Rise and Fall of Newsprint in Ontario, 1894–1932.* University of Toronto Press, Toronto.

Kunisaki, J. (1948 [1798]) *A Handy Guide to Papermaking (Kamisuki Chohoki).* Book Arts Club, Berkeley.

Kurlansky, M. (2017) *Paper. Paging Through History.* W. W. Norton & Company, New York and London.

Kurosawa, T. & Hashino, T. (2012) 'From the Non-European Tradition to a Variation on the Japanese Competitiveness Model: The Modern Japanese Paper Industry since the 1870s'. In J.-A. Lamberg, J. Ojala, M. Peltoniemi & T. Särkkä, eds, *The Evolution of the Global Paper Industry 1800–2050: A Comparative Analysis*. World Forests 17. Springer, Dordrecht, 135–166.

Kurosawa, T. & Hashino, T. (2017) 'Three Markets and Three Types of Competitiveness: Pulp and Paper Industry'. In B. Bouwens, P.-Y. Donzé & T. Kurosawa, eds, *Industries and Global Competition. A History of Business Beyond Borders*. Routledge, Abingdon and New York, 235–259.

Lamberg, J.-A., Ojala, J., Peltoniemi, M. & Särkkä, T., eds (2012a) *The Evolution of Global Paper Industry 1800–2050: A Comparative Analysis*. World Forests 17. Springer, Dordrecht.

Lamberg, J.-A., Ojala, J., Peltoniemi, M. & Särkkä, T. (2012b) 'Research on the Evolution and the Global History of Pulp and Paper Industry: An Introduction'. In J.-A. Lamberg, J. Ojala, M. Peltoniemi & T. Särkkä, eds, *The Evolution of Global Paper Industry 1800–2050: A Comparative Analysis*. World Forests 17. Springer, Dordrecht, 1–18.

Lima-Toivanen, M. B. (2012) 'The South American Pulp and Paper Industry: The Cases Brazil, Chile, and Uruguay'. In J.-A. Lamberg, J. Ojala, M. Peltoniemi & T. Särkkä, eds, *The Evolution of Global Paper Industry 1800–2050: A Comparative Analysis*. World Forests 17. Springer, Dordrecht, 243–284.

Maddox, H. A. (1922) *Paper. Its History, Sources, and Manufacture*. Pitman's Common Commodities and Industries. Sir Isaac Pitman & Sons, Ltd., Bath, New York and Melbourne.

Müller, L. (2014) *White Magic. The Age of Paper*. Transl. from the German by Jessica Spengler. Polity, Malden, MA.

Nara Palace Site Museum (2017) Excavation Site Exhibition Hall, Nara.

Norris, F. H. (1952) *Paper and Paper Making*. Oxford University Press, London, New York, Toronto.

Papermaking. (1968) *Art and Craft*. An account delivered from the exhibition presented in the Library of Congress, Washington D.C. and opened on April 21, 1968. Library of Congress, Washington, DC.

The Paper Trail (2013) Frogmore Mill.

Perkins, P. D. (1940) *The Paper Industry and Printing in Japan*. Japanese Reference Library, New York.

Peteri, R. (1952) 'Pulping Studies with African tropical Woods'. In *Tropical Woods and Agricultural Residues as Sources of Pulp*. Papers Presented at the Fifth Meeting of the FAO Technical Committee on Wood Chemistry, Appleton, Wisconsin, USA. September 1951. FAO Forestry and Forest Product Studies. FAO, Rome, 43–50.

Podder, V. (1979) *Paper Industry in India. A Study*. Oxford & IBH Publishing Co., New Delhi, Bombay and Calcutta.

Pomilio Corporation Limited to Imperial Institute. (24 January 1939) *AY4/2286, Paper Pulp from Bamboo: Details of the Raitt Process. Tropical Products Institute and Predecessors*. The National Archives, Kew.

Roche, M. (2018) 'Technology Transfer and Local Innovation: Pulp and Paper Manufacturing in New Zealand, c.1860 to c.1960'. In T. Särkkä, M. Gutiérrez-Poch & M. Kuhlberg, eds, *Technological Transformation in the Global Pulp and Paper Industry 1800–2018: Comparative Perspectives*. World Forests 23. Springer, Dordrecht, 189–216.

Salvatore, E. (1942) 'Pomilio Continuous Alkali-Chlorine Process'. *Sen-iso Kyo*, 18, 12, 12–19.

34   *The political economy of raw materials*

Särkkä, T., Gutiérrez-Poch, M. & Kuhlberg, M. (2018). 'Technological Transformation in the Global Pulp and Paper Industry: Introduction'. In T. Särkkä, M. Gutiérrez-Poch & M. Kuhlberg, eds, *Technological Transformation in the Global Pulp and Paper Industry 1800–2018: Comparative Perspectives*. World Forests 23. Springer, Dordrecht, 1–10.

Savur, M. (2003) *And the Bamboo Flowers in the Indian Forests. What Did the Pulp and Paper Industry Do?* Vols. I–II. Manohar, Delhi.

Species of Wood Used in Various Processes in Making Paper Pulp (20 March 1937) *AY4/2303, Pinus radiata Wood in South Australia: Paper Pulp Production*. Tropical Products Institute and Predecessors. The National Archives, Kew.

Sundholm, J. (1999) 'History of Mechanical Pulping'. In J. Sundholm, ed, *Mechanical Pulping*. Fapet Oy, Helsinki, 22–33.

Sutermeister, E. (1962[1954]) *The Story of Papermaking*. 2nd printing. R. R. Bowker Company, New York.

Toivanen, H. (2012) 'Waves of Technological Innovation: The Evolution of the US Pulp and Paper Industry, 1860–2000'. In J.-A. Lamberg, J. Ojala, M. Peltoniemi & T. Särkkä, eds, *The Evolution of Global Paper Industry 1800–2050: A Comparative Analysis*. World Forests 17. Springer, Dordrecht, 49–80.

Weatherill, L. (1974) *One Hundred Years of Papermaking. An Illustrated History of the Guard Bridge Paper Company Ltd. 1875–1975*. Guard Bridge Paper Company Ltd., Fife, Scotland.

Weber, T. (2007) *The Language of Paper. A History of 2000 Years*. Orchid Press, Bangkok.

3   The esparto grass trade

The introduction of esparto grass, which constitutes two perennial grasses both endemic to the Western Mediterranean, to the British paper trade in the 1850s offered the first viable solution to the raw material shortage in Britain. Up to the end of the 1950s, as much as 350,000 tons of esparto grass was exported from Southern Spain and North Africa annually to Britain for the manufacture of high-class book and printing paper. Despite being an excellent papermaking material and plentifully available in places in North Africa, it was difficult to assure the continuity of esparto supply at a constant price. The First World War revealed the difficulty in obtaining esparto and Britain's vulnerability in terms of the supply of raw materials, and led to the developments connected to a quest for Empire-grown raw materials to tackle the problems of the lack of indigenous raw materials and the resulting dependence on foreign imports.

In the following, the esparto grass trade is discussed in five sections. The first briefly outlines the developments leading to the quest for a new raw material and the second introduction of esparto grass in the British paper industry. The third endeavours to trace the progress of the esparto grass from its place of growth in North Africa to finished products manufactured in paper mills in Britain. While they are not intended as a comprehensive technical treatise, the fourth and fifth sections outline the basic esparto paper manufacturing process in order to better appreciate the problems involved using esparto as a primary raw material in British mills.

The raw material problem

Since the late eighteenth century, large quantities of Indian and American cottons had been imported into Britain, and the refuse material from cotton mills formed the principal and almost sole source of fibre in British mills. Besides the waste from textile mills, other refuse materials such as thread, string, ropes, burlap, gunny bags, cotton linters, and waste paper were pulped. Raw fibres were but little used in paper manufacture, and only small quantities of cereal straws and cotton stalks were used in some grades of paper. Recycled fibres were preferred over raw fibres because the former had undergone the

36   *The esparto grass trade*

process of semi-manufacture, and therefore, this material could very easily be reduced by simple mechanical means to a mass of fine fibres, which interlaced and formed a continuous, immensely strong, even-textured web. Old garments were especially valued in paper manufacture because, having been exposed to sun and weather and repeatedly washed, all but the most highly resistant material had already been removed from them. Being essentially pure cellulose, it was possible to treat old garments in a very weak alkaline solution by digesting them for a relatively short period of time with little pressure, greatly reducing the need for chemicals and fuel and therefore keeping the costs of treatment low (Herring 1855, 49–55; Routledge 1875; Podder 1979, 92).

The production of handmade papers had been established to satisfy the local demand for paper, but improvements in papermaking technology and the building of a network of canals and railroads made it possible to produce greater quantities for wider markets. As far as refuse materials and cereal straws were concerned, the problem lay in their supply, which could not be assured. Ever faster, wider, and bigger paper units could not depend solely on the raw materials available in the domestic market – rags, waste paper, fabric cuttings, and cereal straws – so they needed to assure their fibre supply through foreign imports.

A growing population contributed directly to the rising domestic demand for paper. The census of 1801 shows that the population of the British Isles was 15 million, whereas 60 years later, it was nearly 29 million (Census records for England and Wales; Scotland; Ireland 1861). New patterns of social interactions, increased literacy, and heightened social consciousness also contributed to the increasing demand for paper. The expansion of education and literature of various kinds, the need for cheap newspapers and serial publications, the increased demand for writing paper for writing and manufacturing, and commercial purposes generally greatly stimulated domestic consumption. In addition, the growth of the industries of the Second Industrial Revolution increased the demand for papers of all kinds. The mechanisation of industry indirectly gave people and institutions more reason to need paper. The early growth of mass communication through new forms of cheap publications was made possible by mechanical printing and papermaking. The single factor that most contributed to the increased demand for paper was the demand generated by the London publishing industry. Penny and half-penny newspapers, journals, magazines, reviews, and cheap editions of books came within the reach of the very poorest members of society. Without paper manufacture, it would not have been possible to bring many of these cheap publications into existence (Coleman 1958, 210–211). To meet the increased demand, within less than 15 years from the abolition of the Customs and Excise duties in 1861, the annual production of paper had more than doubled. The improved productivity, wider markets, and the increased demand for papers meant that a sufficient supply of raw materials became essential to the industry.

The esparto grass trade   37

One of the most pressing problems faced by the British paper manufacturers was failure to supply enough rags to keep up with the increasing demand for paper, and this problem recurred at various times prior to 1861. There were two developments that helped to alleviate the pulp famine. The first was the continued expansion of the cotton textile industry in the nineteenth century and the second was the late seventeenth-century invention, the introduction of chlorine bleaching, which made coloured rags suitable for papermaking. In spite of these developments, Britain continued to need to import 20% of its total rag needs (15,000 tons p.a.) to meet the requirements of its paper industry. By the middle of the nineteenth century, rags were imported to Britain from various ports all over the world, especially from Hamburg. This was not a cost-efficient way to obtain papermaking materials, not only because of the high transport costs involved but also because many nations increased their existing export duties on rags. Owing to increased demand for paper and papermaking materials, the price of rags doubled between 1848 and 1855 (Spicer 1907, 32; Coleman 1958, 214, 338; Shorter 1971, 113–115, 139; Hills 1988, 128, 131; Magee 1997).

In the British paper trade, on average, about half of all running costs were accounted for by raw materials. So it was regarded as essential for the successful introduction of a substitute for rags that the substance should be cheap and available in abundance. In addition, it should be able to be rapidly cleansed and bleached and yield a strong, pliable fibre, which would produce paper possessed of permanent whiteness. Several British papermakers tried out elementary modern processes for separating cellulose from raw fibres. The first attempt, and one of the most important, was made by Matthias Koops, a papermaker from the Neckinger Mill in Bermondsey, London, who started to experiment with wood, straw, and other vegetable fibres as early as 1800 (Koops 1801), but only cereal straws proved to have any commercial value in Britain. Being an easily pulped and readily available material in many regions, the main technical advantage of straw was that pulping required little energy, so the need for fuel was low. In addition, since the cereals are rich in carbohydrates with a low lignin content, with only relatively little chemical consumption they provided a good yield. In terms of paper quality, the main disadvantage of straw as a papermaking material is that it is a short-fibred material, giving the paper it produces a low tear strength (Herring 1855, 55–56; Podder 1979, 60).

On the Continent, the production of pulp from cereal straws preceded the chemical pulping of woods on the industrial scale. In the Netherlands, it was found that winter wheat and rye have the highest mean lengths of fibres, and straw pulps were used for newsprint when expanding consumption demands exceeded the supply of rags then available (Muller 1952, 164–165, 169). In Britain, a sustained supply of straw proved difficult to assure, however, and therefore, the use of straw as a papermaking material remained marginal and temporary. Furthermore, paper mills in any case were usually situated within reasonable proximity to the markets and to the water supply and not close to

38   *The esparto grass trade*

straw-growing areas (where there was likely to be an excess over local farm requirements) (Hebbs 1952, 159). For those reasons, straw was substituted for other raw materials only during major global upheavals when raw material imports waned. Furthermore, since cereal straws are agricultural residues, their availability was conditioned by seasonal variations. Wide fluctuations could occur in straw production due to harvesting conditions. In addition, cereal straws were a liability because of their tendency to deteriorate while in storage. Owing to the consumption of straws for agricultural purposes, the continuity of supply at a constant price was difficult to assure. To economise on the use of straw, it was often pulped with rags. Cereal straws and straw pulp were imported to Britain from the Netherlands and Belgium up to the 1860s, when the commercial manufacture of paper from straw started to wane (Herring 1855, 55–56).

The introduction of esparto grass in the paper trade

The outbreak of the American Civil War, followed by the repeal of the Customs and Excise duties, threatened to cause a cotton famine in the British paper mills. It seemed evident that unless a new raw material suitable for papermaking was speedily introduced, the British paper trade would be seriously crippled. To address this problem, the House of Commons ordered a Select Committee Inquiry into the situation. In its report, the Committee directed its special attention to the possibility of identifying a new raw material which could be utilised directly without having to pass through the process of semi-manufacture (HC Deb 19 July 1864).

As it transpired, it was the introduction of esparto grass that offered the first viable solution to the raw material shortage in Britain. Esparto, two different types of perennial grasses, *Stipa tenacissima* and *Lygeum spartum*, which are both endemic to the Western Mediterranean, constituted the generic papermaking raw material called 'esparto' (in French *sparte*). Esparto grass is indigenous to the sterile, rugged parts of Southern Spain and Portugal as well as to the dry sandy soil of North Africa, and particularly to the foothills of mountainous interior regions in Libya, Tunisia, Algeria, and Morocco. The grass grows in clumps grouped in bushy tufts, often in relatively dense formations in dry or semi-arid Mediterranean areas (with a rainfall between 200 and 400 mm/year), often in poorly developed soils on limestone, and at elevations from sea level up to 1,000 m. above it. The flower-bearing stem is perennial, while the leaves grow annually. The ripening of the new leaves occurs, depending on the habitat, in May or June (Fajardo et al. 2015).

The first papermaker in England who devoted his attention to the use of esparto leaves in the manufacture of paper was Thomas Routledge (1819–87). Having examined various exotics at the Royal Botanic Gardens, Kew, to determine their fibre-yielding potentials, Routledge rented Eynsham Mill, on the River Evenlode in Oxfordshire, where he began to experiment with esparto in 1854. For his initial cooking experiments, Routledge employed a Lancashire Bowling-Keir and a cylindrical boiler of the firm of Bryan Donkin. With these boilers, Routledge managed to reduce esparto into easy bleaching pulp of good yield when cooked with caustic. For the first cook, Routledge used caustic lye composed of soda or potash and lime. Then, the material was washed in a rotating vessel and boiled for a second time in a bath of carbonate of soda (washing soda), known commercially as soda ash. The drained and washed material was then reduced to 'half-stuff' in a beating engine. Next, the stuff was submitted twice to a beaching process and treated with acid. Finally, the material was thoroughly washed to remove any trace of the acid. The resulting product, 'bleached esparto half-stuff', could be made into paper or sold as such for other papermakers (Patent Letter to Thomas Routledge 31 July 1856).

There were two developments in the British paper and chemical industries that assisted Routledge's experiments with esparto. The first was the introduction of the soda process by Burgess and Watt (see Chap. 2), and the second was the increased demand for caustic soda by the textile industry that led to a boost in its production by chemical means (Reed 2016). What Routledge found at the Eynsham Mill was that the soda process could be used for treating esparto. After the introduction of the soda process for pulping, the comparative expense of chemically reducing raw fibres was no longer an obstacle to progress. Routledge patented his process on 31 July 1856, and in the following years, he frequently visited Spain, entering into contracts with grass harvesters for their produce. After being collected, dried like hay, sorted into different qualities, and baled, the grass was ready to be transported to Routledge's works, the Ford Paper Mills, which were situated at South Hylton, on the River Wear, near Sunderland. Up to 1861, Routledge himself was the only paper manufacturer who used esparto. But it did not take long before other British papermakers availed themselves of the new raw material. In 1863, the importation of esparto grass into Britain was about 18,000 tons, and the use of it was estimated to have caused an increased consumption of 4,000 tons per annum of soda ash and bleaching powders (Munsell 1876, 183). Except for the use of more chemicals, there was little cost difference in processing paper from esparto or from rags. Production of enough bleaching powder needed large quantities of chlorine, and the challenge was to find a way of using hydrochloric acid. A significant development took place in the 1860s, when the Weldon (1866–69) and the Deacon (1868–70) processes of bleaching were introduced. After the introduction of these two processes – the first generating hydrochloric acid from the acid towers and the latter from hydrogen chlorine gas – the comparative expense of bleaching raw fibres was no longer an obstacle to progress. The more economical production of chemicals greatly increased the power of production and diminished the cost of manufacturing esparto pulp (CNJIS, 24 December 1875, 299; see also Reed 2016).

British esparto imports rose to 50,800 tons in 1865, and by 1871, they were already 146,300 tons. This increased demand for esparto led to the rapid

40   *The esparto grass trade*

extinction of the Spanish grass, and consequently the demand not being met. In the 1870s, African esparto – which was known to the British paper trade as 'alfa', otherwise 'halfa', derived from the Arabic *halfa maboula* – was substituted for the Spanish imports. Most alfa imports came from Algeria, where the French Government had offered considerable monetary incentives and concessions to Societé Franco Algérienne to induce railway communication with the interior district, where the plant grew abundantly on the mountainous plateaus of Oran. 61,000 tons of alfa was imported into Britain from Algeria in 1874, but the difficulty of procuring labour and the cost of railway carriage added considerable transport costs to British mills. As a result, the price of esparto almost doubled between the early 1860s and 1875. The real cost of the finished paper was even higher because the value of alfa paper was proportionately lower in the market compared to paper made from Spanish esparto. The Spanish grass was described as having long, fine leaves of 12 or even 36 inches in length, while the leaves of the North African grass were smaller and stiffer (Routledge 1875, 15, 19–21, 37–38; Spicer 1907, 13–17, 35, 89–90; Shorter 1971, 141–142; Magee 1997, 118–127).

A new source of alfa supplies was introduced in 1871, when Messrs. Perry, Bury and Co. of Liverpool, then well-known cotton merchants in the Regency of Tunis, commenced exports from Susa (Sousse). Within a decade (by 1881), the British Paper Makers' Association estimated that the Tunisian exports from Susa and Sfax had climbed to 35,000 tons per annum. The combined Algerian and Tunisian alfa exports were estimated to be in the range of 70,000–80,000 tons per annum, which represented a cash value of the produce of £250,000 (The British Paper Makers' Association to Earl Granville, Her Majesty's Principal Secretary of State for Foreign Affairs 16 November 1881; 28 March 1882). Following the French invasion of the Regency in 1881, British merchants' monopoly over the Tunisian esparto trade was abolished by the Bey's Degree of 31 May 1881 (Reade, Thomas F., Consul General, to Earl Granville 22 March 1882). In its place, on 12 June 1881, the Bey of Tunis granted a Concession to the London-based Franco-English Tunisian Esparto Fibre Supply Co. Limited, which had a registered capital of £250,000. The Concession transferred the exclusive right to gather alfa in the mountainous districts of the Ourghemma El Ayacha, Bou Hedma, Heddedj, and Madjoura in the south of the Regency of Tunis and to construct a railway or tramway for the more commercial transport of the merchandise terminating at the Marsa Skira Port (La Skhira) on the Gulf of Gabés (Surtees, R. W., Secretary of Franco-English Tunisian Esparto Fibre Supply Co. Limited to Earl Granville 18 December 1883; Enclosures 13 and 14 June 1881). The concessionaire did not, however, manage to fulfil its obligations to supply a minimum of 30,000 tons of alfa annually, and the company lost its beneficial position with the Bey's Degree of Abrogation on 31 July 1887. In the same year, Tunisian exports of alfa dropped to 13,779 tons. The railway to the interior was not completed until 1902 in virtue of the profitable phosphor deposits found in the interior. Crossing all the major alfa districts, the railway facilitated the more cost-effective transport of much larger amounts of the raw material to Susa and Sfax (McQuarrie 1995, 217–218, 262).

The alfa exports from Tripoli commenced at the same time as those from Susa. Tripolitanian and alfa supplies ranged from nearly 34,000 tons per annum in 1884 to nearly 70,000 in 1888. The value of the merchandise was, however, lower than that from Algeria and Tunisia due to the inferior quality of Tripolitanian alfa (Tripoli of Barbary 1880, 258; McQuarrie 1995, 136–143, 230, 233–234). The exports reached their peak in 1888, with nearly 249,000 tons of esparto compared to 41,000 tons of rags (Routledge 1875, 15, 19–21, 37–38; Spicer 1907, 13–17, 35, 89–90; Shorter 1971, 141–142; McQuarrie 1995, 267–269; Magee 1997, 118–127).

Esparto harvesting and transporting

Esparto was picked by hand, and merely required pulling off the mature esparto leaves – called 'blades' – as near to the ground as possible, leaving the roots behind. These leaves, which could be from 12 to 36 inches long, were removed before the plant reached maturity and while the flower stem was still undeveloped. As the plant gets older, underground rhizomes develop round the edge and they gradually produce a ring structure. The ring then splits at various points and new tufts appear, new growth replacing the old (Esparto Paper 1956, 3). There was some self-seeding, but the conditions were not propitious for expansion through propagation from seed alone. The germination of the seeds takes place in the autumn, and the shoots emerge from the ground in the spring, but it can take up to 15 years until the stems have reached maturity (Messrs. Hawkin, Smalley & Co. to Imperial Institute 19 October 1927; McQuarrie 1995, 130). Being a wild grass, or, botanically speaking, a sedge, propagation from a seed was a slow, laborious, and, from the papermakers' point of view, costly process. Therefore, over-harvesting was a major concern for the esparto paper producers.

Local nomadic or semi-nomadic Arab communities did the harvesting work. The collecting fell to the women. After drying the material in the sun, the pickers tied the grass into small sheaves and gathered them into bundles which were carried on camels or donkeys to alfa yards for weighing and sale. Having weighed and sold the produce, the camel drivers were obliged to transport the material for sorting to the designated collection centres, where the grass was squeezed by hydraulic presses into bales, each weighing from 400 to 500 pounds, and bound by wire, hoop iron, or ropes made from the grass itself. Compression beyond a certain point had to be avoided, however, or the fibre could be badly damaged (Phillips 1915, 635). The bales were transported by rail to shipping stations on the North African coast, where they were loaded on to ocean-going ships. The most important shipping ports in Algeria were Oran, Philippeville (Skikda), Bona (Annaba), and Algiers. In Tunisia, they included Susa, Sfax, Gabés, and Tunis, while in Tripolitania, the sole shipping port was the portal town of Tripoli (Esparto Paper

42 The esparto grass trade

1956; 'Africa – Tripoli' 1871, 261). The principal esparto docks in Britain included those on the Wear (Sunderland), the Tyne (South Shields), and the Dee (Aberdeen) (Palgrave ed. 1894, 620).

The cost of transport and freight to the British markets was the single largest expense of esparto trade. Owing to the high bulk to weight ratio of esparto, vessels were able to carry only 40–48% of their registered tonnage. Export duties were only 1% *ad valorem* in Algeria and Tripolitania, but in Tunisia, duty represented 30–35% of the value of raw material until 1897, when the duties were lowered to the same level as in Algeria and Tripolitania (McQuarrie 1995, 235, 237–238, 255, 262). Esparto grass was imported into Britain in its raw state, which meant roughly 50% of the grass was waste (i.e. the pulp accounted for only half of the bulk of the esparto grass). The shipping of raw esparto was an economically viable method of transport because a large amount of coal was exported from the UK to Italian ports and esparto grass provided a convenient return freight. It was not therefore necessary to consider the question of converting the grass into 'half-stuff' (i.e. unbleached pulp) in situ with the object of saving freight costs, though the saving would have been considerable (Messrs. John Dickinson and Co. Limited, Croxley Mill, Hertfordshire to Imperial Institute 6 October 1916).

Towards the end of the twentieth century, the selling price of esparto in its raw state was coming under increasing pressure in the international market due to the increased availability of cheap wood pulp. From 1880 to 1898, the reported selling price declined from a high of £9 10s (the c.i.f. price of Spanish grass in 1880) to a low of £2 15s (the price of alfa in 1898) (McQuarrie 1995, 222–227). For many years after 1898, up to 1914, the price at the principal British ports was reported by Messrs. Ide & Christie, the Fibre, Esparto, and General Produce Brokers of London, to be constant, varying only from £3 10s to £3 to 15s per ton depending on the place of shipment in Britain (Ide & Christie's Monthly Circular 15 May 1917). During the interwar years, the price was in the order of £3 15s to £4 (Hebbs 1952, 155).

Esparto formed the mainstay of the British paper industry up to 1913, when 208,200 tons was supplied for her esparto mills. The outbreak of the First World War caused a violent disruption to the esparto trade owing to the long and perilous sea route and the lack of shipping capacity. In 1919, the volume of trade was only 29% (71,800 tons) of the pre-war level, but the esparto trade boomed again in the 1920s as the demand for paper products grew. From 1929 to 1939, the volume of trade was in a settled range between 300,000 and 350,000 tons annually. Exports from French Morocco substituted Tunisian exports to some extent after 1932, when the colonial government imposed an export duty of 10% *ad valorem* (W. M. Greenhalgh of Lyddon Co. Ltd. to Imperial Institute 28 April 1932).

The first mill outside the UK using esparto as a primary raw material commenced in Foggia, Italy, in mid-December 1938, producing 20 tons per day with the use of the Pomilio process (Pomilio Corporation Limited to Imperial Institute 24 January 1939). Spanish esparto grass, which had been imported into Britain in large quantities before 1939, assumed considerable importance in Spain during and after the Second World War when Spain could not import wood pulp (Esparto paper 1956, 3; Gutiérrez-Poch 2012, 220). In the UK, esparto supplies dwindled in the first months of the Second World War and entirely cut off after the fall of France in June 1940. The response to this situation was innovation and experimentation with alternative fibres to make new qualities of paper that were considered satisfactory for the wartime emergency. The most important substitute for esparto was straw, which purchased through The Papermakers Straw Trading Co. Ltd., which handled all straw supplies during the war. Up to 350,000 tons per annum was consumed, which equalled the amount of esparto imported before the war (Weatherill 1974, 95). Besides straw, waste paper also entered into the fibre furnish, representing approximately 25% of the total during the war (Sykes 1981, 294). Annual consumption of straw for pulping in the UK was 127,000 tons p.a. in 1941, 249,000 in 1942, 303,000 in 1943, 328,000 in 1944, and 346,000 in 1945. Straw continued to be used regularly after the war, until esparto supplies were fully established. In 1949, 360,624 tons of esparto was supplied compared to 186,000 tons of straw (Hebbs 1952, 156–157). The use of straw brought with it severe technical problems. Straw required substantially longer cooking than esparto, and at least half as much caustic soda, while yielding only 33% on the dry weight of the raw material, compared with 40–42% on grass. Straw was also bulkier than esparto, and its haulage to paper mills necessitated the use of extra equipment and labour, which were already depleted due to the wartime requirements (Weatherill 1974, 96). In 1949, esparto was available at an average price of £14 10s, or, say, £16 delivered in Britain. However, since then the price of esparto rose substantially, reaching an average of £33 per ton by the first half of 1951, with quotations between £45 and £50 per ton by 1952 compared to straw at about £7 per ton delivered. In spite of such a substantial price difference, straw remained relatively unattractive to the esparto mills because of decreased output of paper, increased fuel, and alkali consumption, and perhaps most important of all, esparto pulp had superior characteristics for the writing and printing paper grades which these mills were producing (Hebbs 1952, 158).

Papermaking in British esparto mills

In the interwar years (before 1939), there were 41 paper mills in Britain producing esparto pulp by the conventional pressure cooking method using caustic soda. The Association of Makers of Esparto Papers had 20 member companies, whose mills were distributed from the south-west coast of England to the north-east coast of Scotland and often still occupied the same sites where they had been initially established – on the banks of rushing rivers or streams and at close proximity to major conurbations. These mills naturally varied in size, but with the arithmetic mean at no more than 7,000 tons of grass per mill per annum or producing about 3,000 tons of pulp (Hebbs 1952,

44   *The esparto grass trade*

155), it will be realised in Chap. 7 that the capacity of the average esparto mill was very small by the standard wood pulp capacities of the time.

The situation was still largely unchanged up to the beginning of the 1950s. In 1951, there were 282 mills in Britain producing paper and board (CP 1955). The vast majority of the British paper mills delivered their raw material in rough sheet form and operated only the machinery of a paper mill. Leaving out the three strawboard mills, 54 of the 279 paper mills were equipped with some kind of pulping capability. Only two were specially equipped for operating pulping machinery to yield cellulose from wood by using the sulphite process. The remaining 40 or so mills specialised in pulping esparto and also straw, which continued to supplement the raw material base of British mills some years after the war. Seven largest pulp mills produced just over 100,000 tons of pulp per annum between them (Hebbs 1952, 155–156).

The esparto mills were distinctive in Britain in that each of them was in fact an integrated pulp and paper mill. The first of these isolated the vegetable fibres from their natural encrusting matter through a suitable combination of mechanical and chemical means. The second felted the fibres together to an even-textured web and then subjected the web to various finishing processes that rendered the paper suitable for delivery to printers or for other specific purposes. As papermaking is an ancient craft, the esparto mill employees – Engineers, Machinemen, Beatermen, Men at the Edge Runner, Men at the Disintegrator, Sizemen, Reelers, Cutters, Finishers, Packers, and Sorters – still regarded themselves as craftsmen rather than factory workers.

Although research and development work made tremendous improvements in production techniques possible over time, the esparto papermaking process itself did not change in its essentials since Thomas Routledge first patented his invention in 1856. However, over the course of a century of esparto papermaking in Britain, research and development work as well as production control in accordance with modern scientific methods and usage of modern technology were applied throughout the whole series of processes in papermaking. Even if small by wood pulp mill standards, the typical esparto mill of 1956 was a self-contained unit with heavy demands for supplies of raw material, water, coal, and chemicals. In 1956, it was estimated that the average esparto mill consumed annually as much water as a community of 15,000–20,000 inhabitants. In terms of fuel, the average esparto mill consumed two and a half tons of coal for every ton of esparto paper produced. Fuel was needed for pumping raw material, water, and chemicals from process to process and within the processes themselves, and it was needed too for the chemical recovery plant. Esparto mills habitually had their own power plants comprising a battery of water tube steam boilers to generate steam for chemical processing and large turbo-generators to produce electricity for driving the heavy machinery (Esparto Paper 1956).

Esparto grass was received at the mills in the same form as it had been shipped, in bales, weighing, from 400 to 500 pounds each, and composed of a large number of sheaves. Dusting the raw esparto was the first process in the conversion of the raw esparto grass into pulp. The bales were burst and the sheaves fed to a duster where, by means of vacuum, the sand and the dust were removed. The purpose of the process was to separate the grass from any extraneous impurities and from surface dust, and to collect the dust. The dust was extracted and used as an ingredient in various types of polishes and wax mixtures with either montan or paraffin for making carbon-paper ink (Esparto Paper 1956). The dusted esparto grass was originally taken to the boilers by a conveyor belt, but in the 1890s, the belt was replaced by a system of blown air to transfer the grass to the tops of boilers (Weatherill 1974, 19).

The basic chemical treatment esparto received – i.e. cooking the grass with caustic soda in a grass boiler or 'digester' at a high temperature and under pressure for some hours – did not vary in essence during the 100 years of the esparto grass trade. Two-and-a-half to five tons of esparto was boiled in one batch with 13–15% of caustic soda (NaOH on its air-dry weight) in a Sinclair grass boiler. Steam was required for the digestion, which lasted from two-and-a-half to five hours depending upon the amount of pressure and caustic soda used. After the cooking or digesting was finished, the runoff soda was recovered for the next cook in a recovery plant, where most of the caustic soda used in the boiling grass or rags was recovered for further use, reducing the costs of boiling as well as dealing with the disposal of effluent (Weatherill 1974, 21). The successful application of evaporators and recovery furnaces and the economic reuse of expensive chemicals were essential by the early 1950s, when the greater part of the caustic soda used in the grass boiling process was being recovered. In 1952, the recovery rate of soda averaged 78% (Hebbs 1952, 156). While the recovery process was a vital factor in the economic operation of an esparto plant, it was also an indispensable asset in the prevention of river pollution. Another benefit of soda recovery was that it did not involve the extremely disagreeable odours caused by the organic sulphur compounds, such as was typical of the sulphate wood pulp digestion process (Esparto Paper 1956, 4).

The brownish green esparto pulp was washed with copious supplies of fresh water and discharged for further cleansing. Then, the esparto pulp passed over sand traps and through slowly circulating slotted strainers leaving grit and coarser particles behind. Before bleaching, the sulphite pulp sheets were broken up by various mechanical means and with water to a suitable consistency so they could then be blended in the desired proportion with the washed esparto pulp. The pulp was mixed with a solution of calcium hypochlorite, made at the mill from milk of lime and chlorine. After passing through a series of bleaching towers for several hours, the pulp emerged bleached to a creamy tinge. Variations of the process such as carrying out part of the bleaching by the use of chlorine in a similar manner as in wood pulp bleaching were also tried from time to time, but owing to the absence of lignin, chlorine bleaching was not widely adopted in esparto mills (Esparto Paper 1956, 5).

46   *The esparto grass trade*

In the condition of combined 'half-stuff', the two fibres were relatively stiff, and before they could be made into a satisfactory sheet of paper, they required further modification. This was done in the beater house, which was the heart of an esparto mill. The minute fibres of cellulose were beaten in Hollander beaters and refined in refiners which could be used separately or in combination. The beating and refining processes ensured the length and flexibility of the fibre according to the type of paper required. During these processes, China clay, otherwise known as kaolin (derived from the Chinese village Gaoling), was added to the pulp for 'loading' – helping to close the interstices between the fibres to produce a more heterogeneous surface in the paper; rosin size was added for 'sizing' – regulating the rate at which paper absorbs water or ink; and dyes and certain chemicals were also added. After a final mixing and straining in machine drum strainers to filter out impurities from the pulp, esparto was in a state of virtually pure cellulose and so was ready to flow forward to the paper machine. In its passage from beater to paper machine the slurry of fibres, the 'stock' will be passed through a consistency regulator, where water is added and the fibre content is reduced to about 1% (Esparto Paper 1956, 6–9).

The commonest type of paper machine used was the Fourdrinier of which there were many varieties, depending on the type of paper to be made. Their output varied from eight tons per hour in the case of the 260-inch wide newsprint machine running at 1,500 ft. per minute, to a few cwt. produced by the small machines using the highest class of esparto or rag papers. In both, however, the principle was the same (Clapperton 1967). The Fourdrinier consisted of several sections, but essentially, it was divided into a 'wet end' and a 'dry end'. The wet end was centred about the 'endless wire' – a continuous moving belt of bronze wire mesh gauze supported by a frame on which the sheet was formed. To achieve good formation, the stock had to be delivered on to the wire at approximately the same speed as the belt was travelling. The fibres settled quickly so a lateral shaking motion was applied to the wire frame, so that the fibres on the wire were properly felted into a web of randomly interwoven sheet of fibres. The sheet now had a mirror-like appearance. As the wire carried the stock along, automatic devices for creating suction drew the water steadily out of the material. The sheet was then sufficiently strong to bridge the gap of a few inches as it passed to the first woollen wet felt, no longer as pulp but paper. Along felts and a series of press rolls, which removed further water and progressively consolidated the sheet, the paper passed to the first press section of steam-headed drying cylinders, where the sheet was then dried and 'calendered' between chilled calender bowls. This compacted the sheet still further, creating a glossy finish as required. Finally, the paper was reeled up ready for cutting, examining, counting, bundling, and despatching (Esparto Paper 1956, 10–11).

A substantial part of esparto paper was sold in a sheet form. Paper was first split lengthwise and then chopper crosswise in a paper cutter and finally collected in stacks. In the finishing house, otherwise *salle*, a well-lit, large room, paper was inspected sheet by sheet, requiring a considerable number of the typical esparto mill's employees to be engaged in 'overhauling' or 'sorting' the finished paper. Paper was then counted into reams of 500 sheets or half reams of 250 sheets and cut down in the guillotine to smaller sizes. The final processes of packing the paper into bales of 20 reams and labelling it with the manufacturer's brand were done prior to despatch.

In 1956, 200,000 tons of esparto paper was manufactured in the esparto mills, much of it for export overseas. This amount, which represented, very roughly, 8% of the total make of paper and board in Britain (CP 1955), highlights the fact that esparto paper was a speciality product for quality printing finish. Books and magazines printed on esparto paper tended to be found at the top end of the price range and were normally lavishly illustrated with lithographs, for which the esparto paper was admirably suited. Seminal works printed on esparto paper included, for instance, Winston Churchill's history of the First World War, *The World Crisis* (1923–31), the first English edition of which was published by Thornton Butterworth Limited as a '5- in-6 volumes' set with navy cloth blocked blind on the cover. It is regarded by many connoisseurs of Churchill and knowledgeable booksellers as a pinnacle of his published works. Equally lavish was *The Times Atlas of the World. Mid-Century Edition* (1955–59), issued by The Times Publishing Company Limited in a five-volume set of 19" by 12" elephant folio atlases with 120 plates in eight colours and over 200,000 names. It is also a testament to the quality of esparto paper that many of the high-quality reprints of such classics as Charles Darwin's *On the Origin of Species* and Axel Munthe's *The Story of San Michele* were habitually printed on esparto up to the 1950s. Other books typically printed on esparto paper included travelogues of notable individuals such as *The Ascent of Everest* (1953) by Colonel John Hunt, the leader of the famed 1953 British Mount Everest Expedition, whose account of the first ascent of Mount Everest by Sir Edmund Hillary and Sherpa Tenzing Norgay was first published by Hodder and Stoughton.

Esparto – the fibre and the medium

British cellulose experts examined and tested the esparto fibre in numerous laboratory and service tests to better understand its inherent characteristics. In its report, dated 1 July 1910, Olive & Partington Limited, Turn Lee Mills, Glossop described the ultimate fibre as short, cylindrical, and tapering to a point at both ends. The length of the fibre was reported to be from 0.012 to 0.12 inch, the average being 0.045 inch (Olive & Partington Limited to Professor Wyndham R. Dunstan, the Director, Imperial Institute 1 June 1910). These characteristics of the fibre contributed to the quality of the esparto paper. A well-beaten sheet was closely woven and could be relied on to take an excellent finish without undue pressure and consequent loss of bulk. The paper had a velvety finish and even texture, with a feel of considerable softness, elasticity, and firmness. Moreover, esparto paper

48   *The esparto grass trade*

had a very considerable inherent resistance to changes in atmospheric humidity. All machine-made paper tended to shrink in width and stretched in the direction of flow during the passage over the different sections of the papermaking machine, but, other things being equal, an esparto finish was less affected than other pulp qualities. This high degree of dimensional stability was a factor of great importance to the printers of Britain due to the rapidly fluctuating atmospheric humidity in the country. It ensured that the paper did not tend to become wavy or to stretch before or during printing. Thus, the competitive advantage of costly esparto paper lay in its bulk, opacity, dimensional stability, absorbency, but perhaps above and beyond everything else, printability – a crucial feature for printing paper due to the popularity of lithographs for book and magazine illustrations (Esparto Paper 1956).

From the wartime experience of straw pulping for papermaking, it was recognised that the use of straw involved a higher alkali and fuel consumption than esparto pulping for the following reasons: (a) straw is relatively more bulky than esparto so that a five-ton grass boiler could be charged with only three tons of uncut straw; (b) while esparto could be cooked by adding 13–15% of caustic soda on its weight, cereal straws required 22–25%; (c) the yield of cellulose from straw was not more than 33–35% on unbleached air-dry grass as compared with 42–45% from esparto; (d) because straw pulps tended to be relatively wet and slow draining compared with esparto, less liquor could be removed from the digesters. Surveys made during wartime showed that the alkali recovery was averaging no more than 46% in mills processing straw compared with 78% recovery when pulping esparto. The alternative approach was the production of high-yield pulps using relatively low concentrations of alkali and without a recovery plant. Several such straw pulping plants were started during the war years and were still running, the bulk of the straw being pulped in Britain, at the beginning of the 1950s. The waste liquor from such processing resulted in a very substantial increase in Biochemical Oxygen Demand (BOD) effluents (Hebbs 1952, 157–159). The BOD discharges were the reasons for the death of fish and caused severe damage to the river ecosystem (Bergquist & Söderholm 2018, 68), making pulping straw an unattractive substitute for chemical wood pulp deliveries in time.

Esparto fibre had more advantages over the numerous other exotic plants examined by the Imperial Institute in comparison with it. Firstly, the small thickness of the fibre offered little resistance to liquid penetration, thereby improving the paper's ink absorbency when used for printing. Secondly, the structure of the plant, without knots or seed heads, gave a uniform pulp, which imparted an even texture to the finished product. Thirdly, the chemical composition of the plant made the isolation of the fibres from their natural encrusting matter possible at low steam pressures, or even at atmospheric pressure, improving the fuel efficiency of the pulping process. Finally, the yield of esparto was found to be habitually higher (it varies from 42 to 45% on unbleached air-dry grass to even 50–58% on the absolutely dry grass) than with most other exotic plants tested (Olive & Partington Limited to Professor Wyndham R. Dunstan, the Director, Imperial Institute, 1 June 1910; Hebbs 1952; Esparto Paper 1956).

The main disadvantage of esparto (as it was the case with straw) was that it lacked the necessary tearing resistance and foldability of the sheet owing to its short fibre. This was why esparto pulp was normally blended with coniferous sulphite or sulphate wood pulp to meet these specifications. It was therefore not possible to substitute the chemical wood pulp imports entirely with esparto. The drastic increase in the price of esparto in the 1950s affected the rapid development of the reversion to other imported raw materials. The last British esparto mills were closed down in the 1960s as the companies could not operate economically and the producers lost faith in their viability in the business environment (Hills 1988, 142).

Conclusions

The story of a 100 years of esparto papermaking tends to have a romantic tenor. We have seen how the resourcefulness and persistence of Thomas Routledge enabled high-grade paper to be made from esparto in the 1850s, just before wood pulp begun to dominate the world of papermaking. It might have been thought that the vast scale of the coniferous wood resources of Canada and Scandinavia released for papermaking purposes so soon afterwards would have ousted esparto completely. That this did not in fact occur was largely due to the inherent characteristics of the esparto fibre, capable of producing paper that offered competitive advantages to the ever-increasing printing industry (Esparto Paper 1956).

Esparto was the mainstay of the British paper industry for a century, offering her the only genuine alternative to wood pulp. In spite of its supplementary role, esparto managed to fortify its position as the raw material of choice for quality printing paper. The use of esparto as a raw material was a distinctive feature of the British paper industry, so esparto – the fibre and the medium – was the yardstick by which other raw materials and their papermaking qualities were measured. To enter the British market, any raw material had to be equal to esparto in terms of quality and price in order to be considered as a real alternative. No matter how low the cost of harvesting a cheaper raw material was, for there to be profit for the producer after the cost and charges for converting it into stock and transporting to Britain, the price ended up as high, or nearly as high, as the price of esparto. The importers had been prepared to sell their stock as cheaply, or nearly as cheaply, as esparto, and the buyers also had to have the inducement of superior quality. It will be seen in Chap. 6 that these requirements proved very difficult to assure in colonial contexts.

50   *The esparto grass trade*

References

Bergquist, A.-K. & Söderholm, K. (2018) 'The Greening of the Pulp and Paper Industry: Sweden in Comparative Perspective'. In T. Särkkä, M. Gutiérrez-Poch & M. Kuhlberg, eds, *Technological Transformation in the Global Pulp and Paper Industry 1800–2018: Comparative Perspectives*. World Forests 23. Springer, Dordrecht, 65–90.

The British Paper Makers' Association to Earl Granville, Her Majesty's Principal Secretary of State for Foreign Affairs (16 November 1881; 28 March 1882) *FO 102/158, Claim of Esparto Fibre Company (1881–1884)*. The National Archives, Kew.

Census Records for England and Wales; Scotland; Ireland (1861) *The Online Historical Population Records (Histpop)*. Available at http://www.histpop.org/ohpr/servlet/. Accessed 26 June 2020.

The Chemical News and the Journal of Industrial Science (CNJIS) (24 December 1875), 32, 839, 299.

Churchill, W. (1923–31) *The World Crisis*. Vols. I–V. Thornton Butterworth, London.

Clapperton, R. H. (1967) *The Paper-Making Machine: Its Invention, Evolution and Development*. Pergamon, Oxford.

Coleman, D. C. (1958) *The British Paper Industry, 1495–1860*. Clarendon Press, Oxford.

Dictionary of Political Economy (1894) R. H. Inglis Palgrave, ed, Palgrave Macmillan, London.

Enclosures (13 and 14 June 1881) *FO 102/158, Claim of Esparto Fibre Company (1881–1884)*. The National Archives, Kew.

Esparto Paper (1956) The Association of Makers of Esparto Papers, London.

Fajardo, J., Verde, A., Rivera, D., Obón, C. & Leopold, S. (2015) 'Traditional Craft Techniques of Esparto Grass (*Stipa tenacissima L.*) in Spain'. *Economic Botany*, XX, X, 1–7.

Gutiérrez-Poch, M. (2012) 'Is There a Southern European Model? Development of the Pulp and Paper Industry in Italy, Spain and Portugal (1800–2010)'. In J.-A. Lamberg, J. Ojala, M. Peltoniemi & T. Särkkä, eds, *The Evolution of the Global Paper Industry 1800–2050: A Comparative Analysis*. World Forests 17. Springer, Dordrecht, 211–242.

HC Deb (19 July 1864) vol 176 cc1711–49. *Report from the Select Committee of Paper (Export Duty on Rags)*. Available at https://api.parliament.uk/historic-hansard/index.html. Accessed 27 July 2020.

Hebbs, L. G. S. (1952) 'Cereal Straw Pulping in the United Kingdom'. In *Tropical Woods and Agricultural Residues as Sources of Pulp*. Papers Presented at the Fifth Meeting of the FAO Technical Committee on Wood Chemistry, Appleton, WI. September 1951. FAO Forestry and Forest Product Studies. FAO, Rome, 155–161.

Herring, R. (1855) *Paper & Paper Making, Ancient and Modern*. Longman, Brown, Green, and Longmans, London.

Hills, R. L. (1988) *Papermaking in Britain 1488–1988. A Short History*. Athlone Press, London and Atlantic Highlands, NJ.

Hunt, J. (1953) *The Ascent of Everest*. Hodder and Stoughton, London.

Ide & Christie's Monthly Circular (15 May 1917) *AY4/2197, Paper Pulp Industry. Uganda. Elephant Grass*. Tropical Products Institute and Predecessors. The National Archives, Kew.

Koops, M. (1801) *Historical Account of the Substances Which Have Been Used to Describe Events, and to Convey Ideas, from the Earliest Date to the Invention of Paper*. Jaques and Co., London.

Magee, G. (1997) *Productivity and Performance in the Paper Industry. Labour, Capital, and Technology in Britain and America, 1860–1914.* Cambridge Studies in Modern Economic History 4. Cambridge University Press, Cambridge.

McQuarrie, G. (1995) *European Influence and Tribal Society in Tunisia during the Nineteenth Century: The Origins and Impact of the Trade in Esparto Grass 1870–1940*, unpublished PhD thesis. Department of Geography, University of Durham.

Messrs. Hawkin, Smalley & Co. to Imperial Institute (19 October 1927) *AY4/2243, Materials: Empire Sources of Supply.* Tropical Products Institute and Predecessors. The National Archives, Kew.

Messrs. John Dickinson and Co. Limited, Croxley Mill, Hertfordshire to Imperial Institute (6 October 1916) *AY4/2197, Paper Pulp Industry. Uganda. Elephant Grass.* Tropical Products Institute and Predecessors. The National Archives, Kew.

Muller, F. M. (1952) 'Developments in Straw Pulping in the Netherlands'. In *Tropical Woods and Agricultural Residues as Sources of Pulp*. Papers Presented at the Fifth Meeting of the FAO Technical Committee on Wood Chemistry, Appleton, WI. September 1951. FAO Forestry and Forest Product Studies. FAO, Rome, 162–169.

Munsell, J. (1876) *Chronology of the Origin and Progress of Paper and Paper-Making*. 5th ed. J. Munsell, Albany, NY.

Mokyr, J. (1990) *The Lever of Riches. Technological Creativity and Economic Progress.* Oxford University Press, Oxford.

Olive & Partington Limited to Professor Wyndham R. Dunstan, Director, Imperial Institute (1 June 1910) *AY4/2196, Bromelia Leaves for Paper Making.* Tropical Products Institute and Predecessors. The National Archives, Kew.

Patent Letter to Thomas Routledge (31 July 1856) *British Patent 1816.* The British Library, London.

Phillips, S. C. (1915) 'The Empire's Resources in Paper-Making Materials'. *Journal of the Royal Society of Arts*, XLIII, 3261, 613–636.

Podder, V. (1979) *Paper Industry in India. A Study.* Oxford & IBH Publishing Co., New Delhi, Bombay and Calcutta.

Pomilio Corporation Limited to Imperial Institute (24 January 1939) *AY 4/2286, Paper Pulp from Bamboo: Details of the Raitt Process.* Tropical Products Institute and Predecessors. The National Archives, Kew.

Reade, T. F., Consul General, to Earl Granville (22 March 1882) *FO 102/158, Claim of Esparto Fibre Company (1881–1884).* The National Archives, Kew.

Reed, P. (2016) *Entrepreneurial Ventures in Chemistry: The Muspratts of Liverpool, 1793–1934.* Routledge, Abingdon.

Routledge, T. (1875) *Bamboo Considered as a Paper-Making Material with Remarks Upon Its Cultivation and Treatment.* E. & F. N. Spon, London.

Shorter, A. H. (1971) *Paper Making in the British Isles. An Historical and Geographical Study.* David & Charles, Newton Abbot.

Spicer, A. D. (1907) *The Paper Trade. A Descriptive and Historical Survey of the Paper Trade from the Commencement of the Nineteenth Century.* Methuen, London.

Surtees, R. W., Secretary of Franco-English Tunisian Esparto Fibre Supply Co. Limited to Earl Granville (18 December 1883) *FO 102/158, Claim of Esparto Fibre Company (1881–1884).* The National Archives, Kew.

52 *The esparto grass trade*

Sykes, P. (1981) *Albert E. Reed and the Creation of a Paper Business 1860–1960.* X.525/ 5617, unpublished manuscript. The British Library, London.

The Report on the Census of Production for 1951 (CP) (1955) Volume 10, Trade F, Paper and Board. Her Majesty's Stationery Office, London.

The Times Atlas of the World. Mid-Century Edition (1955–59) J. Bartholomew, ed, Vols. I–V. The Times Publishing Company Limited, London.

'Tripoli of Barbary' (1880) Report by Consul Jones on the Commerce of Tripoli for the Year Ending 30 June 1879. In *Report Upon the Commercial Relations of the United States with Foreign Countries for the Year 1879*, Vol. I. Government Printing Office, Washington, DC, 255–271.

Weatherill, L. (1974) *One Hundred Years of Papermaking. An Illustrated History of the Guard Bridge Paper Company Ltd. 1875–1975.* Guard Bridge Paper Company Ltd., Fife, Scotland.

W. M. Greenhalgh of Lyddon Co. Ltd. to Imperial Institute (28 April 1932) *AY4/2284, Bamboo and Sisal Pulps from Kenya.* Tropical Products Institute and Predecessors. The National Archives, Kew.

4   The pursuit of wood pulp

This chapter considers the role of wood pulp in the British paper trade up to 1960. By the paper trade, we mean those establishments engaged primarily in the manufacture of newsprint. Establishments engaged primarily in manufacturing printing and writing paper and board or converting paper into paper products as well as allied trades, such as bookbinding and printing (i.e. the art of transferring ink from printing plate to paper to give a permanent copy of the original), are by and large excluded from consideration, although the distinction is not always feasible.

The years from 1861 to 1960 in the British paper trade will be divided as follows. The introduction of the free trade principle on 1 October 1861 created the world's largest and freest paper market in the world. The period from 1914 to 1919 was interrupted by the First World War. The nineteenth-century belief in free trade and in an unlimited extension of markets with a corresponding extension of production capacity was shattered by the experience of the war. Britain failed to take part in the world boom of 1925–29 and then sank in 1931 with the rest of the world into the Great Depression. For 70 years, Britain had been the world's chief free market for pulp and paper, but was now forced to abandon the free trade principle which had been close to a national ideology (Trentmann 2008). The economic depression was at its worst in the third quarter of 1932, but thereafter, everything pointed towards a strong upward trend, leading up to the boom of 1937. The Second World War caused a violent disruption to British production capacity, and it was not until 1950 that raw material rationing was repealed. The Korean War led to a continued boom in the paper market in the 1950s. Tables 4.1–4.3 provide the particulars of the Accounts Relating to Trade and Navigation quoted below.

The introduction of wood pulp

As the supply of esparto and rags started to wane, wood pulp began its steady rise to prominence in the British raw material markets. Wood emerged as the predominant source of fibre in the 1880s, when international breakthroughs in the production of chemical wood pulp had made the product available for

54 *The pursuit of wood pulp*

British manufacturers. Wood pulp began its steady rise to prominence initially at the expense of esparto but then later at the expense of both esparto and rags (Coleman 1958, 342–343; Shorter 1971, 114; Hills 1988, 150–153). The first establishment to adopt wood pulping in Britain on a large scale was the Ekman Pulp and Paper Company's Northfleet Mill in Kent, in 1886 (Sykes 1981, 40–41). But in the absence of readily available domestic wood resources, British papermakers quickly availed themselves of Scandinavian wood pulp, and there were several reasons for this development. These included its close proximity, the suitability of the pulp for newsprint, and finally the low cost of the product compared to other available materials. Norway was a particularly appropriate location for the manufacture of mechanical pulp since the country had bountiful spruce forests and abundant waterfall resources for the power-intensive grinding process. The short sea passage and all year-around ice-free ports were added advantages over Norway's main competitor, Sweden, where similar resources could be tapped, or over the British colony of Newfoundland where even better wood and waterpower resources were available.

From 1877 to 1886, wood pulp imports rose by 100,000 tons (from 18,000 to 118,000 tons p. a.), while rags rose only 19,000 tons (from 17,000 to 36,000 tons p.a.) and esparto the same amount (from 176,000 to 195,000 tons p. a.). The development accelerated after 1890, as in 1900 esparto imports had risen by 17,000 tons (from 200,000 to 217,000 tons p. a.) and wood pulp imports by a whopping 351,000 tons (from 137,000 to 488,000 tons p. a.) (TN, 1882–1964; Sykes 1981, 40, 57). A similar tendency can be observed by analysing mill level figures. At Snodland Paper Mill, Kent, wood pulp emerged as the primary raw material in a matter of just ten years. In 1884, its fibre furnish mainly constituted raw fibres obtained from cereal straws (62%), esparto (17%), and wood pulp (9%), together with waste paper (12%). In 1894, by far the largest raw material was wood pulp (94.7%), while waste paper (3.8%), rags (1.1%), esparto (0.4%), and straw (0.04%) had dwindled to a minimal role at the Snodland Mill (Funnell 1985, 43).

Publishers as well as papermakers were dependent on large, uninterrupted supplies of wood pulp, and the terms on which they acquired it were crucial to the health of their enterprises. These requisites persuaded British printing and publishing houses to engage in the pulp and paper business. An illustrative example of this business pattern is Edward Lloyd's publishing empire, which included the *Daily Chronicle*, a halfpenny daily, which by the outbreak of the First World War had built up a steady circulation of 750,000 copies, and, during the war, sold more copies than *The Times*, the *Daily Telegraph*, the *Morning Post*, the *Evening Standard*, and the *Daily Graphic* combined (Lee 1976). To reach his market, Lloyd had to find far more paper than any previous publisher had ever needed. This encouraged Lloyd to build his own paper mills. By 1902, the Daily Chronicle Mills in Sittingbourne, Kent, had 11 paper machines with a weekly output of 1,000 tons of newsprint and other grades of paper. Interestingly, Lloyd determined to control raw material

The pursuit of wood pulp 55

supplies as well. He bought esparto grass cutting rights from Southern Spain and Algeria, and, in 1892, a pulping plant, Hønefoss Træsliberi from Norway, in order to ensure a ready supply of wood pulp. Eventually, Lloyd had a stake in every stage of the publishing business, from making pulp to selling 'news' (Reader 1981).

In 1905, another major British newsprint manufacturer Albert E. Reed & Company acquired a pulp mill at Hønefoss, Follum Træsliperi. Reed calculated that the price of mechanical pulp made in the British-financed Norwegian mill was significantly lower than that of mechanical pulp bought directly from Norwegian-owned mills (Sykes 1981, 99–104). Before long, however, opposition to British investments began to mount in Norway. In October 1909, a bill before the Storting, the supreme legislative body of Norway, became law, which prohibited foreign companies from acquiring any forest land without a Royal Concession and stipulating that they could not in no case acquire more than 250 acres in any one commune. Despite this regulation, Norway emerged as the prime supplier of wood pulp to the British paper mills, which had amounted already to 218,000 tons by 1903, i.e. 65% of the total imports of wood pulp trade (TN 1882–1964; Fasting 1967; Sykes 1981, 99–100; Moen 1998; Järvinen et al. 2012).

During the pre-1914 era, Canada and Newfoundland were the only pulpwood-producing countries of the British Empire. The Dominion of Canada with its vast forest resources possessed an enormous amount of fibre wealth, with manufacturing potentials yet hardly realised. The Forest Products Laboratories of Canada had been established in 1913 under the jurisdiction of the Forestry Branch of the Department of Interior and in cooperation with McGill University in Montreal (Kuhlberg 2012, 112). The investigation of indigenous species of wood, and of many products which could be manufactured from them, was one of the laboratories' most important functions, and in Britain, there were high hopes that in the domain of wood pulp manufacture, a real service to the paper industry could be rendered. The fundamentals of the political economy of raw materials affected the outlook of the Canadian pulp and paper industry. The country had very ample timber and waterpower resources for grinding mechanical wood pulp, and the large US markets for both mechanical pulp and newsprint, but little forthcoming capital for the manufacture of kraft (Kuhlberg 2012, 107–108, 2018, 133–134).

Of the 15 groups of industries listed in the *Canada Year Book 1913* (1914, 186–187), that of 'Timber and Lumber and Re-Manufacturers' was easily the most important when measured by the amount of capital invested, the number of people employed, and the total sum of wages paid. In 1913, the following quantities (cords p.a.) of spruce and other woods were used in the manufacture of pulps in Canada: white spruce 754,858; balsam fir 283,292; hemlock 47,360; jack pine 19,383; and poplar 4,414 – making a total of 1,109,034 cords. Of this figure, over half (600,000 cords) were converted into mechanical pulp, a third (367,105 cords) into sulphite, less than a tenth (136,569 cords) into sulphate, and the rest (5,144 cords) into soda pulp.

56   The pursuit of wood pulp

The white spruce (*Picea glauca*) was by far the most important of the Canadian timber trees. It grew in a very wide area from the south to as far north as the Yukon, and its high yield of cellulose (c. 56%) as well as long, tough, and colourless fibres rendered it particularly suitable for papermaking purposes. White spruce had also a considerable value as lumber, and the manufacture of pulp could therefore be integrated with sawmills in a similar manner as in Scandinavian countries. The balsam fir (*Abies balsamea*) was steadily increasing favour for pulp manufacture, while hemlock (*Tsuga canadensis*) figured third in the list of woods used in Canada for pulp making purposes. Hemlock's advancement was largely due to its increased use in British Columbia, where its utility for pulp manufacture was first demonstrated by Norman K. Brokaw of the Kankama Fibre Company, the first company to produce sulphite pulp from hemlock. Further service tests in the USA showed that when in the proportion of 25% hemlock sulphite pulp to 75% jack pine mechanical pulp, the standard 'news' quality could be manufactured from hemlock, allowing the use of hemlock in a commercially viable manner in Canada. The jack pine (*Pinus banksiana*) was another wood which was being increasingly used for pulp manufacture. This wood was being used in soda and mechanical pulp mills, though to a lesser extent than hemlock. The Maritime Provinces were the sole source of supply of pulp manufactured from poplar (*Populus tremuloides*), which had up to then been considered a non-commercial three. The poplar was the only wood still treated by the soda process, but it had already been demonstrated that the American aspen could also be used for making a very tenacious mechanical pulp (Phillips 1915, 617–621; Species of Wood Used in Various Processes in Making Paper Pulp 20 March 1937).

Several London based companies which aimed to exploit the Dominion's vast timber and waterpower resources were registered on the Stock Exchange in the 1900s. The usual method adopted by a London-based firm engaged in overseas raw material business was to court investment, primarily from British individuals but also from imperial sources. After this initial establishment period, it was usual to leave technical and production matters in the hands of local managers who ran operations in the host countries with the help of engineering firms and raw material suppliers. The board exercised complete financial control with the support of the corporate secretary and the financial and marketing services provided by commercial and financial City firms.

An illustration of this business pattern is The Oriental Power and Pulp Company, which was registered in 1903 to exploit the attractive conditions created by the Land Act Amendment of 1901 passed by the Government of British Columbia. The Act granted extremely favourable timber licences in British Columbia for the manufacture of pulp and paper, and it resulted in a rush of 15,000 licences in just two years before new licences could no longer be applied for. The Oriental Power and Pulp was one of the first in the rush and managed to secure 84,180 acres on the Princess Royal Island and the mainland opposite, together with waterpower rights and some freehold land. In May 1906, a new company to take over the technical and production responsibilities, the Canadian Pacific Sulphite Pulp Company Ltd., was floated. The Prospectus of the Canadian Pacific Sulphite, based on reports of Canadian and British cellulose experts, drew attention to the location at Swanson Bay, near Yule Lake, where it was claimed there were enough waterpower and timber for producing 700,000 tons of pulp together with sawnwood. A sawmill was built first, and the pulp mill soon followed and was in production by 1909. Swanson Bay had numerous advantages as a mill site. It was on the fairway for steamers running north from Victoria and Vancouver, and despite being very remote from the British markets, it was 5,000 to 7,000 miles closer to the booming Japanese markets than any mill site in the UK. The climate was mild and humid, allowing pulping operations to be carried out all year round with little danger from the damaging forest fires which were common in several other Canadian Provinces. The local Finnish and Norwegian settlers along with the indigenous population provided a ready, acclimatised workforce for logging operations. Ultimately, the real obstacle proved to be the absence of a railway, which the railway operators decided to build at Prince Rupert instead of at Swanson Bay. As a result, the Canadian Pacific Sulphite Company failed, and none of the subsequent operators trying to operate at Swanson Bay was never profitable (Canadian Pacific Sulphite Pulp Company Ltd. 1906; Sykes 1981, 113–115).

A similar fate was experienced by the Dominion Pulp Company Ltd., which was founded in 1897 to make sulphite pulp in the Canadian Province of New Brunswick on the Atlantic for Albert E. Reed's paper mills in the UK. The Company went into liquidation in 1930 with liabilities of CAD\$650,000 (Dominion Pulp Company Ltd. 1897; Carruthers 1947, 374–375; Parenteau 1992, 12–13). The fate of the early London-based wood pulp ventures in Canada highlights that it was not a simple matter to set up a pulp company in the Empire countries, and to successfully manage the operations from the London Head Office, thousands of miles from the mill site, however luring the outlooks were. The tangled histories of Canada's forestry industry, involving papermakers, company promoters, railway magnates, and political parties, highlight the challenges brought by the quest for imperial raw materials. It was much less problematic to transport finished wood pulp from Scandinavia than to be tangled with political controversies in the faraway Provinces of the Dominion of Canada.

Since 1904, Newfoundland, England's oldest colony, was in the limelight by reason of the development of its vast pulpwood resources by two British newspaper proprietors, Alfred and Harold Harmsworth – later Lords Northcliffe and Rothermere, respectively, the owners of London's *Daily Mail* family of newspapers. The Harmsworths' Company, The Anglo-Newfoundland Development Co., Ltd., was floated to build and operate the largest pulp mill of the time in the world, the Grand Falls Mill, on the Exploits River, in the central region of the island of Newfoundland, which went into operation on 9 October 1909. Grand Falls had great potential due to easy access to the surrounding virgin black spruce (*Picea mariana*), balsam fir, and pine stands

58   *The pursuit of wood pulp*

which predominated in Newfoundland forests. The mill had enough energy for the power-intensive grinding process, and a natural deep-water port for ocean-going vessels was available in nearby Botwood, which was connected to Grand Falls by a railway. Two years later, another London-based project, A. E. Reed of Newfoundland, Co., Ltd., established a pulp mill at Bishop's Falls, some 11–12 miles upstream from Grand Falls on the Exploits River. The Company had been incorporated on 26 April 1907 with a nominal capital of £400,000, making the Newfoundland venture almost as large as its parent company, Albert E. Reed & Company of England. The first pulp was made at Bishop's Falls on 18 April 1911, realising 100 tons per day with nine grinders. Although a significant amount at the time, the production fell short of the target output needed at the time for Reed's paper mills in England (40,000 tons per annum, expressed on an air-dry basis) (Phillips 1915, 621–622; Sykes 1981, 107–108, 111–112; Hiller 1982, 1990).

Before 1914, British papermakers used various expansion strategies within the Empire to address their fibre challenge. We have seen how London-based companies tried to ensure they had a supply of wood pulp by acquiring logging and waterpower rights in the Dominion of Canada, and how these companies were forced to abandon their schemes one by one. Similar expansion strategies in Newfoundland only led to limited success – they were unable to alleviate the raw material shortage to any great extent. By the outbreak of the First World War, the British paper industry had grown increasingly dependent on wood pulp imports to maintain its rate of growth. In 1913, British raw material imports totalled about 1,249 million tons. The share of mechanical and chemical wood pulp was 79.6% (993,600 tons), while the import of esparto and other fibrous vegetable materials (mostly cereal straws) constituted 18% (225,400 tons) and rags a mere 2.4% (30,000 tons) (Table 4.1). Of the total tonnage of wood pulp imports, roughly 40% came from Norway (mainly mechanical pulp), while Sweden supplied nearly the same amount of chemical pulps. Newfoundland supplied 101,900 tons, which represented 10.3% of total pulp imports into Britain, and the Dominion of

Table 4.1 Raw Material Imports 1913–1959 (1,000 tons and %)

Year	Rags	Wood pulp	Esparto	Other fibrous vegetable materials	Total
1913	30.0	993.6	208.2	17.2	1,249.0
1919	6.6	952.9	71.8	1.3	1,032.6
1929	20.0	1,664.5	317.7	9.7	2,011.9
1939	15.5	1,147.0	225.0	15.7	1,404.1
1949	20.7	1,326.0	366.4	20.6	1,733.7
1959	n.a.	2,263.6	n.a.	26.2	2,289.8
Total 1913–59	92.8	8,347.6	1,189.1	90.7	9,720.2
% of total	1.0	85.9	12.2	0.9	100.0

Source: TN (1882–1964).

Canada provided much of the rest wood pulp for the British markets (TN, 1882–1964; Sykes 1981, 131–133).

The introduction of the free trade principle

While Britain led the field in papermaking, the momentum of being the first nation successfully to mechanise the production of paper was gradually lost to overseas competitors by the close of the nineteenth century (Magee 1997), not least because of the raw material shortage that threatened to cripple the development of the British paper industry. In overseas trade, Britain was committed to mercantilism up to 1861. Domestic industry was protected by tariffs, and the little that Britain exported went to her overseas colonies. However, in the course of the nineteenth century, British paper industries had come to a greater extent to depend on exports to maintain their rate of growth. In an evolving business environment, mercantilist policies seemed not only unnecessary but even harmful to an export industry that needed to access a wider range of markets than the British colonies could offer. For the paper industry, the most important duties levied by 'Customs and Excise' included duties on imported paper and raw materials, the Excise Duty on paper manufactured in Britain, and the licences which had to be taken out by papermakers. The Customs and Excise duties in force influenced both the supply of exported foreign paper and the volume of domestic production (Spicer 1907; Coleman 1958; Owen 2000).

The introduction of the free trade principle in October 1861 caused the paper industry for the first time to become an object of general public discussion in Britain. The British papermakers had traditionally supported import duties to compensate for export duties on rags and had opposed the excise duty on paper. The influential campaigners for the abolition of excise included *The Times* (see, for instance, 17 February 1860) that was connected with influential papermaking families, and *Economist*, which lamented that the industry had not grown to be a major national industry like that of cotton manufacturing due to the repressive 'Taxes on Knowledge' (10 March; 12 and 19 May; 2 June; 4 August 1860) – so called because the Government was claimed to levy taxes in an effort to keep newspapers out of the reach of the masses (Kurlansky 2017, 204). The papermakers saw themselves as being sacrificed to the dogma of free trade as they were forced into the ironic position of opposing the repeal of excise against which they had been campaigning for 150 years. These questions brought on the first papermakers' clubs, and later, in 1872, The British Paper Makers' Association came into being (Coleman 1958). Its aim was to fix prices at a generally profitable level and to bring a greater degree of stability in times of falling prices and intensifying competition (Muir 1972).

As it turned out, the British paper industry was not ruined by the removal of the protective tariff wall. However, the repeal of customs duties on the export of rags in 1861 led to an increase in exports of these raw materials

60 *The pursuit of wood pulp*

as well, rising from only 1,000 tons in 1861 but already 24,000 tons in 1870 (Spicer 1907; Coleman 1958; Shorter 1971; Hills 1988; Magee 1997). Another consequence of the introduction of the free trade principle was foreign competition on British markets, which became a major feature of the paper trade after 1861. Firstly, the biggest importer of paper and board as well as printing and packing paper was Germany. In the early twentieth century, the share of German imports fell due to growing competition from Canadian and Scandinavian producers, which could readily make use of wood pulp as the primary raw material (Spicer 1907; Bartlett 1980; Magee 1997). The quantity of imports rose rapidly and was already 644,093 tons by 1913. The removal of the tariff wall in Britain did not lead to similar decisions elsewhere in Europe. Quite the opposite. Protective tariffs continued to be enforced throughout Western Europe. As a result, British orientation towards the Empire in the paper trade remained strong. In 1913, exports were 174,976 tons, of which over 70% went to the British Colonies and Dominions, countries like Australia, the Union of South Africa, British India, and New Zealand (Magee 1997) (Table 4.2).

The end of the free trade era

The British paper industry entered the war poorly prepared to as it did not have adequate means to address the sudden halt of wood pulp and esparto imports. Because of their bulk, the main problem of getting raw materials was shipping. No Spanish grass was received after the beginning of 1917 (Weatherill 1974, 79), and the raw material shortage worsened further when the Swedish Government banned foreign companies from acquiring forest land in Sweden (Hedberg & Häggqvist 2019; Karlsson 2019). The supply of wood pulp and paper from Canada and Newfoundland continued, but the volumes of trade were limited due to a lack of shipping for the long transatlantic crossing. The combined effect of these problems was that the use of available raw materials in 1918 represented 20% of the reported pre-war level (TN 1882–1964). The amounts of raw materials received were monitored by the Royal Commission on Paper, which operated for the two years, from 1 March 1916 to 8 March 1918. It was replaced by another regulatory body, the Controller of Paper, which regulated both raw material imports and the use of domestic refuse materials (e.g. waste paper) and annual plant fibres

Table 4.2 Imports and Exports of Paper and Board 1913–1959 (tons and %)

	1913	1919	1929	1939	1949	1959	Total 1913–59
Imports	644,093	381,076	996,647	823,464	463,919	1,203,684	4,512,883
Exports	174,976	46,796	252,366	118,671	188,475	244,705	1,025,989

Source: TN (1882–1964).

The pursuit of wood pulp   61

(i.e. cereal straws) until March 1919, when the Government lifted all restrictions (Sykes 1981, 146–8, 154).

Britain was formally off the gold standard from March 1919 (*de facto* from the outbreak of the war), but by April 1925, the pound had reached its pre-war parity with the dollar, and it returned to the gold standard. It has been estimated that the pre-war parity was over-valued to the extent of 10%. Such a significant price differential encouraged imports, while it handicapped the export trade (Pollard 1965; Youngson 1967; Table 4.2). Canadian paper in particular was increasingly exported to Britain. A new thread emerged from Finland, where the Finnish Pulp and Paper Association (Finnpap) was established in 1918 to search for new markets from the West to replace the formerly lucrative duty-free export trade with imperial Russia. The collapse of the Russian Empire and the continued Allied blockade of trade in the Baltic blocked Finnish producers' traditional export market, Germany, leading to efforts to open up British markets for their products. Devaluation of the Finnish Mark in 1919 gave Finnish producers an advantage over Norwegian and Swedish producers in the British markets, thus forming the main market area for Finnish producers (Circular 83. Finnpap; Heikkinen 2000, 58–64; Jensen-Eriksen & Ojala 2015).

The Nordic countries (Finland, Sweden, and Norway) were collectively the dominant suppliers of wood pulp to Britain; for instance, they delivered 1,300,000 tons in 1929. In the same year, British wood pulp producers, which sourced their pulpwood from Norway and Newfoundland, and, to a small extent from forests in the British Isles, stood at 209,000 tons, which represented 13.9% of total wood pulp use (LN 1938–1939). The collapse of the Russian Empire offered fresh business opportunities and perhaps less entangled bureaucracy for British papermakers in Finland, which was open to a dialogue with British money interests. Peter Dixon & Son Ltd., which operated two paper mills, one in Grimsby and the other in Oughtibridge, Sheffield, provides an example of this business pattern. Peter Dixon & Son Ltd., which was one of the pioneers in the use of wood pulp in Britain, tried to control the supply of wood pulp by launching a company (Toppila Ltd.) to operate a pulp mill in Meri-Toppila, Oulu, Finland. The Toppila Mill, situated at the farthest northern reach of the Bay of Bothnia, went into production in 1931 to produce chemical sulphite and mechanical pulp for Dixon's paper mills in the UK. The Toppila Mill was surrounded by luxuriant virgin coniferous forest stands. Compared to the British-owned mills in Norway, the main disadvantage was the longer distance. Another disadvantage was that the port was not ice-free all the year around, but had to be kept open by icebreakers during the direst months of the Arctic winter. Despite these drawbacks, the business pattern chosen by Peter Dixon & Son Ltd. proved successful. The Toppila Mill supplied wood pulp for Dixon's paper mills until 1985 (Kainua 1981).

The dependency on Scandinavian wood pulp imports put British papermakers into a difficult situation in their trade negotiations with the major

62   *The pursuit of wood pulp*

wood pulp suppliers. What was worse, the Nordic countries themselves were becoming important papermakers and exporters of paper to the British and Empire markets. In 1930, the Nordic trio produced 616,000 tons of newsprint, which was only 59,000 tons less than the British paper mills manufactured in the same year (675,000 tons) (Scanticon 13 April 1931). The Scandinavian paper mills were operating with significant natural advantages on their side, due to their abundant raw material and hydroelectric power resources and in many cases cheaper labour costs. Thanks to these natural advantages, output per employer and per paper machine tended to be higher in Scandinavian mills than in British ones (Järvinen et al. 2012). This allowed the Scandinavian producers, backed by natural advantages, to implement a price policy; *viz.*, they were selling relatively cheap paper and relatively dear pulp to put pressure on the profit margins and viability of British mills, and, therefore, to further their dominance over the British markets (WPTR 19 October 1961).

The protection of the British markets was first extended for wrapping and packing paper grades, on which import duties were imposed in 1926 under the Safeguarding of Industries (Customs Duties) Act. This was a defensive tariff intended to grant protection to British industries if foreign imports compared with domestic products enjoyed unfair advantages such as subsidies or bounties or if imported goods were sold below the cost of production (HC Deb 5 December 1927). Then, following the economic upheaval of 1931, Britain went off the gold standard and sterling depreciated in value by nearly 28%. Almost immediately, however, Sweden, Norway, and Finland each followed suit by devaluing their currencies, thus redressing the short-lived advantage (Sykes 1981, 254–255; Häggman 2006; Järvinen et al. 2012, 30). Further apprehension was caused by the acquisition of the Star Paper Mills near Blackburn in Lancashire by a major Finnish forestry industry operator, Kymin Oy in 1930 (Ahvenainen 1976).

The Abnormal Importations (Customs Duties) Act was passed to impose duties up to 100% *ad valorem* to prevent a sudden surge in imports in anticipation of later duties in December 1931 (HC Deb 4 December 1931). Finally, in February 1932, the Import Duties Act, which imposed a general revenue duty of 10% on imports received from countries outside the British Empire, inaugurated the protectionist era in the British paper and board industry (Pollard 1963). From 1 January 1933, printing and writing papers were protected by a 20% *ad valorem* duty, while a 50% *ad valorem* duty was levied from wrapping papers and boards under the Abnormal Importations Act of 1931 (HC Deb 4 December 1931 vol 260 cc1419–86; Sykes 1981, 257–258, 260). Wood pulp and newsprint were among the manufactured articles exempted from duty, subject to limits on quantity, signifying the strong British dependence on these articles.

The end of the free trade era signified the establishment of the Sterling Area in the form of the Imperial Preference system, aimed at expanding trade among the members of the British Commonwealth in a world of shrinking commerce and rising trade barriers. Imports from Empire countries were exempted from the Import Duties Act of 1932, and in an Imperial Economic Conference, assembled in Ottawa in July–August 1932, it was hoped to expand trade among the members of the British Commonwealth (Pollard 1965). However, the pre-1861 mercantilist conception of an industrialised mother country linked with primary produce countries had become grossly anachronistic by 1932. After difficult negotiations, small preferences were secured from Newfoundland, India, and the Union of South Africa, and those already safeguarded from Australia and New Zealand were confirmed and extended. No preferential treatment was received from Canada, which was determined to protect its industries even against Britain (HL Deb 26 October 1932; Sykes 1981, 259). Ultimately, the introduction of the Imperial Preference did not increase trade volumes as such but it directed the paper trade to the Empire. This had significance for the British newsprint producers, which had a large export market for its products in the Empire countries, but it did not alleviate British dependency on imports for a large proportion of the nation's supply of wood pulp and paper from Scandinavia.

In early 1933, the Kraft Paper Agreement with Norway, Sweden, and Finland was published. The British and Scandinavian mills, importers, and agents who were the signatories to the Agreement were bound to certain price levels, terms of sale, and minimum profits among many other rules (Kraft Convention 4 November 1932). The Kraft Paper Agreement and a corresponding agreement covering kraft paper bags were held up as models of their kind and led to numerous similar trade agreements covering various grades of pulp and paper in the 1930s (e.g. Minutes of the Meetings of the European section of the Ticon, 24 and 25 February 1930, FP2691; Sykes 1981, 262, 265–266). The signatory bodies of these trade agreements were the Paper Makers' Association of Great Britain and Ireland and their Scandinavian counterparts, the Swedish Paper Mills Association, the Norwegian Papermakers' Association, and the Finnpap. These three Nordic sales organisations, similar in organisation and structure, united as a single Scandinavian body, the Scan-organisation, which aimed (1) to ensure the stabilisation of adjusted prices to the maximum extent possible, (2) to keep advancing prices reasonably under control in times of exceptional demand, and (3) to assist the maintenance of reasonable prices when demand declined and manufacturing costs tended to advance as a result of a fall in production (Sykes 1981, 265; Järvinen et al. 2012, 30; see also Heikkinen 2000). The Scan-organisation was, in effect, an export cartel.

How were these trade policy measures reflected in tonnages and prices of wood pulp and paper? Between 1931 and 1933, there was in fact a substantial increase in the tonnage of imported raw materials, from 1,750,000 tons to 2,223,000 tons, together with a fall in the average price from 5.7 to £4.2 per ton, indicating increased paper production in Britain, and giving British papermakers strong bargaining power over Scandinavian wood pulp producers. The evidence from imports of paper and board is less clear. In the same

64 *The pursuit of wood pulp*

period, imports fell from 1,200,000 to 893,000 tons, but increased again to 949,000. Owing to strong competition over the British markets, the price of imported newsprint fell from £16 5s to £14 10s. By 1935, the price of newsprint hit rock bottom, £9 15s per ton, which was the lowest price realised since 1914 (TN 1882–1964; Sykes 1981, 260, 264).

By the outbreak of the Second World War, the British paper industry had assumed an important role in the country's economic life. Owing to Britain's strong economic growth, British paper consumption doubled from 1924 to 1938 (from 1.8 million tons to close 3.6 million tons), and the share of imports dropped from 42% in 1930 to 29% in 1938 (Owen 2000). In 1938, the apparent paper consumption was 3,395,490 tons, of which two-thirds (2,501,230) came from domestic production and a third (1,070,696) from imports – a ratio of trade that was more or less constant over many years. In 1938, the British consumption of raw materials totalled 3,036,000 tons. Wood pulp imports were 1,618,000 tons, pulpwood 322,000 tons, esparto 311,000 tons, and all the other fibrous raw materials 34,000 tons, making a total of 2,286,000 tons. Of the domestic raw materials, in the order of 750,000 tons were recovered fibres from waste paper. The imports of paper and board came essentially from Scandinavia, Continental Europe, and Canada. Despite the Imperial Preference, exports had fallen to 7% (176,436 tons) of the total paper production, signalling intensified competition in the traditional markets of the Empire (TN 1882–1964; Sykes 1981, 274–276, 280).

Effects of global upheavals

On the outbreak of the Second World War, prices, raw materials, labour, markets, and production became subject to the orders of the Paper Control, a governmental body set up by the Board of Trade on 3 September 1939. The Paper Control regulated the supply of raw materials by acquiring all pulp stocks and became responsible for allocating future paper supplies. The buyers were issued with licences to purchase specific quantities of paper, with H. M. Stationery Office and the War Office taking priority over its use before commercial use for it (Weatherill 1974, 94; Chater 1977, 46; Funnell 1985, 69–70).

The war affected the British paper industry in numerous negative ways. Above all, wood pulp and newsprint imports were severely restricted. The outbreak of the Winter War between Finland and the Soviet Union on 30 November 1939 ceased all pulp and paper deliveries from Finland, since all her human and material resources were now committed to the war effort (Nykänen 2018, 44–49). Sweden managed to retain her neutrality, but in April 1940, Germany attacked Norway. A consequence of the German invasion of Norway was that the rest of the trade between Scandinavia and Britain was blocked. Wood pulp and newsprint imports ceased from that direction until Germany was defeated, and all future imports would have to make the long hazardous passage across the North Atlantic.

The raw material shortage of the British paper continued in the years immediately following the war. In 1946, the import of raw materials had not risen even to half its pre-war level (TN 1882–1964). Some of the reasons for difficulties lay on the supply side. Due to the war over the sovereignty of Finland, which had emerged as one of the chief sources of paper, pulp, pulpwood, and timber for the rest of Europe (Järvinen et al. 2012), the country's ports, railroads, machinery, and mills had been severely damaged. Furthermore, the annexation of Eastern Karelia by the Soviet Union represented a loss of 12% of Finland's forest area and a reduction of about 25% of her forest industry capacity. Post-war reconstruction raised domestic timber requirements, and in addition, Finland was required to make large war reparations to the Soviet Union, including shipments of various forest products as well as paper and pulp machinery until September 1952. Shortages of coal and oil imports constituted another limiting factor, and increased domestic fuelwood needs restricted the country's capacity to supply industrial wood. The combined effect of these factors was that Finland's 1946 shipments of wood were reduced by 20% from what they had been in 1939 (Forestry and Forest Products 1948, 19–20; Nykänen 2018, 44–45).

The situation was much better in Sweden, where the war had not caused direct damage to the forests, infrastructure, or mills. At the end of hostilities, Sweden had large stocks of timber and pulp on hand, and was able to avail itself quickly of opportunities in the export market. The Norwegian forest industry also came through the war in a sound condition, in spite of the German occupation. After the war, the Norwegian Government started planting Sitka spruce (*Picea sitchensis*) as a first step towards rehabilitating its depleted forests (Forestry and Forest Products 1948, 19–20).

In Britain, the road to peacetime conditions started on 1 January 1949, when newspapers were freed from control of circulation. Imports, however, continued to be limited for balance-of-payments reasons (Ahvenainen 1976; Reader 1981). A rising demand for paper was frustrated by the weakness of the British economy, and in September 1949, Britain announced a substantial devaluation of sterling in acknowledgement of the extent to which its financial position had deteriorated during the war while that of the USA had strengthened. There was no adequate source of domestic raw materials, and the lack of dollars prevented the import of either raw materials or newsprint. Strict Paper Control measures lasted until 1 April 1950, when the purchasing of wood pulp, esparto, and pulpwood reverted to private companies. Overall, the effects of the wartime economy lasted until 1951, when production returned to the pre-war level. However, the lifting of the Paper Control restrictions on newsprint volume was delayed until 1954, when the paper industry could again determine its own selling price (FAO 1954, 75–76; Sykes 1981, 285–286).

In the global market, due to requirements of the Korean War of 1950–53, there was a general shortage of pulp, causing skyrocketing prices. In February 1952, the British Government, in concert with some European governments,

66 *The pursuit of wood pulp*

imposed artificial 12–25% cuts in pulp prices, varying according to the category of pulp. The combined effect of this agreement together with improved production capacity was that prices plummeted. Mechanical pulp dropped about a half, from £50 to £27 by September. The price of unbleached chemical pulp sank proportionally even more, by two-thirds, from £120 to £40. For the British papermakers, who were forced to buy pulp in great bulk as stock, the sudden fall of prices, and, in general, the volatility of the pulp market, caused great financial problems. For the Albert E. Reed, the largest purchaser of wood pulp in Europe, 1952 was the direst financial year in the company's nearly 100 years long history (Sykes 1981, 346–347).

Before the war, the prices of pulp and paper had been agreed in bilateral negotiations with the Scandinavian sales organisations. But in the new postwar economic reality, such a pattern of trade was no longer feasible. At the onset of the Cold War, the political map of Northern Europe dramatically altered. Norway was embracing the Western Block, and the country joined the North Atlantic Treaty Organization in its inception in 1949. Sweden continued to enforce its policy of neutrality and enjoyed her increasing international prestige within the United Nations (UN), while Finland, badly scarred by the ravages of war, was wavering between the Eastern and Western Blocks, trying to fend off the Soviet Union's attempts to undermine her sovereignty (Nykänen 2018, 49–51). In this political reality, the British companies returned to their pre-1914 strategy and tried to make contracts directly with the Scandinavian producers. One example of this revived strategy is Albert E. Reed's long-term contract with the Norwegian Sande Træsliperi, which led to the erection of a new pulp mill, Sande Paper Mill in 1961–62 (Sykes 1981, 348–349).

From Empire to Europe

On 1 January 1948, the General Agreement on Tariffs and Trade (GATT), to which the British Government had subscribed, became in force in world trade. Following GATT, the extension of preferential tariffs was prohibited and the import duties on paper and board were reduced, events which were met with great disappointment among British papermakers (Sykes 1981, 380–382). Inflation, combined with the general liberalisation of trade around the world, ended the formal system of Imperial Preference. However, the Empire continued to dominate the geographical horizons of the British export trade. About a half of Britain's exports went to her dominions and colonies in 1949, with the major export countries being Australia (28% share of the total exports of paper and board), the USA (15%), the Union of South Africa (8%), New Zealand (6%), the Irish Republic (6%), and India (5%). In 1959, the major export countries were, respectively, Australia (33%), New Zealand (12%), the Union of South Africa (9%), and the Irish Republic (6%) (TN 1882–1964).

The pursuit of wood pulp   67

In the economy at large, the British Government began to see the advantages of cooperation instead of competition with Europe. At the Stockholm Convention on the European Free Trade Association (EFTA) in November 1959, Britain was one of the signatory countries together with Sweden, Denmark, Norway, Switzerland, Austria, and Portugal (Sykes 1981, 386). In 1961, Finland was brought into association with EFTA and shared the advantages of free trade to the full (Jensen-Eriksen 2007). In the EFTA system, the British market was left open to the Nordic importers – Sweden, Finland, and Norway – as the tariff wall was gradually dismantled by the end of 1966. The signatory countries, however, retained their autonomy in deciding their separate national tariffs against imports from the rest of the world. British entry into EFTA had a largely negative impact on the country's paper industry. The reasons were obvious, and they in turn determined the attitude taken by British papermakers towards the EFTA. The volume of paper and board exports rose 30% from 1949 (188,475 tons) to 1959 (244,705 tons). At the same time, imports rose significantly more, 159.5% from 1949 (463,919 tons) to 1959 (1,203,684 tons) (Table 4.2). In 1959, paper imports already stood at about 1.2 million tons and exports at only about 0.25 million tons, so it was obvious that the tariff reductions favoured imports more than they encouraged exports. The major importers were Canada along with the Nordic countries (Finland, Sweden, and Norway). In 1949, the share of the Scandinavian trio of the total imports of paper and board was 54.5% (252,808 tons), while Canada's share was 24% (111,219 tons). In 1959, Canada and the Nordic countries had each a 36.3% share of the total imports of paper and board (Table 4.3).

Table 4.3 Imports of Paper and Board by Country in 1949 and 1959 (tons and %)

	1949	*%*	*1959*	*%*
Canada	111,219	24.0	436,842	36.3
Other Commonwealth countries and the Irish Republic	2,468	0.5	23,760	2.0
Finland	55,480	12.0	183,757	15.3
Sweden	144,782	31.2	180,467	15.0
Norway	52,546	11.3	72,289	6.0
Western Germany	–	0.0	9,660	0.8
Netherlands	70,032	15.1	116,901	9.7
Belgium	786	0.2	2,573	0.2
France	784	0.2	2,867	0.2
Austria	5,107	1.1	2,634	0.2
USA	17,505	3.8	163,742	13.6
Czechoslovakia	964	0.2	–	0.0
Other foreign countries	2,248	0.5	8,192	0.7
Total	463,921	100.0	1,203,684	100.0

Source: TN (1882–1964).

68   *The pursuit of wood pulp*

British paper mills lost their edge over their competitors because production in Scandinavia was in integrated mills which could use wet pulp manufactured on the spot that no longer had to climb the tariff wall. In 1959, the additional cost to manufacture a ton of paper at a non-integrated British mill compared to an integrated Scandinavian mill was estimated to be at a range of 7 to £10. The tariffs on papers and boards, which had remained almost unchanged since 1926, and applied to all paper grades, excluding newsprint, and to all counties except British Dominions and Colonies, had effectively offset Scandinavian producers' cost advantage and enabled British producers to compete with Scandinavian paper mills. But now, the imminent reduction of tariffs threatened to subject the British paper industry and its domestic markets to even more intensive competition. Compared to the removal of protective tariffs a hundred years earlier, in 1861, the situation was more serious for the British papermakers, because overseas producers were now in a much stronger competitive position compared to them. British paper companies were under great price pressure due to the increased imports by the Nordic paper producers, which were working in a much more cost-effective environment than the British papermakers. At the onset of the tariff reductions imposed by EFTA, the manufacture of bulk papers and boards, which had been protected by the tariffs, became economically unviable and their production was greatly reduced or stopped altogether in British paper mills. Only those produced from waste paper remained reasonably viable. Therefore, the removal of the tariff wall meant not only losing much of the profit margin and intensified competition in the form of imports, but it also meant that there was great deal of rationalisation and mill closure in Britain as manufacturers lost their faith in their business environment. It also meant a loss to the country's balance of payments as well, because British-made paper, even from imported pulp, was a major currency saver in Britain (Sykes 1981, 387).

The dismantling of the tariff wall revealed also a more deep-rooted problem. The British paper industry was historically deficient in terms of the industry's fibre resources and was forced to satisfy its domestic demand for pulp through imports. At the end of the 1950s, only 1% of wood pulp was manufactured from wood logged from British forests, which meant that nearly all wood pulp required by the industry had to be imported in the form of either 'half-stuff' or pulpwood. The development of the wood pulp industry base on domestic wood resources, with a few exceptions, was a relatively new business idea in Britain. The timber did not exist in sufficient quantities and on a guaranteed scale for the necessary capital investments to be forthcoming. However, in the late 1960s, the Forestry Commission, a body established in 1919 to acquire and afforest land for the creation of a national timber reserve, had high expectations for the use of British-grown coniferous wood resources and the use of fertilisers in planting. The supply of British-grown coniferous wood was expected to rise from 2.3 million tons in 1970 to 7.8 million tons in 2000 (wet wood with bark) (Hummel and Grayson 1969). Even though these expectations proved to be false, they prompted the promotion of several

The pursuit of wood pulp   69

new pulp mill ventures in the 1960s. For example, in 1963, Wiggins, Teape & Co. Ltd. tried to counter competition by building an integrated pulp and paper mill in the Scottish Highlands at Fort William, which exploited British-grown timber resources (MacKenzie 2018). The bold experiment made by Wiggins, Teape, was never profitable, and the pulping unit at Fort William was closed in 1980.

Conclusions

Before 1914, British papermakers used various expansion strategies within the Empire to address their fibre challenge. We have seen how London-based companies tried to ensure they had a supply of wood pulp by acquiring logging and waterpower rights in the Dominion of Canada, and how these companies were forced to abandon their schemes one by one. Similar expansion strategies in Newfoundland only led to limited success – they were unable to alleviate the raw material shortage to any great extent.

In the absence of readily available domestic or imperial wood resources, British manufacturers quickly availed themselves of Scandinavian timber. By the early twentieth century, the British paper industry had grown increasingly dependent on wood pulp imports to maintain its rate of growth. The British companies' dependency on wood pulp allowed Scandinavian cartel-like sales organisations to make various types of market sharing arrangements relating to the UK markets. During the interwar period tariffs, quotas and price-fixing agreements spread widely to the paper industry. As a consequence, free competition, which had hitherto characterised the paper trade, nearly disappeared from the British business scene.

In the early 1950s, the British paper industry's consumption of raw materials surpassed pre-war amounts for the first time, and the demand for paper was steadily rising. The relative cost of esparto and wood was important in determining their proportion, though quality was always the first consideration, especially in making fine print paper. The Nordic countries were collectively the dominant suppliers of wood pulp to Britain. Among the countries of the Empire, Newfoundland was the main source for wood pulp and pulpwood. For instance, within the Bowater Organisation, the sources of supply were in Scandinavia for mechanical pulp and in Newfoundland for pulpwood and sulphite pulp (Reader 1981, 209, 245). Esparto was sourced from Algeria, Tunisia, and Morocco. Of the domestic raw materials, waste paper, rags, waste cotton, and threads from textile mills were used as supplementary materials with other fibres. From 1913 to 1959, the proportion of wood pulp to all the other raw materials increased to an average of about 86% (Table 4.1).

In 1959, when the apparent consumption of paper in Britain was estimated to stand at five and a half million tons (Green 1963, 14), the British papermaking industries imported over two million tons of raw materials (2,289,800 tons). The share of wood pulp had risen to nearly 100% of the total imports of raw materials (Table 4.1), and the paper mills in Britain depended entirely

70   *The pursuit of wood pulp*

on imports of pulp for their survival. In this vital regard, the situation remained unaltered throughout the research period. Raw material dependency had been the problem when rags were the principal raw material, and it was even more of a problem in the case of esparto, and overwhelmingly so as the British paper mills switched to wood pulp.

References

Accounts Relating to Trade and Navigation of the United Kingdom (TN) (1882–1964).

Ahvenainen, J. (1976) *The History of Star Paper, 1875–1960.* Studia Historica Jyväskyläensia 13. University of Jyväskylä, Jyväskylä.

Bartlett, J. N. (1980) 'Alexander Pirie & Sons of Aberdeen and the Expansion of the British Paper Industry, c. 1860–1914'. *Business History,* 22, 1, 18–34.

Canada Year Book 1913 (1914) Ottawa, J. de L. Tache.

Canadian Pacific Sulphite Pulp Company Ltd. (1906) *BT 31/11543/88998, Board of Trade (BT), Companies Registration Office, Files of Dissolved Companies.* The National Archives, Kew.

Carruthers, G. (1947) *Paper in the Making.* Garden City Press Co-operative, Toronto.

Chater, M. (1977) *Family Business. A History of Grosvenor Chater 1690–1977.* Grosvenor Chater, St. Albans.

Circular 83. *FINNPAP2851, Suomen Paperitehtaiden Yhdistys – Finska papersbruksföreningen (Finnpap).* Central Archives of United Paper Mills, Valkeakoski.

Coleman, D. C. (1958) *The British Paper Industry, 1495–1860.* Clarendon, Oxford.

Dominion Pulp Company Ltd. (1897) *BT31/15783/52666, BT, Companies Registration Office, Files of Dissolved Companies.* The National Archives, Kew.

Economist (10 March 1860; 12 May 1860; 19 May 1860; 2 June 1860; 4 August 1860).

FAO. (1954) *Wood Pulp and Paper Resources and Prospects.* A survey prepared by the Food and Agriculture Organization in co-operation with the secretariats of the United Nations Educational, Scientific and Cultural Organization (UNESCO); the Economic Commission for Europe (ECE); and the Economic Commission for Latin America (ECLA). AO, New York.

Fasting, K. (1967) *Den norske papirindustris historie. 1893–1968.* De norske papirfabrikanters felleskontor, Oslo.

Forestry and Forest Products World Situation 1937–1946 (1948) Stockholms Bokindustri Aktiebolag, Stockholm.

Funnell, K. J. (1985) *Snodland Paper Mill. C. Townsend Hook and Company from 1854.* C. Townsend Hook and Company Limited, Snodland, Kent.

Green, T. (1963) *Yates Duxbury & Sons, Papermakers of Bury 1863–1963,* Newman Neame, London.

Häggman, K. (2006) *Metsäteollisuuden maa. Suomalainen metsäteollisuus politiikan ja markkinoiden ristiaallokossa 1920–1939. Metsän tasavalta.* Suomalaisen Kirjallisuuden Seura, Helsinki.

Hedberg, P. & Häggqvist, H. (2019) 'Wartime trade and tariffs in Sweden from the Napoleonic Wars to World War I'. In J. Eloranta, E. Golson, P. Hedberg & M. C. Moreira, eds, *Small and Medium Powers in Global History: Trade, Conflicts, and Neutrality from the 18th to the 20th Centuries.* Perspectives in Economic and Social History 54. Routledge, Milton Park, 116–138.

The pursuit of wood pulp   71

Heikkinen, S. (2000) *Paper for the World: The Finnish Paper Mills' Association – Finnpap, 1918–1966*. Otava, Helsinki.

Hiller, J. (1982) 'The Origins of the Pulp and Paper Industry in Newfoundland'. *Acadiensis* XI, 2, 42–68.

Hiller, J. (1990) 'The Politics of Newsprint: The Newfoundland Pulp and Paper Industry, 1915–1939'. *Acadiensis* XIX, 2, 3–39.

Hills, R. L. (1988) *Papermaking in Britain 1488–1988. A Short History*. Athlone Press, London and Atlantic Highlands.

House of Commons Debates (HC Deb). (5 December 1927) vol 211 cc956–7; (4 December 1931) vol 260 cc1419–86. Available at https://api.parliament.uk/historic-hansard/index.html. Accessed 27 July 2020.

House of Lord Debates. (26 October 1932) vol 85 cc819–86. Available at https://api.parliament.uk/historic-hansard/index.html. Accessed 27 July 2020.

Hummel, F. C. & Grayson, A. J. (1969) 'The Future of Wood Supplies in Great Britain'. In J. A. Dickson & P. J. Dixon, eds, *Pulpwood Supply and the Paper Industry*. Report of a Conference of the British Paper and Board Makers' Association, Forest Record, 68. Forestry Commission, London, 4–16.

Järvinen, J., Ojala, J., Melander, A. & Lamberg, J.-A. (2012) 'The Evolution of Pulp and Paper Industries in Finland, Sweden and Norway 1800–2005'. In J.-A. Lamberg, J. Ojala, M. Peltoniemi & T. Särkkä, eds, *The Evolution of Global Paper Industry: 1800–2050. A Comparative Analysis*. World Forests 17. Springer, Dordrecht, 19–48.

Jensen-Eriksen, N. (2007) *Metsäteollisuuden maa. Metsäteollisuus kasvun, integraation ja kylmän sodan Euroopassa 1950–1973*. Läpimurto. Suomalaisen Kirjallisuuden Seura, Helsinki.

Jensen-Eriksen, N. & Ojala, J. (2015) 'Tackling Market Failure or Building a Cartel? Creation of an Investment Regulation System in Finnish Forest Industries'. *Enterprise & Society*, 16, 3, 521–555.

Kainua, L. (1981) *Osakeyhtiö Toppila – Toppila Oy (Toppila Ltd.) 1927–1974*. Toppila Oy (Toppila Ltd.), Oulu.

Karlsson, B. (2019) 'Two Cartel Regimes. Swedish Paper Cartels and the EEC in the 1970s'. *Scandinavian Economic History Review*, doi: 10.1080/03585522.2019.1704858.

Kraft Convention. (4 November 1932) *FP2693, Finska Paperskontoret (FP)*. Central Archives of United Paper Mills, Valkeakoski.

Kuhlberg, M. (2012) 'An Accomplished History, An Uncertain Future: Canada's Pulp and Paper Industry since the Early 1800s'. In J.-A. Lamberg, J. Ojala, M. Peltoniemi & T. Särkkä, eds, *The Evolution of Global Paper Industry: 1800–2050: A Comparative Analysis*. World Forests 17. Springer, Dordrecht, 101–134.

Kuhlberg, M. (2018) 'Natural Potential, Artificial Restraint: The Dryden Paper Company and the Fetters on Adopting Technological Innovation in a Canadian Pulp and Paper Sector, 1900–1950'. In T. Särkkä, M. Gutiérrez-Poch & M. Kuhlberg, eds, *Technological Transformation in the Global Pulp and Paper Industry 1800–2018: Comparative Perspectives*. World Forests 23. Springer, Dordrecht, 133–160.

Kurlansky, M. (2017) *Paper. Paging Through History*. W. W. Norton & Company, New York and London.

Lee, A. J. (1976) *The Origins of the Popular Press in England, 1855–1914*. Croom Helm, London.

MacKenzie, N. G. (2018) 'Creating Market Failure: Business-Government Relations in the British Paper-Pulp Industry, 1950–1980'. *Business History Review*, 92, 4, 719–741.

72 *The pursuit of wood pulp*

Magee, G. B. (1997) *Productivity and Performance in the Paper Industry. Labour, Capital, and Technology in Britain and America, 1860–1914*, Cambridge Studies in Modern Economic History 4. Cambridge University Press, Cambridge.

Minutes of the Meetings of the European section of the Ticon (24 and 25 February 1930) *FP2691, Finska Paperskontoret (FP)*. Central Archives of United Paper Mills, Valkeakoski.

Moen, E. (1998) *The Decline of the Pulp and Paper Industry in Norway, 1950–1980: A Study of a Closed System in an Open Economy*. Scandinavian University Press, Oslo.

Muir Augustus. (1972) *The British Paper and Board Makers' Association 1872–1972*. The British Paper and Board Makers' Association, London.

Nykänen, P. (2018) 'Research and Development in the Finnish Wood Processing and Paper Industry, c. 1850–1990'. In T. Särkkä, M. Gutiérrez-Poch & M. Kuhlberg, eds, *Technological Transformation in the Global Pulp and Paper Industry 1800–2018: Comparative Perspectives*. World Forests 23. Springer, Dordrecht, 35–64.

Owen, G. (2000) *From Empire to Europe. The Decline and Revival of British Industry since the Second World War*. HarperCollins, London.

Parenteau, B. (1992) 'The Woods Transformed: The Emergence of the Pulp and Paper Industry in New Brunswick, 1918–1931'. *Acadiensis*, XXII, 1, 5–43.

Phillips, S. C. (1915) 'The Empire's Resources in Paper-Making Materials'. *Journal of the Royal Society of Arts*, XLIII, 3261, 613–636.

Pollard, S. (1965) *The Genesis of Modern Management. A Study of the Industrial Revolution in Britain*. Edward Arnold, London.

Reader, W. J. (1981) *Bowater. A History*. Cambridge University Press, Cambridge.

Scanticon. (13 April 1931) *FP2691, Finska Paperskontoret (FP)*. Central Archives of United Paper Mills, Valkeakoski.

Shorter, A. H. (1971) *Paper Making in the British Isles. An Historical and Geographical Study*. David & Charles, Newton Abbot.

Species of Wood Used in Various Processes in Making Paper Pulp. (20 March 1937) *AY4/2303, Pinus Radiata Wood in South Australia: Paper Pulp Production*. Tropical Products Institute and Predecessors. The National Archives, Kew.

Spicer, D. A. (1907) *The Paper Trade. A Descriptive and Historical Survey of the Paper Trade from the Commencement of the Nineteenth Century*. Methuen, London.

Statistical Year-Book of the League of Nations (LN) (1938–1939).

Sykes, P. (1981) *Albert E. Reed and the Creation of a Paper Business 1860–1960*. X.525/5617, unpublished manuscript. The British Library, London.

The Times (17 February 1860).

Trentmann, F. (2008) *Free Trade Nation. Commerce, Consumption, and Civil Society in Modern Britain*. Oxford University Press, Oxford.

Weatherill, L. (1974) *One Hundred Years of Papermaking. An Illustrated History of the Guard Bridge Paper Company Ltd. 1875–1975*. Guard Bridge Paper Company Ltd., Fife, Scotland.

The World's Paper Trade Review (WPTR) (19 October 1961) 156, 16, 1439–1442.

Youngson, A. J. (1967) *Britain's Economic Growth, 1920–1966*. George Allen & Unwin, London.

5 Bamboo for papermaking

Bamboo can be considered as an ideal raw material for papermaking. Under favourable conditions of climate and soil, the plant produces a heavy crop with minimal care and cost. In terms of quality, the bamboo stem possesses a high-quality fibre, capable of withstanding considerable wear and tear, and therefore, the plant is especially suitable for paper manufactured for printing. Despite being an excellent papermaking material as well as plentifully available and easily cultivable in the Tropics, the use of bamboo as a papermaking raw material has remained sporadic and marginal. India, which is the setting of this chapter, is the only country in the world where bamboo has been used on a large scale for papermaking. This chapter maintains that the main reason for this can be found from the path-dependent nature of the paper industry. Paper manufacture is a highly capital-intensive industry, which is characterised by rather inflexible combinations of inputs of investments, knowledge, and technology, and breaking the 'path' demands both capital and the knowledge of the properties of the fibre, as this chapter illustrates.

Bamboo as a fibre-yielding plant

Bamboo is a grass, which can be propagated by seed or transplanting. In its natural habitats, the plant does not seed annually but periodically at long intervals, varying with different species and different climates and soil, from 30 to 60 years. The culms die after ripening their seed, and usually, the underground rhizomes die as well (Pearson 1912, 24). Bamboo forests vary a great deal according to the atmospheric, climatic, and edaphic influences. In wet evergreen forests, the stems emerge from the ground in their full width (i.e. the stem does not increase in girth while it grows upwards) and grow so fast that they attain full height in a matter of few weeks, or, during the Monsoon season, in months. The temperate varieties of bamboo, being kinds of large grasses, grow in a more continuous manner. The number of culms put out by a single clump varies with the different species and according to the age and size of the plant. The culms of *Bambusa arundinacea* (also known in India as Kyathaung) and *Bambusa polymorpha* (also known in India as Daugi), the two tall, elegant species that occur gregariously in wet evergreen forests

74   *Bamboo for papermaking*

throughout the Indian Peninsula and which are of close concern in discussing the Indian pulp and paper industry, grow in thick clusters or clumps, each holding 30–100 culms varying in height from 50 to 150 feet from the ground (Watt 1908, 99–100; Sindall 1909; Bamboo Pulp for Paper Making 17 July 1916; Raitt 1928, 155–165).

The main benefit of bamboo as a papermaking material is that under favourable conditions of climate and soil, the plant produces a heavy crop with minimal care and cost. The degree of facility and the cost of removal from the forest to the mill depend on the plant's size, weight, and other physical features (Pearson 1912, 27). 'Branches' of *B. arundinacea* are 'thorny' and its culms tended to get tangled at the top (Watt 1908, 99–100; Sindall 1909). This feature made extraction, bearing in mind the weight and size of the culms, an expensive and difficult matter (Savur 2003, I, 25). On the other hand, the great size compensated for the extra expenditure, so that the actual cost of harvesting one ton of dry material of *B. arundinacea* worked out the same as the cost of the lighter and the more easily handled species found in the Peninsula. Another significant feature was the thickness of the stem walls and the hardness and size of the nodes (i.e. the bamboo stem is a hollow culm or stem with solid joins called nodes). For instance, the culms of *B. polymorpha* grow nearly as large as the culms of *B. arundinacea*, but owing to their thinner walls and smaller nodes, the first mentioned species could be much more easily reduced by crushing to a tow-like substance. *B. polymorpha*, therefore, had an advantage as a fibre-yielding plant over *B. arundinacea*, except that it did not yield the same quantity of raw material per culm (Pearson 1912, 15; Bamboo Pulp for Paper Making 17 July 1916).

Both *B. polymorpha* and *B. arundinacea* flower at long intervals. For instance, *B. arundinacea* of the West Coast of the Peninsula has a 34-year life cycle and a 12-year reproduction period. A clump throws out 15–20% new shoots every year. Thus, old plants were cut every fifth year. Gregarious flowering presented further challenges in view of the plant's commercial use. When the plant flowered, the whole bamboo stock in that area died, and the mill could be left without any supplies from that source for five to ten years before the area was regenerated by self-seeding (Podder 1979, 53). There were, however, certain factors that made it possible to rely on a continued supply of raw material. Firstly, normally more than one bamboo species occurred in every virgin forest and the chances that they all flower at the same time were very remote. Secondly, the catchment areas of the mills were typically so vast that raw material was always available from other localities. Finally, the period during which the new crop was growing could be partly tided over by extracting the dry culms to supply the mill (Pearson 1912, 24–25; Bamboo Pulp for Paper Making 17 July 1916).

In terms of quality, bamboo fibres are extremely silky, fine, and long, varying in length up to 4 mm. The long fibres are arranged in the internodes in regular parallel lines forming vascular bundles. Owing to these fibre characteristics, bamboo paper is capable of withstanding considerable wear and tear, so it is an especially suitable raw material for the manufacture of printing papers. In terms of quantity, air-dried bamboo yields 42–50% of unbleached air-dried pulp, depending on the species and pulping method used (Raitt 1912, 15–16, 30; Bamboo Pulp for Paper Making 17 July 1916). Based on a yield of 45%, the manufacture of one ton of pulp necessitated the treatment of 2.5 tons of air-dried bamboo. Consequently, it was estimated in 1909 that a mill producing 300 tons of dry pulp per week would require an annual supply of 35,000 to 36,000 tons of bamboo (Sindall 1909, 31).

The introduction of bamboo to the Indian paper industry

In Britain, the likelihood of a pulp famine and the consequent increase in the price of esparto were among the factors that first raised interest in the possibility of making commercial volumes of good-quality pulp from bamboo. From the very beginning, it was obvious that it would not be commercially viable to import raw bamboo in large quantities into Britain owing to the bulkiness of the material and its relatively low value. Furthermore, the plant's tendency to be damaged from fermentation made the importation of fresh succulent bamboo stems problematic. Even if dried, underdeveloped means of shipping in all-purpose ocean-going vessels and the high costs of carriage for relatively low-valued plant fibres made imports commercially unviable. It was evident, therefore, that to ensure a continuous supply of bamboo pulp, it would have to be reduced to fibrous paper stock where it was grown. This development led to the need to export capital into India, where the abundance of bamboo stock provided a seemingly inexhaustible supply of raw material.

Bamboo has been subject to a new processing treatment since 1875, when Thomas Routledge initiated the first serious attempt to make use of bamboo as a regular source of supply for pulp at the Ford Paper Mills on the River Wear, at South Hylton, Sunderland. Routledge, who suggested it as an ally to esparto, conducted a series of pulp preparation trials at his works, with the stems of *Bambusa vulgaris*, a variety growing in Demerara (British Guiana), which he had received from the Royal Botanic Gardens, Kew. The modest experiments preceding Routledge's trials had failed both technically and commercially, for the reason that the bamboo stems had been cropped and treated without regard to their age. Owing to the presence of a large quantity of silica, and the extreme hardness of the woody stem, the only possible means of converting dry bamboo stems into pulp was to subject them to a prolonged digesting in very strong solutions of caustic alkali at elevated temperature and under high pressure. By this means, pulp had been produced but at a disproportionate cost (due to the large consumption of processing chemicals for the digesting process and of coal for energy) and under perilous conditions (caused by cooking the material under a high pressure). The chief conclusion Routledge established was that cutting the stems at an early stage of the plant's growth (i.e. shoots of the season), when bamboo may still

76 Bamboo for papermaking

be termed as a succulent vegetable (i.e. before the cellulose and lignin have become indurated and silica deposited), would allow bamboo to be processed using only a mild alkali treatment (Routledge 1875, 2–5).

The report of Routledge's trials was published in a pamphlet *Bamboo, Considered as a Paper-Making Material* (1875), which was extensively circulated in India through the India Office. In India, the topic was first brought to the agenda of the Forest Conference held at Simla in October 1875 (Report 1876, 110–111). Thenceforward, the bamboo question occupied the attention of Indian Forest Officers and frequently filled the pages of *The Indian Forester*.[1] Dr. Dietrich Brandis (1824–1906), the noted German forester who was the Inspector-General of Forests in India, was not very sanguine about the success of converting bamboo into paper stock in India. Brandis succeeded in convincing Routledge that cropping the young shoots from virgin forests and transporting them to the mill would not be commercially viable for two reasons. Firstly, the yield of cellulose that could be obtained from fresh succulent shoots constitutes only a very small proportion to their original weight, and secondly, fresh succulent shoots are of too high a specific gravity to float. Instead of rafting bamboo stems down rivers, the manufacturers would have to use the more expensive river steamer transport or the even more expensive rail transport to their mills, which would increase the already high transport costs of relatively low-value bamboo stems (Brandis 1899, 24).

The appointment of Brandis as the Superintendent of Forests in Pegu (Burma) in 1856 and the first Inspector-General of Forests in India in 1864 had marked the commencement of scientific forestry in British India. Routledge's proposal to reserve large areas of virgin bamboo forests for paper mills contradicted Brandis' notions of developing forestry on scientific lines and for planned forest management. Instead, Brandis made a proposal that the Government should establish industrial bamboo forest plantations on a large scale for the purposes of pulp manufacture. By means of manure and irrigation, the bamboo clumps could be induced to produce larger numbers of fresh shoots, and not at one season only, but throughout the year. Industrial plantations would be assured a constant supply of raw material at a certain fixed price, independent of the open market price of bamboo offered for sale at commercial centres for construction and other purposes. From the paper manufacturers' point of view, a further advantage would be a regular supply of bamboo of uniform growth and age (Brandis 1899).

In 1876–77, Dr. George King, the Superintendent of the Royal Botanic Gardens, Calcutta (Kolkata), conducted the first propagation and cultivation trials with *Bambusa balcooa*, a thick-walled variety native to Bengal. The purpose of the trials was to yield a succession of crops of young shoots throughout the year. By a judicious cropping method, a continuous and reliable supply of raw material irrespective of the season could be assured (King 1877, 1027). King's cultivations trials resulted in utter failure, however. After the areas in which harvesting of bamboo had been carried on for some years had been inspected, it was concluded that the clumps had been damaged by over-felling. The number of new stems the clumps propagated had been reduced owing to the intensity of cutting. But ultimately, the clump seemed to recover, if given even a short period of rest (Routledge 1879, 2–11). The chief finding from the propagation and cultivation trials was that in order to determine the optimal cropping rotation for bamboo, it was necessary to know how many stems were put out on average each year by the different varieties, and how many stems could be cut from each culm without damaging the plant (Pearson 1912, 18–23).

For nearly 30 years, Routledge devoted his attention to the raw material question, and for about seven years, from 1880 to 1886, he was working under the auspices of the Royal Society of Arts. Routledge devoted himself especially to the study of the bamboo exceedingly rich in fibres that was omnipresent in the Pegu area of Burma, which was chosen on account of its ideal climatic conditions, with its particularly large amount of rainfall, as much as 160–200 inches per annum. In some parts of Pegu, rain or showers fell nine months out of twelve, creating conditions very favourable to the rapid growth of bamboo. The process devised and patented by Routledge reduced the material into a tow-like state, which could be then compressed into an ordinary freightage article, like jute or cotton. Routledge calculated that when bamboo was treated as he proposed, the cost of bamboo to the main British ports would be about the same as Algerian alfa, the cheapest imported raw material in the market at the time. Routledge also believed that bamboo besides being a potential papermaking raw material would ultimately form an important textile material for the British textile industry. The versatility of bamboo was illustrated in that fact that the Burmese made not only rope from it, but also the houses they lived in, the masts and spars of their vessels, and many other everyday necessities (JSA 27 May 1881, 584–585).[1]

After lengthy negotiations, in 1880, Routledge managed to obtain a Concession from the Government, but the terms on which it was granted were not particularly liberal. The Government offered him a Concession for five years, and he would have to pay a royalty of one rupee (2s) per ton for bamboo fibre exported to the British market. By way of comparison, the French Government granted the exclusive right to the Societé Franco Algérienne for collecting alfa over one million acres for 99 years on payment of only 15 centimes (1.5d) for every ton exported (Routledge 11 October 1880). Ultimately, Routledge's Burma bamboo pulp scheme floundered, for partly technical and partly commercial reasons. Though thoroughly suitable for papermaking purposes, bamboo, after cutting and collecting, required a considerable outlay for crushing and drying, and a somewhat costly manipulation to reduce it to a transferrable (merchantable) condition.[2] Another problem was that Routledge never managed to secure very warm support from the Indian Government in Burma. The Chief Commissioner, the Inspector-General of Forests, and Conservators of Forests, with whom he was in communication, viewed the bamboo scheme as a potential source of revenue for the British

78 *Bamboo for papermaking*

Government in Burma, not as a panacea for the British papermakers' pulp famine (Bernard 19 January 1881).

It took nearly 20 years before the Government of India decided to follow up Routledge's experiments on a commercial basis. In 1905, the Government asked Robert Walter Sindall, a consulting chemist to the wood pulp and paper trades, to conduct experiments in order to determine conditions under which pulp might be manufactured in Burma. Sindall's investigations, carried out in Burma under the auspices of the Government in 1905–6, and the subsequent laboratory investigations conducted in London, on the suitability of bamboo as a papermaking raw material, demonstrated the technical possibility of manufacturing soda pulp bamboo in Burma (Sindall 1906).

In 1908, some eight to nine tons of Burmese *B. polymorpha* was shipped to Britain where it was subjected to service tests by Messrs. Thomas & Green Ltd. at Soho Mills on the River Wye, in Wooburn Green, Buckinghamshire. The service tests gave highly satisfactory results. The yield was over 50% on the weight of air-dried material, and the use of 8 to 10% bleach gave the pulp considerable brightness. The manufacturer reported that the raw material worked exceedingly well on the paper machine, and the paper produced was capable of withstanding considerable wear and tear, and therefore was admirably suitable for printing purposes. Some specimens of the bamboo paper were later sent to the North of Ireland Paper Mill Company for lithographic printing trials, which gave equally satisfying results (Sindall 1909, 44–47).

Encouraged by these positive results, research and development work for ascertaining a pulping process suitable for bamboo continued at the cellulose and paper branch of the Imperial Forest Research Institute, Dehra Dun (Dehradun). The Forest Research Institute was established in conjunction with the Imperial Forest School in 1906 with six officers – the Imperial Silviculturist, the Imperial Superintendent of Forest Working Plans, the Imperial Forest Zoologist, the Imperial Forest Botanist, the Imperial Forest Chemist, and the Imperial Forest Economist (100 Years of Indian Forestry 1961, I, 80). The correct identification of plants (Forest Botany) was not only of scientific importance but was also a prime necessity for almost all aspects of scientific forestry – silviculture, wood anatomy and technology, cellulose chemistry, and entomology were all dependent on it. Since 1881, when J. S. Gamble published his mammoth *A Manual of Indian Timbers*, Indian foresters had been helping with the correct identification of Indian plants for commercial purposes (Gamble 1881). Gamble's work was followed in 1911 by R. S. Hole's study of Indian grasses, *On some Indian Forest Grasses and their Oecology* (Hole 1911; Progress Report 1911).

Scientific forestry had a special significance during the First World War, when it helped to find several indigenous substitutes for many imported wood products, and many new or little-known indigenous plants were brought to the market (100 Years of Indian Forestry 1961, II, 181). In this respect, the responsibilities of the Forest Economist in the charge of the Economic Branch of the Forest Research Institute were imperative. The Forest Economist made 'a special study of the best methods of rendering forest produce of all kinds available at the smallest cost to consumers'. The Forest Economist also kept in touch with 'the commerce in India with the view of fostering and meeting the demand for forest products' (Progress Report 1908, 2).

The history of pulp and paper development work at the Forest Research Institute can be traced back to the year 1910, when William Raitt, the Mill Manager of the Bengal Paper Mills Co. at Raniganj, was hired as the first research worker at the Forest Research Institute to conduct laboratory tests into developing a pulping process suitable for bamboo.[3] Raitt's trials were of a practical nature, and they were carried out under the same working conditions experienced in the manufacturing process on an industrial scale (Progress Report 1911, 9). Raitt's report on the pulping trials was published in 1912, and the general impression it presented was that bamboo was a difficult material to treat, both mechanically and chemically. At the time, there were three possible methods by which bamboo could be reduced to chemical pulp: by sulphite, by sulphate, and by the well-known soda process, which had already been experimented with in connection with bamboo by Routledge and Sindall. Of these chemical processes, Raitt employed the acid, of which the sulphite process was typical, and the alkaline treatment, exemplified by the soda process. The alkaline treatment of bamboo for the manufacture of soda bamboo pulp was similar to that used for the manufacture of esparto pulp. The main challenge in digesting bamboo lay in the removal of its starchy carbohydrates, which required a large amount of alkali. To overcome this difficulty, Raitt employed a preliminary treatment with hot water to remove the excessive starchy matter. Then, the crushed bamboo in the form of fine shredding was heated in rotary digesters with a solution of caustic soda. The non-fibrous constituents of the material were dissolved, and portions of brown-coloured cellulose in a more or less pure condition were obtained. The spent liquors were preserved, and the soda recovered to be used over again (Raitt 1912, 27; Bamboo Pulp for Paper Making 17 July 1916).

In the sulphite process, the crushed bamboo was cooked in a solution of bisulphite of lime, or, when dolomite limestone was used, a mixture of the bisulphites of lime and magnesia. In connection with bamboo, Raitt noted that the sulphite process exercised a less destructive effect on the fibre than the soda process. The yield was slightly higher, and the process did not degrade the soluble material to a brown colour which stained the soda pulp. Instead, the pulp was of yellowish white colour in the unbleached state and could be used for cheaper grades of newspaper without further bleaching. However, this advantage was largely lost when better paper grades were required. The pulp required 5–10% of bleach to obtain a sufficient degree of whiteness. Despite some definite advantages, Raitt found the ordinary sulphite method unsuitable for work in the tropical conditions of India. The reason was that sulphur dioxide is a volatile gas and its successful absorption in limewater was adversely affected either by the high temperature or by the high atmospheric pressure (Raitt 1912, 20–21).

80 Bamboo for papermaking

The main mechanical challenge was related to the vexed question of how to make the bamboo nodes reducible. Cellulose experts at the time were of the opinion that the bamboo nodes and internodes could not be treated together (Pearson 1912, 34–35). The nodes are a prominent feature of all grasses, but in annual grasses and cereal straws, they are so small and slightly lignified that they did not cause trouble in manufacturing pulp. Initially, cutting the bamboo nodes out by means of a circular saw was experimented with but it proved to be too a process that was too time-consuming and costly. It meant not only a considerable loss of raw material but also additional expenditure on cutting apparatus as the hard, siliceous cuticle proved very destructive on the steel cutting edges of the saw (Raitt 1912, 6). If both nodes and internodes could be treated together, much labour and time could be saved (Pearson 1912, 34–35).

Throughout the report, Raitt's calculations of yields of dry bamboo were based on the assumption that the nodes and internodes could in fact be treated together. This Raitt demonstrated in laboratory experiments with crushed bamboo, which was obtained by passing culms split in half (i.e. split once longitudinally) through the heavy cane crushing rollers of a sugar plant (Raitt 1912, 16, 35, 9–10). To obtain practical proof of the commercial viability of the process, 80 tons of bamboo of four different species (*B. polymorpha, B. arundinacea, Melócanna bambusoides,* and *Cephalostachyum pergracile*) was dispatched to Titagarh Mill, through the courtesy of Messrs. F. W. Heilgers & Co., the Managing Agents to the Titaghur Paper Mills. Messrs. Bryce, the General Manager, and J. Thomson, a Paper Engineer, supervised the service tests at the mill, where the bamboo consignment was converted into pulp and eventually into paper (Pearson 1912, 3–4, 33).

The manufacturing process began by transporting the raw material to the factory, where the stems were then passed through the heavy crushing rolls in order to split and flatten them, and at the same time, to crush the nodes. Before digesting the material, which was now a tow-like substance, a preliminary treatment with hot water was necessary to remove unwanted starchy matter. Then the material was tightly packed in a digester where it was cooked for a period of six to seven hours with caustic soda at considerable strength. After the cooking process had been finished, the material was put through the washing and beating engine which reduced it to pulp. Finally, the thoroughly washed fibre was dried and baled up in hessian for storage or export (in a similar manner as cotton or jute in the textile industry). Using this method, the Titagarh Mill succeeded in manufacturing bamboo pulp by the soda process on a limited scale but the process did not work satisfactorily enough for commercial production (BPC, CLC/B/022, MS28965:1/241, 281; Sindall 1909; Clapperton & Henderson 1947). To be a commercially viable process, it was necessary for a crushing plant to turn out a large quantity per annum. This of course involved a large supply of raw material, which in view of the undeveloped means of transport proved difficult to ensure.

A decisive step in the commercial utilisation of bamboo as a papermaking material was taken on 27 July 1911, when Samuel Milne of Messrs. Bertrams Ltd., the paper mill engineers of St. Katharine's Works, Sciennes, Edinburgh, patented a new type of bamboo crushing machine that was able to break the nodes without destroying the fibre (Milne 27 July 1911). This work resulted in an improvement in crushing technology and the more economic use of chemicals in treating the pulp. It meant that bamboo stems could be treated whole. The obvious advantage was that it saved the expense of cutting the nodes off, and there was also a saving in raw material. Furthermore, crushing the nodes before digestion allowed for easier chemical treatment, and the period of digestion was shortened owing to the greater speed with which the cooking liquors penetrated the pulp. It also permitted the use of a weaker solution of cooking chemicals.[4]

In 1911, Bertrams equipped two mills (Việt Trì and Hải Phòng) of the Tonkin Pulp and Paper Co., which operated in French Indochina (Vietnam), with Milne's crusher. The bamboo pulp manufactured in these mills emerged during the First World War on the French market at Bordeaux, where it was offered at the equivalent of about Rs.187 per ton in gunny, hydraulically pressed and hooped bales of 400 pounds each. The unbleached pulp was manufactured from young shoots by using the soda process, and it was suitable for printing cheaper grades of newspaper. In terms of quality, the pulp was said to have good resisting and felting qualities. It could therefore be adopted for all 'the fine qualities of paper requiring feel and suppleness'. The pulp compared favourably with cotton rag pulp and was superior to alfa pulp (Bamboo Pulp for Paper Making 17 July 1916).

A further step in the development work on 16 March 1916, when two Scottish papermaking and cellulose experts, James Lockhart Jardine of Esk Mills, Penicuik, in cooperation with Thomas A. Nelson of Parkside Works, Edinburgh, patented a process for the production of an acid magnesium sulphite solution for the extraction of cellulose from bamboo. The patentees found that the sulphite process was cheaper than the sulphate or the soda processes. They also found that the sulphite process produced paper with more enduring whiteness. The acid process was similar to that employed on coniferous wood, but instead of calcium bisulphite, it used magnesia bisulphite after calcium was found to be too acidic for bamboo (Jardine & Nelson 16 March 1916). Jardine's and Nelson's modification required a careful adjustment of cooking temperature. Moreover, the process was particularly devised for bamboo and could not be applied satisfactorily to other raw materials (Bamboo Pulp for Paper Making 17 July 1916).

In order to ascertain the suitability of the sulphate process in the conversion of bamboo into chemical pulp, a series of trials and experiments were carried out at the Thunes Mekaniske Værksted's Paper technological Laboratories, Oslo, Norway, in 1921. The trials revealed the technical possibility of making sulphate pulp from bamboo. The laboratory's report suggested that the sulphate process possessed definite economic advantages over the

82   *Bamboo for papermaking*

soda process. The cost of production by the sulphate process was reduced by 10–15% compared to the cost of the soda process. The working lines, chemicals used, and machinery were about the same in both processes. The main difference was that in the sulphate process, the lost alkali was replaced by cheaper sodium sulphate instead of caustic soda (Bamboo Pulp for Paper Making 17 July 1916).

The results of the cooking trials conducted over a period of a decade or so (1910–1921) had thus established definite commercial possibilities for manufacturing pulp from bamboo. Ultimately, the whole bamboo raw material question came to depend on the cost of production. Although it was sufficiently demonstrated that using a properly adapted treatment made it possible to obtain good-quality soda pulp from bamboo, papermakers in India received no encouragement from financiers for commercial production. Competing in markets against wood pulp and finished paper imports was impossible in India unless financiers were assured that bulk supplies could be delivered to a mill at rates that would permit the finished paper to be sold at a profit. To be commercially viable, it was necessary that a mill should process a large quantity of raw material annually. The output from any given locality depended on the size of the area from which bamboo could be exploited and the size and density of the crop (Pearson 1912, 30, 37–38).

Following Raitt's laboratory experiments at Dehra Dun, in 1912, Captain (later Sir) Ralph Sneyd Pearson (1874–1958), the Imperial Forest Economist,[5] commenced investigations in several bamboo areas on the West Coast of the Indian Peninsula and Lower Burma with a view to ascertaining whether bamboo existed in commercially exploitable quantities (Pearson 1912, 2). As a result of his investigations, in 1914, the Forest Department started negotiations with Thomas A. Nelson, one of the patentees of the bisulphite process devised for bamboo, to build a mill in Beypore, but it appears that no agreement was made. Further investigations into the cost of cutting and transporting bamboo were made in 1917, but these, too, proved to be in vain (Marsden 1922, 39). To induce investors, concessions for the extraction of bamboo were ultimately granted to two firms, Bamboo Pulp Mills Ltd., Tavoy, Burma (the Tavoy River Bamboo Pulping Concession) (Raitt 20 January 1922; Raitt 1929), and The Titaghur Paper Mills Co., but the start of the manufacturing was postponed, owing largely to a labour shortage.

After a considerable delay caused by the repercussions of the First World War, the Government of India followed up the initial success of the Forest Research Institute in the production of bamboo pulp by setting up a pilot plant. The plant was equipped with a digester of approximately 15 cwt. capacity, an up-to-date 36-inch experimental paper machine, and various fittings, which the Government managed to purchase with considerable difficulty from England, Canada, and the USA in 1921–22 (Progress Report 1924, 71). The plant went into operation using the soda process in March 1924 (Progress Report 1925, 64).

Experiments with bamboo on a commercial and organised basis

The factor that most decidedly increased interest towards the use of bamboo as a papermaking material was the experience of the First World War. During the conflict, a shortage of shipping caused trade between India and the rest of the world to collapse. The difficulty of obtaining wood pulp and paper because of the war forced manufacturers in India to switch to indigenous raw materials instead (Marsden 1922, v). The war revealed India's vulnerability in terms of the supply of overseas imports. The decreased imports and the consequent increase in prices meant that Indian mills were not in a position to meet the demand for paper. The effects of the war therefore provided the necessary economic incentive for the papermakers in India to utilise bamboo for large-scale paper manufacture.

The progress of forestry in India on scientific lines had a special significance during the war, as the war made enormous demands on the Empire's forest resources (Barton 2002). The demands of the war and the shortage of imported products and the virtual cessation of production in many important pulp and paper-producing countries made it necessary to develop the use of the Empire's indigenous raw materials (Oosthoek 2018, 138). With the help of forestry, several indigenous substitutes could be found for imported wood pulp and wood-based paper and board, and subsequently, many new or little-known indigenous plants were brought to the market (100 Years of Indian Forestry 1961, II, 181).

Capital and entrepreneurship

Before 1914, most of the capital employed in the Indian paper industry was controlled by two British managing agency houses, Messrs. F. W. Heilgers & Co. and Messrs. Balmer Lawrie & Co. The former controlled the largest Indian producer, The Titaghur Paper Mills Co., and the latter the second largest, the Bengal Paper Mills Co. Such a large degree of concentration of capital facilitated the smooth working of Indian paper markets through various price and market-sharing arrangements (Bagchi 1972, 134, 158–159, 175–176, 178, 391–392). At the beginning of the twentieth century, there was no sharp distinction between the commercial and industrial interests of the managing agents. Typically, managing agency houses acquired a diverse group of subsidiary companies and built up a portfolio of investments primarily in British companies. Whether a subsidiary company was registered in London or Calcutta depended primarily on the business acumen of the managing agents (Bagchi 1972, 162, 200; see also Jones 1992).

The Bamboo Paper Company was the first London-based company that was established to carry on the business of manufacturing and dealing in pulp from bamboo in India. On 27 January 1919, the incorporated company was freestanding in the sense that it had limited managerial resources, and it

84 Bamboo for papermaking

operated with the support of the financial and marketing services provided by commercial and financial City firms (Wilkins 1988, 264). The Bamboo Paper Co. was a private company under the meaning of the Companies Acts of 1908–1917. Its investments were made through channels other than the Stock Exchange, and no invitation was made to the public to subscribe for any shares, debentures, or debenture stock of the company. The capital invested in the Bamboo Paper Co. constituted reinvested profits and capital raised from their partners, Andrew Yule & Co., a managing agency firm which had its registered offices in Calcutta (BPC, CLC/B/022, MS28961).

After its establishment, the Bamboo Paper Co. left technical and production matters for the India Paper Pulp Co., which was incorporated on 4 April 1918 by Andrew Yule & Co. According to an indenture, which was made on 4 November 1919 between the Bamboo Paper Co. and the India Paper Pulp Co., the latter company got exclusive rights to the use of inventions relating to improvements in making bamboo pulp and the authority to manufacture and sell it. In return, the India Paper Pulp Co. allotted and issued 3,800 fully paid-up shares of its capital to Bamboo Paper Co. (i.e. 20% of the equities) (BPC, CLC/B/022, MS28963).

The Bamboo Paper Co. did not invent the process for extracting cellulose from bamboo using acid sulphite but had acquired the patent rights by assignment from the original patentees, Thomas Nelson, his brother Ian Nelson and James Lockhart Jardine, who acted as the company's paper and cellulose experts. The patents covered two principal areas: the actual pulping process by which it was possible to manufacture high-grade pulp on a commercial basis and the machinery for crushing bamboo (BPC, CLC/B/022, MS28964:1/126, 241). Thomas Nelson & Sons, Ltd., which had its registered premises at Parkside Works, Dalkeith Road, Edinburgh, acted as the patent agents for the Bamboo Paper Co. The former tried to eliminate potential competitors in the field by securing foreign and colonial patents for the sulphite pulping process and the crusher.

According to the requirements of the Patent Office, working on a commercial scale should have been carried out within four years of the issue of the patent but this provision was suspended during the war and the period for complying with it was extended until 1922. A certain amount of crushing, pulping, and paper manufacturing was initially done at the works of James Brown & Co., Ltd., the Esk Mills, Penicuik, Midlothian (BPC, CLC/B/022, MS28964:1/335; MS28964:2/178). For the commercial development of the process, the India Paper Pulp Co. required a large plant, which it started to construct in 1919 on the East bank of the River Hooghly, at Hazinagar, near Naihati, Eastern Bengal Railway, 30 miles from Calcutta. The experimental and development work was carried out over the next four years at the Naihati Mill, and this resulted in improvements in the mechanical treatment as well as the economic use of chemicals in treating bamboo. The mill started to pulp bamboo by using the sulphite process in 1922 (ITB 1924, 312; Podder 1979, 8–9, 55–56) (Figure 5.1).

Bamboo for papermaking 85

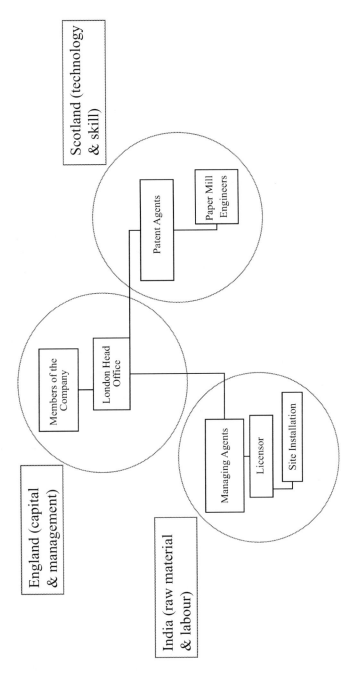

Figure 5.1 Business Structure of the Bamboo Paper Company.
Source: Compiled by the author from the Records of the Bamboo Paper Company Limited (BPC, CLC/B/022).

86   Bamboo for papermaking

The essential conditions for successful bamboo pulp and paper industry

In considering the commercial value of bamboo in its application to papermaking, the following points needed to be considered concerning the construction of the Naihati Mill. Firstly, to reduce transport costs, it was imperative that the mill be located close to the source of the raw materials. The amount of raw material needed was calculated by estimating the quantity of bamboo required for the manufacture of a stated annual amount of finished, air-dried pulp, and the area of land that was estimated to be necessary for the production of that quantity. Air-dried bamboo typically yielded 42–50% pulp on its weight, depending on species exploited. On the basis of a 45% yield, the manufacture of one ton of pulp necessitated the treatment of two and a quarter tons of bamboo (Sindall 1909).

Initially, the India Paper Pulp Co. adopted a business model in which the supply of raw material was ensured by cropping and cultivating the Kasalong Bamboo Reserve (located in Chittagong Hill Tracts), which the company leased from the Government. By gradually harvesting the older growth for the manufacture of certain qualities of pulp and introducing a system of cropping, it was possible to control the growth of bamboo and thus ensure a permanent supply of raw material. The bamboo was procured by first cutting it and then floating it in rafts down to the company's crushing and baling plant in Chittagong (Chattogram). The capacity of this crushing plant was approximately 24 tons of raw bamboo per day. The crushed material was then transported by steamer to the Chittagong Jetties and finally delivered by rail to the Naihati Mill (the total distance from the bamboo reserve to the mill was 470 miles). Working the concession directly proved to be too costly, however, and before long, the company started to obtain its raw material directly from contractors in Assam as well as Chittagong (ITB 1924, 312, 362, 1931, 40, 45). Although this approach was cost-effective, its obvious disadvantage was that it was difficult to ensure the uniformity of the raw material.

Secondly, the location of the mill needed to be considered. Up to the late 1930s, Indian paper mills were almost entirely dependent on imports from abroad for their requirements of machinery, machine tools, and processing chemicals (Bagchi 1972, 434). To ensure the delivery of the supplies of raw material, coal for energy and various chemicals and loading materials and the transfer of the finished paper, a railway siding and a port contiguous to the mill had to be built. In wood pulping, hydroelectric energy resources were essential in choosing a location for the mill, but this consideration did not apply to the Naihati Mill, which obtained electric power from a steam-driven power station situated in the mill. Coal was brought by rail from the Raniganj Coalfield (a distance of 150 miles) (BPC, CLC/B/022, Letter Book, MS28964:2/197).

The technology in connection with the crushing process was perfected in Edinburgh at the Leith Walk Foundry of Messrs. James Bertram & Son, Ltd., which supplied the crushing plant. The same company delivered a 98-inch wide paper machine to the mill together with various fittings. Besides the actual machinery needed for the production of pulp and paper from bamboo fibre, the equipment for the Naihati Mill varied widely and included, among other items, corrugated roofing materials from the British Everite & Asbestilite Works, Ltd. of Manchester, a Turbo-Generator from Messrs. Bruce, Peebles & Co. of Edinburgh, an engine from Belliss & Morcom, Ltd. of Ladywood, Birmingham, and a steam turbine from Ljungström Steam Turbine Co. (Aktiebolaget Ljungströms Ångturbin) of Sweden (BPC, CLC/B/022, MS28964:2/197). The supplies of heavy chemicals and minerals included, for instance, 50 tons of refined rock sulphur per month from Sicily, together with volumes of bleaching powder, China clay, dyes, and magnesite. In terms of the latter, which was imperative for the extraction of cellulose from bamboo, the company relied on supplies from the Salem Mines, located in Kancheepuram, near Chennai (BPC, CLC/B/022, MS28965:1/246, 273, 325). It also considered acquiring its own magnesite deposits in India (ITB 1924, 315).

Finally, the total operating costs, which would determine whether the finished paper could be sold at a profit, needed to be considered. Reliable cost estimates were difficult to make because of various factors. To begin with, enormous demands for all kinds of machinery, equipment, and chemicals had to be taken into account. But there were problems with industrial supplies both in Britain and India, including a serious shortage of building materials. Furthermore, there was a shortage of suitable shipping, which was part of more general difficulties with communication (for instance in 1921 cables from London to India frequently took from seven to eight days) (BPC, CLC/B/022, MS28965:1/317).

In particular, fluctuations in the exchange value of the rupee created difficulties for the India Paper Pulp Co. Between 1898–99 and 1919–20, the value of the rupee was maintained at the fixed rate of 1s. 4d. The breakdown of the pre-war monetary mechanisms and the inability of the Government of India to introduce a paper currency to replace the old silver rupee meant that the fixed value of the rupee became linked to the soaring price of silver (Bagchi 1972, 64–65). Fluctuations in the rupee's exchange value combined with intense competition from abroad cast a dark shadow over the potential development of the bamboo pulp and paper industry. In 1919, it was estimated that total expenditure on the Naihati Mill was Rs.750,000 (£50,000 when the exchange value of the rupee was 1s. 4d) (BPC, CLC/B/022, MS28965:1/275–277). This was significantly higher than Sindall's estimate some ten years earlier. In 1909, the cost of a dry-pulp plant, which had a weekly output of 200 tons pulp, had been in total about £36,000 (Sindall 1909).

The estimated production cost at the Naihati Mill was Rs.80 per ton of wet pulp and Rs.140 per ton of paper (BPC, CLC/B/022, MS28965:1/273). These estimates were exclusive of labour costs, which amounted to 38% of the total production costs in the UK, but were significantly lower in Bengal,

88 *Bamboo for papermaking*

where cheap and abundant Indian labour was one of the main assets of the pulp and paper industry (ITB 1924, 311; Bagchi 1972, 152–153). In general, from the mid-1920s onwards, there was abundant labour in most of India's major industrial centres. Since working conditions in mills were much better than in mines and plantations, and wages were higher, particularly for skilled workers, it was not necessary for the managing agents to make any special effort to recruit labour (Bagchi 1972, 135, 138). In 1924, it was estimated that the Naihati Mill employed some 800–1,000 labourers (exclusive of those workers who were extracting and collecting raw material) (ITB 1924, 315). The wages of Indian workers varied from Rs.190 per month at the high end of the scale (i.e. the Head Mechanic) to Rs.14 per month at the low end (i.e. a 'Boy') (ITB 1924, 318). These wages were significantly higher than average monthly wages of Indian workers in the Calcutta Jute Mills, where work-ers earned between Rs.12 and Rs.20 a month (Bagchi 1972, 126–127). The management at the Naihati Mill was European and earned approximately 50% more than the average wage that would have been drawn in England (ITB 1924, 318).

The paper and pulp trades and Indian tariff policy

Up to 1914, the Government of India pursued the policy of free trade and non-intervention in industry, and there was virtually free trade as far as im-ports into India from other countries were concerned. This pattern of trade primarily served the British imperial system; Britain had a large market, in which Lancaster and Manchester piece goods (i.e. fabrics woven in standard lengths for sale) and other industrial products in demand in India such as machinery and hardware entered duty-free at the time when other markets in the world were closing against them. On the other hand, Britain was the largest purchaser of raw materials and manufactured jute from India. The system's smooth functioning was facilitated by the fact that the Indian money market was directly linked to the City, the world's chief money market before 1914, and also by the fact that there was little industry in India in comparison with trade (Bagchi 1972, 5, 48–50, 58–59).

An early attempt in the Indian paper industry at finding a suitable sub-stitute for imports was choked off before the First World War by the rapid progress of the wood pulping processes in Europe and North America. The war caused a violent disruption to the trade owing to the lack of shipping capacity. By 1918–19, the amount of wood pulp imported into India had recovered to merely 2,090 tons, causing soaring prices. At this time, the Ra-niganj Mill of the Bengal Paper Mills Co. was buying imported sulphite pulp at the very high price of £20 a ton. Its average manufacturing costs from all materials was £14 a ton (BPC, CLC/B/022, MS28965:1/198–199). By the end of 1922, competition from European papermakers had started in earnest, so prices fell rapidly. In this regard, competition was most intense from the UK, Norway, Sweden, Finland, Germany, and the Netherlands. In terms of wood pulp, Sweden, Finland, and Norway were the main suppliers to the Indian markets (ITB 1924, 321). The average price of imported Scandinavian pulp was in the neighbourhood of £10–15 a ton. By way of comparison, the price of Scandinavian wood pulp at an English mill was reported to be approximately £9 a ton (ITB 1931, 19, 90). A factor which favoured the use of imported wood pulp over indigenous materials was that it took a much larger quantity of bamboo to produce the same quantity of paper (it took between two and a half and three tons of bamboo to make a ton of pulp). Furthermore, the cost of imported wood pulp went down in relation to that of indigenous raw materials (Bagchi 1972, 395–396, 398; ITB 1931 68).

The first step in erecting a tariff on imported pulp and paper occurred in June 1923 when the Indian Paper Makers' Association submitted its claim for protection to the Government of India. The question was referred to the Indian Tariff Board (ITB) one year later. The ITB considered it inadvisable for the Government to commit itself firmly to the protection of the bamboo pulp and paper industry until the bamboo pulping process had really proved itself commercially. Instead, the ITB suggested that the Government support the India Paper Pulp Co. by providing capital either in the form of loans or by guaranteeing a public issue of debentures for an extension of its capacity. Secondly, it recommended that, in place of the existing 15% *ad valorem* duties on printing and writing paper, a specific duty of one anna per pound should be imposed on all writing paper and on all writing paper other than newsprint containing 65% or more of mechanical pulp. Newsprint was exempted from the protective duty on the grounds that mechanical pulp had never been made from either sabai grass or bamboo and that the existence of cheap newsprint on the Indian markets depended on imports. However, the Government rejected the ITB's recommendation to provide financial assistance to the India Paper Pulp Co. for three reasons. Firstly, the India Paper Pulp Co. was a private company. Secondly, the sulphite process was covered by patent rights held by Jardine and the Nelsons, who were members of the company. And finally and most importantly, it was stated that financial assistance to the Indian paper industry should assist all competitors within the industry equally and not benefit the India Paper Pulp Co. alone, thereby giving it an undue advantage over its rivals (ITB 1931, 3; Bagchi 1972, 397).

Ultimately, the ITB ended up endorsing protection instead of financial assistance to the India Paper Pulp Co. because it considered that bamboo could serve as the raw material for the long-term development of the Indian paper industry. The two major producers of paper in India, the Titaghur and the Bengal Paper Mills, did not have promising prospects, on the one hand, because the supplies of sabai grass from known sources were rather limited, and on the other because both companies' mills were situated far from the known sources of sabai. The Bamboo Paper Industry Protection Act of 1925 marked the end of the free trade era. It imposed an import duty of one anna per pound on printing and writing paper, and on all writing paper other than newsprint containing 65% or more mechanical pulp. Papers made from

90 *Bamboo for papermaking*

bamboo were protected for seven years (up to 31 March 1932) (ITB 1931, 3–5; Bagchi 1972, 5, 396–397; Podder 1979, 56).

The protective duty for the bamboo pulp and paper industry in India had numerous effects. The bamboo pulping process, although known theoretically since the mid-1870s, entered the period of commercial production only in 1922 and developed in an economically viable manner only after tariff protection had become effective. The technology was first developed at the Naihati Mill, but was later adopted by the other Indian mills in response to the increased cost of other indigenous raw materials (e.g. sabai grass) (Bagchi 1972, 419). In 1923, the Titaghur Paper Mills Co. and the Bengal Paper Mills Co. had 12 paper machines all told (with an aggregated capacity of 31,000 tons). The India Paper Pulp Co. had initially only one paper machine (its capacity was 6,000 tons and it installed a second machine in 1927) with which it had managed to produce (by using only their own bamboo pulp) 4,228 tons of paper by the end of 1924 (ITB 1924, 311, 1931 10). Although it had started production only in 1922, it already showed lower production costs than its competitors in Bengal. Including labour, its costs were Rs.485.27 a ton of paper for 1923–24 (ITB 1924, 335). In 1930–31, the costs were approximately one-third lower (Rs.330.65 a ton) (ITB 1931, 54). The fall in costs is attributable to the growing familiarity with bamboo as a papermaking material, the employment of contractors as opposed to using men who were on the company's payroll to work the concession, and improved efficiency in production, which led to a reduced need for coal (ITB 1931, 63, 65–66).

The tariff protection was not much of a success in terms of increased production of bamboo paper in relation to India's total output of paper. The rate of growth of the bamboo paper industry under tariff protection was initially very modest. Production of 2,500 and 5,000 tons was recorded in 1925 and 1931, respectively, while the total output (from all materials) of the Indian mills increased from 25,000 to 40,000 tons. In 1925, the protected bamboo paper industry represented 14.7% of total Indian paper production and dropped to a mere 8% in 1931 (ITB 1931, 18, 25). Protection was primarily effective in restricting the consumption of certain grades of paper, but a substitution of unprotected for protected varieties took place. The total Indian consumption of all grades of paper increased from 112,000 tons in 1924–25 to 154,300 in 1930–31, and the consumption of tariff-protected paper increased from 43,300 tons in 1924–25 to 49,000 in 1930–31 (ITB 1931, 105).

One of the unintended effects of protecting the bamboo pulp and paper industry was a rise in the proportion of imported wood pulp used in the manufacture of paper. This was a natural outcome because the bamboo pulping process developed very slowly. At the time of the 1931 enquiry by the ITB, apart from the India Paper Pulp Co., only the Titaghur Paper Mills Co. seemed to have succeeded in developing a truly effective bamboo pulping process. Titaghur relied first on the soda process but later applied the improved fractional system of digestion with the sulphate of soda method along with other Indian mills. Only the India Paper Pulp Co. continued to rely on the sulphite process it had devised for bamboo (ITB 1931, 47, 106). Between 1924–25 and 1930–31, the use of both indigenous and imported materials increased, but there was a drastic decline in the ratio of indigenous compared to imported materials used. All the major companies were using a higher percentage of imported wood pulp in 1930–31 than they had done in 1924–25. In the case of the India Paper Pulp Co., for example, in 1924–25, wood pulp accounted for 21% by weight of the finished paper it produced. In 1930–31, wood pulp accounted already for 63% by weight of the finished paper produced and bamboo some 30%, with the rest coming from recycled fibres. The total quantity of wood pulp imported into India in 1930–31 was 22,715 tons, which was equivalent to nearly 20,000 tons of finished paper or about half of total Indian paper production (ITB 1931, 55, 87, 93; Bagchi 1972, 402).

The Bamboo Paper Industry (Protection) Act of 1932 extended protection by another seven years since the withdrawal of the protective duty would have meant the disappearance of bamboo as a raw material for the manufacture of paper. The ITB estimated that without tariff protection it would be far too expensive for the mills to use bamboo pulp. It would have wasted all the development work, left indigenous raw material resources undeveloped, and kept the Indian paper industry dependent on imported wood pulp. During the First World War, the scarcity of wood pulp had nearly crippled the paper industry and highlighted the importance of having a domestic pulp industry (ITB 1931, 82–84; Bagchi 1972, 45). From 1932 to 1937, India's total production increased every year. This was due to the better utilisation of existing production capacity under the stimulus of higher duties. The protective duty on paper was raised in 1932 from 18.75 to 30% *ad valorem*, with a preferential duty for grades manufactured in Britain (Bagchi 1972, 402). This was a result of the imperial preference system, created at an Imperial Economic Conference in Ottawa in July–August 1932, which aimed at expanding trade among the members of the British Commonwealth in a world of shrinking commerce and rising trade barriers (see Chap. 4).

A period of seven years (1932–39) afforded the Indian paper industry an opportunity to consolidate its position and encouraged it to undertake further expansion. It also made considerable progress in substituting bamboo pulp for wood pulp. This was primarily the result of the imposition in 1932 of a specific duty of Rs.45 per ton on imported pulp by the Bamboo Paper Industry Act of 1932. Since all protective duties were subject to the revenue surcharge imposed in November 1931, the effective rate of specific duty on imported pulp came to Rs.56.25 per ton. The replacement of imported pulp by domestically produced pulp was also facilitated by resolving the problems involved in the mechanical treatment of bamboo (ITB 1931, 95–96; Bagchi 1972, 399).

The monetary incentive given by the Bamboo Paper Industry Protection Act of 1932 was enough to introduce bamboo into the paper industry. As it transpired, bamboo raw material provided the basis for the long-term

92 Bamboo for papermaking

development of the Indian paper industry. Between 1936 and 1939, five new mills using bamboo as a primary raw material for making paper appeared on the business scene: Star Paper Mills (Bengal) in 1936, Mysore Paper Mills in 1937, Orient Paper Mills (Orissa) and Sirpur Paper Mills (Hyderabad Deccan) in 1938 as well as Rohtas Industries (Bihar) in 1939.

Creating a national bamboo pulp and paper industry in India

The Second World War created a shortage of pulp and paper and prices were soaring, thereby precluding the import of wood pulp into India at competitive rates. After the transfer of power, India was short of cellulosic raw material, which it could not afford to import. At this juncture, the bamboo pulp and paper industry came to play a very important role in the Indian national economy, and the country's bamboo forests proved indispensable for the pulp and paper industry. India was passing through a phase of rapid industrialisation and modernisation, and the bamboo pulp and paper industry was considered a strategic industry for increasing literacy. *B. arundinacea* and *Dendrocalamus strictus* were the main species that were exploited, and the moist dense forests in the 'paper belt', *viz.* mountain ranges and hill slopes of the Western and Eastern Ghats, the Vindhya and the Satpura ranges, the Assam hills and the Eastern Himalayas, were the main areas of their extraction. Several other species were also exploited locally in limited quantities (Savur 2003, I, 1–12).

The factors that most influenced increased cultural paper consumption in India were the rising numbers of literate people and school pupils. Demand for industrial papers increased as a consequence of improved national income and industrial production. The total consumption of paper was 355,000 tons in 1956–57, which represented an increase of almost a third compared to 1948–49 (238,000 tons). At the same time, paper was produced progressively more in India than it was imported. In 1948–49, the domestic production of paper was 98,000 tons, which was over 40% of the total consumption in that year. After this, the Indian bamboo pulp industry developed rapidly, and self-sufficiency improved in all the major grades of paper, with the single exception of newsprint. By 1956–57, domestic production had increased to 224,000 tons, which represented 63% of the total consumption. During the period 1948–57, the self-sufficiency rate was at its highest in printing and writing paper (81%), board (80%), wrapping paper and special varieties (45.2%), but it was only about 4% in newsprint (Demand Forecast 1965, 1, 5).

An adequate raw material base and the availability of indigenous fibre-yielding raw materials continued to be a matter of concern for the future growth of the industry. After the transfer of power, the significance of developing a pulp industry based on an indigenous raw material was emphasised from the perspective of national economic performance. The choice for suitable raw material naturally devolved to bamboo because it was plentiful compared to other available domestic papermaking materials such as grasses, waste paper, rags, bagasse, and all other papermaking materials. Another benefit of bamboo as a papermaking material proved to be the fact it can also yield viscose rayon, for which pulping trials were initiated by the Birla Group of Companies in 1954 (100 Years of Indian Forestry 1961, II, 49; Savur 2003, I, 21).

In terms of their paper equivalents, from 1948 to 1954, the domestic production of raw material was as follows: bamboo (52%), grasses (14.1%), waste paper (12.8%), wood pulp (7.4%), rags (4.5%), straw (4.1%), sugarcane bagasse (2.6%), and all others (2.5%). In the following years, the importance of bamboo increased even further, and, by 1959, bamboo accounted for about two-thirds (67%) of the fibre furnish (Demand Forecast 1965, 1–2; Podder 1979, 66, 177). However, this did not alleviate the production of newsprint because normally 75 to 85% of it was produced from mechanical pulp for which production bamboo was not suitable. In general, underdeveloped countries like India imported most of their newsprint from the outside world. The situation started to improve in 1956–57, when National Newsprint and Paper Mills, Ltd., which had gone into production in the previous year, achieved 30,000 tons, which represented almost a third of the total newsprint consumption in the same year (Demand Forecast 1965, 1, 5; Podder 1979, 177, 196).

Bamboo harvesting and transporting

In 1952, there were in total ten mills using bamboo for papermaking in India: Titaghur Paper Mills (2 production units); India Paper Pulp Co. Ltd; Bengal Paper Mills; Rohtas Industries Ltd. (Bihar); Orient Paper Mills (Orissa); Sirpur Paper Mills (Hyderabad Deccan); Mysore Paper Mills; Andhra Paper Mills; and Punalur Paper Mills (Travancore). In 1957, their aggregated annual capacity stood at 158,600 tons of paper (Table 5.1), which represented 78.8% of the total annual rated capacity of the Indian paper industry in the same year (201,200 tons) (Demand Forecast 1965, 22–23).

Table 5.1 Annual Rated Capacity of Bamboo Pulp and Paper Mills in India 1957 (tons)

State	Mill	Location	Capacity
Bengal	Titaghur Paper Mills (2 units)	Calcutta	42,000
	India Paper & Pulp	Naihati	6,600
	Bengal Paper Mills	Raniganj	14,000
Bihar	Rohtas Industries	Dalmianagar	29,000
Orissa	Orient Paper Mills	Brajrajnagar	36,000
Andhra	Sirpur Paper Mills	Sirpur	15,000
	Andhra Paper Mills	Rajahmundry	2,000
Mysore	Mysore Paper Mills	Bhadravati	8,000
Kerala	Punalur Paper Mills	Punalur	6,000
Total			158,600

Sources: Paper Production of Bamboo from India 18 April 1952; Demand Forecast 1965, 22–23.

94 Bamboo for papermaking

The Titaghur Paper Mills Co., Ltd. formed the largest paper-manufacturing group in India, producing over one-third of the paper made in the country. The company's two mills consumed about 90,000 tons of bamboo (c. 96% of the total fibre furnish) and 3,500 tons of sabai grass (c. 4%, respectively) annually. Sabai grass had been the primary indigenous raw material for papermaking at the Titaghur Paper Mills for many decades, but the quantity available had become very restricted. The final choice rested with bamboo, which at time was the cheapest and most readily available indigenous raw material. The quantity available in West Bengal was relatively small, however, because the bamboo areas in this State had suffered from the effects of over-cropping due to its prolonged industrial use. Therefore, the amount of locally available bamboo tended to be very limited and the price is unreasonably high. To alleviate the problem, Messrs. F. W. Heilgers & Co. Ltd., the Managing Agents of the Titaghur Paper Mills, laid out a plantation of *Bambusa balcooa* in Bengal. Incidentally, the area was requisitioned two and a half years later by the Royal Air Force, which started to build Asansol Airfield following the conquest of Burma by the Imperial Japanese Army. The company therefore clear-felled the area. A yield of six tons of bamboo per acre was achieved due to the combination of the bamboo being planted systematically, the fertility of the agricultural land, and an annual rainfall of 65 inches (Paper Production of Bamboo from India 18 April 1952).

The company therefore had to look further afield for new supplies for papermaking from leased virgin bamboo forests, which were widely separated from each other in East and West Bengal, Assam, Bihar, Orissa, and Madhya Pradesh (Demand Forecast for Bamboo Sulphate Pulp 1965, 11). It was quite difficult to estimate the size of the catchment area which would be necessary to keep the mills in full production. As already pointed out, several factors affected the yield per acre of bamboo. The chief factors were the varieties of bamboo, the topography of the land, the nature of the soil, and the annual rainfall. In its natural habitats, bamboo rarely formed pure crops but was found growing in proximity to trees, and the yield per acre naturally varied according to the number of the clumps as well. Three of Messrs. F. W. Heilgers & Co.'s six leased areas were similar in regard to variety, the topography of the land, and the nature of the soil. As regards the varieties of bamboo grown in these areas, they varied from the thick-walled, heavy stemmed to the thin-walled, hollow varieties. The managing agents estimated that the yield per acre, where the forest consists purely of different varieties of bamboo, was one ton per acre per harvest. Where bamboo was mixed with trees, the yield per acre could be as low as 0.2–0.5 tons per harvest (Paper Production of Bamboo from India 18 April 1952).

If an area was clear-felled, i.e. every single shoot was cut, it could take anything from 5 to 10 years before the clumps regenerated through self-seeding. Therefore, in normal circumstances, clear-felling of clumps has never been done, and the expression 'intensive cutting' associated with wood logging did not apply to bamboo harvesting. According to the Indian Forest Department's silvicultural rules, in normal circumstances, the bamboo clumps were worked on a felling cycle of once every three or four years depending on local factors. So the bamboo forests were correspondingly laid out in three or four compartments to form blocks. In felling, fresh culms, which are shoots of that year, were not cut. Of the older culms, about six to ten stems were left untouched, depending on the size of the clump, and well distributed in the clump to support the immature stems. The cut was made not less than 12 inches from the ground, and in clump clearing, any broken or malformed stems were removed. The Forest Department insisted that the cutting should be carried out only on a four-year rotation basis in order to avoid deterioration in the vigour of the clumps (Paper Production of Bamboo from India 18 April 1952).

The Forest Department's silvicultural rules enable us to make an estimation of the size of the catchment area required to keep a mill in full production throughout the year. If the capacity of a pulp mill was 10,000 tons per annum, an area yielding 30,000 tons of air-dried bamboo was required. Assuming that the yield of bamboo was 0.5 ton per acre, an area of at least 60,000 acres would have been required to keep the mill in full operation throughout the year. This was only for one year, but if the system of harvesting once in every four-year rotation was adopted, an area of about 240,000 acres would be required. In India, and elsewhere, where the large reserves of bamboo occurred, the bamboo did not occur on its own, as there were normally various species of trees in the bamboo forests. Therefore, that 240,000 acre catchment area is a conservative estimate. There is, of course, also the fact that bamboo flowers gregariously. Admittedly, this occurs only between at long intervals (every 30–60 years), but when it did occur, the whole of the bamboo in that area died, with the consequent risk that the mill would be left without any supplies from that area for five to ten years (Paper Production of Bamboo from India 18 April 1952).

Three main methods of transporting raw bamboo from the forest were (1) by rafting down rivers, (2) by river steamers, and (3) overland by road and rail. Rafting provided the cheapest means of transport for bamboo, but its application was limited to those forests which were close enough to rivers of sufficient magnitude. At the same time, there had to be facilities for receiving and handling raft-borne traffic. A large river frontage was required, especially on the river upon which the paper mill stood, but this condition did not obtain at the mills of the Titaghur Paper Mills as its mills were laid out primarily for railway traffic, which was the most convenient means of transporting sabai grass (Paper Production of Bamboo from India 18 April 1952), the principal indigenous raw material of the mill up to 1930.

Forests from which raw bamboo could be transported by means of rafting down rivers to a convenient railhead occurred in certain forests of Orissa and Assam. In Orissa, the cost of transporting 3,000 bamboo stems (about eight tons) 100 miles by raft worked out to be of the order of Rs.30 per ton. In Assam, bamboo forests constituted mainly the thin-walled, hollow bamboo

96 *Bamboo for papermaking*

varieties and river rafting was the first method of transport attempted by Messrs. F. W. Heilgers & Co. But this proved a costly proposition since a large portion of stems was lost on the way, so the company switched to river steamers instead. However, the cost of river steamer transport was found to be very high, being approximately Rs.60 per ton over the whole journey from Assam to the mills in West Bengal. River steamer transport was more suitable to valuable and more compact commodities such as tea and jute rather than to bulky and heavy bamboo, which was essentially a low-cost raw material (Paper Production of Bamboo from India 18 April 1952).

The greater proportion of Titaghur Paper Mills' bamboo deliveries were handled by road-cum-rail, which was the most convenient means of transport for bamboo. Most of the forest areas of Bihar, Orissa, and Madhya Pradesh were served by roads of varying quality, and sometimes stretches of 100–120 miles had to be traversed before a suitable railhead, from which the bamboo could be conveyed to the mills by rail, was reached. Bamboo harvesting went on throughout the year, but extraction from forests by vehicular traffic was not possible during the Monsoon rains from July to September and for a further month to six weeks until the forest roads had dried up sufficiently. Bullock carts were used prior to the war, but by the 1950s, motor lorries had largely replaced the carts, though the bullock and cart did retain the advantage of being able to move through forests inaccessible to mechanical vehicles. Nonetheless, the slow speed on account of the payloads largely militated against the use of the bullock carts in the 1950s (Paper Production of Bamboo from India 18 April 1952).

Until 1 October 1948, bamboo enjoyed a preferential tariff on the railways, but after that, this advantage was progressively withdrawn, as the following will indicate. Prior to 1 October 1948, on the Bengal–Nagpur Railway (distance 250–300 miles), the cost of bamboo was Rs.15 per ton. From 1 October onwards, the cost rose to Rs.25 per ton, and at the latter rate, the cost of the freight exceeded the cost of the bamboo. While bamboo was heavier than sabai grass, it was also a much bulkier raw material. The full length of bamboo stems, which could be up to 45 feet long depending on the variety, was cut into convenient lengths of six feet and bundled and packed into railway wagons. Up to 11 tons of bamboo could be loaded on to a broad gauge wagon, depending on the variety of the bamboo and the floor area of the wagon. Since the satisfactory packing of the wagons was a matter of the first importance, serious consideration was given to the feasibility of establishing crushing centres so that hydraulically pressed bales of crushed bamboo could be more economically moved by rail as was done in the grass trade. The innumerable areas from which the supplies were drawn were so widely scattered, however, that the scheme had to be abandoned. To make a more economic use of space, Titaghur Paper Mills also tried to split stems longitudinally before hauling, but that proved only to increase transport costs even further due to the increased use of labour. However, the general shortage of railway wagons in India rendered the use of these alternative means of packing wagons imperative for future large quantities of bamboo (Paper Production of Bamboo from India 18 April 1952).

Although there still were large untapped tracts of bamboo forests in India in the 1950s, the difficulties of transport hindered any immediate large-scale expansion in bamboo operations. The problems were technical and economic by nature. Since 1939, the cost of bamboo steadily rose due to increased labour and freight charges. In 1939–40, the cost of two and a half tons of bamboo necessary to produce one ton of pulp was Rs.65, whereas in 1952, it was Rs.225 by means of road-cum-rail transport. There seemed little likelihood of any reduction being achieved in the cost of either extraction or railway freight. So it proved very difficult to bring the raw bamboo from the different parts of India to the paper mills situated in West Bengal. It was much less problematic to transport finished pulp than import raw bamboo because the raw material loses about two-fifths in weight during the pulping process (Paper Production of Bamboo from India 18 April 1952).

Conversion of bamboo into pulp

Of the ten mills that were using bamboo for papermaking in India in 1952, only the Naihati Mill of the India Paper Pulp Co. was still using its well-tried sulphite process specially devised for bamboo. The rest of the mills employed the sulphate process using the fractional method developed at the Forest Research Institute. Bamboo pulping involved crushing, chipping, cooking, bleaching, beating, and sizing before it was ready to be made into paper. Roughly speaking, two and a half to three tons of bamboo stems was required to turn one ton of paper. Firstly, the stems, cut in six feet lengths, were fed into a crusher, where it passed between series of serrated, heavy rolls, which split and crushed the material. Then, the flattened and crushed material was fed into a revolving drum with fixed knives. This reduced the material to half-inch chips, which were then conveyed into a pipe leading to the loft of the digester house. From the loft, the chips were fed into vertical digesters of eight tons capacity each, where they were cooked (i.e. digested) in two stages at an elevated temperature under steam pressure. Coal was the basic fuel in the industry for raising temperature and making steam. For instance, both mills of the Titaghur Paper Mills Co. used slack coal for their Turbo-Alternators. Some electricity was also purchased from the Calcutta Electric Supply Corporation. The power consumed within the mills was therefore mainly electric, though there were still a few steam engines in use (Paper Production of Bamboo from India 18 April 1952).

Digestion separated the cellulose (or fibre) from the lignin, silica, waxes, and resins. The first cook lasted four hours at 40 lbs. pressure. After the cook was completed, the black liquor was blown under steam pressure to the caustic recovery plant, where a proportion of caustic soda was recovered for future use. Other effluents were released untreated into rivers, often

98 *Bamboo for papermaking*

causing serious environmental problems. Besides pollution of water and the river ecosystem, the organic sulphur compounds, which were formed during the cooking process, polluted the air, causing extremely disagreeable odours. In the case of the Titaghur Paper Mills Co., the untreated effluents were released into the Hooghly, which is a tidal river. The mill operated day and night throughout the year, and when the height of the tide was at its lowest, the effluents lingered on the river until the next tidal current carried suspended solids and organic matters into the Bay of Bengal (Paper Production of Bamboo from India 18 April 1952).

For the second cook, which lasted for four and a half hours at 80 lbs. pressure, fresh cooking liquor was used containing about 9% caustic soda and 1% sodium sulphate. When the second cook had been completed, the cooking liquor was blown under steam pressure to a storage vessel, where it remained until it was required for the first cook of the next digest. The green pulp resulting from the digestion was washed and pumped into cylindrical tanks for storage. From the storage tanks, the pulp was fed into a series of vacuum filters. As the pulp left the last filter, calcium hypochlorite bleaching liquor was added continuously, and the pulp mixed with bleach was circulated through a series of vertical bleaching towers, where the green pulp was bleached white. From the last tower, the bleached pulp was pumped into a sand table, into which pieces of uncooked bamboo, nodes, and other particles fell, and from there through a series of cylindrical strainers to remove finer uncooked material. Thereafter, the pulp was passed through another vacuum filter, which removed excess water and discharged the pulp which was now known as 'bleached bamboo half-stuff' (Paper Production of Bamboo from India 18 April 1952).

The pulp was next fed into Hollander beaters for further processing before it was ready to be made into paper. The Hollanders shortened the length of fibres and crushed or fibrillated them (i.e. broke fibres into fibrils) according to the degree of beating to which the pulp was subjected. During beating, sizing agents were added so that the finished paper could be written on with ink. Pigments, dye, rosin size, and kaolin were also added to the stock during the beating process. Kaolin helped to close the interstices between the fibres and produced a more heterogeneous surface in the paper and rosin size regulated the rate at which paper absorbs water or ink. When the pulp had been beaten to the requisite degree for the quality of paper of which it was intended, the beaten stock was dropped by gravity to the stuff chests, where agitators kept it stirred so that the heavier ingredients did not settle out and the stuff remained uniform throughout. From the stuff chests, the stock was pumped to the head box, which regulated the amount of stock that was permitted to go forward to the paper machine. At this stage, the stock was further diluted with water before passing over sand tables (Paper Production of Bamboo from India 18 April 1952). The stock having been cleaned in this way was ready to be made into paper, by applying in principle the same methods used with esparto pulp (Chap. 3).

Demand forecast for bamboo pulp by 1960

The entry of new firms into the industry depended on Government Policy, particularly with respect to licensing new bamboo areas for harvesting. In 1957, a new company called the Assam Pulp Mills Ltd. of the Managing Agency firms Messrs. Balmer Lawrie & Co., Ltd. and Andrew Yule & Co., Ltd. explored the forest belt of Assam, that was endowed with rich bamboo resources, with a view producing sulphate bamboo pulp in the state for their paper mills in Calcutta. Up to then, the Assam Pulp Mills Ltd. was the only industrial venture that had been officially sanctioned by the Paper Panel constituted in the Planning Commission for the manufacture of bamboo sulphate pulp in India. The Assam Pulp Mills Ltd., which was expected to go into production by 1960–61 with a rated capacity of 35,000–40,000 tons per annum, was a new type of bamboo pulp venture in India in that it hoped to obtain export markets for its produce from neighbouring countries, including Ceylon, Burma, Malaya, South Vietnam, Indonesia, the Philippines, and Australia, whose markets looked particularly promising due to large domestic pulp consumption (291,000 tons in 1957), of which nearly a third was imported (96,000 tons in 1957) from New Zealand, the USA, Canada, Norway, Sweden, and Finland (Demand Forecast 1965, 8, 12, 14).

Although India's bamboo groves were vast, little was known about the exact extent of forests or the total availability of raw material in different regions. No precise historical data regarding bamboo resources of different regions in the country is available. Data collected by the State Governments for the Central Government gives a rough picture of the estimated bamboo resources and the extent to which bamboo was used by existing mills in 1956. According to the data, 385,118 tons of bamboo was utilised in 1956, which represented 21.5% of the total sustained annual yield in India (1.789 million tons). Bihar and West Bengal utilised their resources most heavily, while in seven States, bamboo forests were still untapped. Up to then, there had been no scientific survey of the bamboo resources of India, and the Central Government admitted that considerable confusion arose out of some of the figures submitted by State Governments. For instance, Bihar reported that its total sustained annual yield was 54,000 tons, while its utilisation exceeded 6,848 tons (12.7%) of the sustained annual yield. This was due to the fact that the major bamboo pulp producers, such as the Titaghur Paper Mills, sourced their bamboo from neighbouring Bihar and that the sustained annual yield in West Bengal was merely 9,400, of which 7,500 (78.9%) was utilised annually. On the other hand, the figures for the bamboo resources included areas incapable of being exploited economically, which could easily amount to be one-third of the total (Demand Forecast 1965, 28–30). In 1961, another estimate placed the total extent of bamboo resources at 36,000 sq km, but this figure included the very considerable areas of teak forests where different varieties of bamboo occurred, usually in the second storey (100 Years of Indian Forestry 1961, II, 49). In the same year, K.P. Sagreiya, President of the Forest Research

100   *Bamboo for papermaking*

Institute and Colleges at Dehra Dun, noted that even the existing mills were finding it difficult to get raw materials on a sustained basis (100 Years of Indian Forestry 1961, I, ix).

The introduction of eucalypts for papermaking in India

After the transfer of power, wood pulp imports into India decreased temporarily but recovered by 1956 to 120,000 tons, which represented 35% of the total pulp consumption (343,000 tons) in that year. The remaining 65% (223,000 tons) of India's pulp requirements were met by domestic supply (mostly bamboo pulp) (Demand Forecast 1965, 26). As paper manufacturing is a highly capital-intensive industry and is characterised by rather inflexible combinations of inputs of investments and knowledge and technology, Indian paper mills could not respond to the threat of wood pulp imports and the lack of indigenous raw materials either by producing produce wood pulp cheaply in India or by the extensive substitution of labour for capital (or chemicals) in the manufacture of paper. Besides, Indian timber resources were poor from the point of view of developing a low-cost wood pulp industry. Although the growth of spruce (*Picea morinda*) and silver fir (*Abies pindrow*) was abundant in the hill belt between the Northern Indian Plains and the Great Himalaya Range, and those species are thoroughly suitable for papermaking, their fibres being long, tenacious, and of good colour, woods grew for the most part in the accessible hill tract areas from which extraction was uneconomical (Bamboo Pulp for Paper Making 17 July 1916; Podder 1979, 46).

In 1953 and 1956, respectively, the Food and Agricultural Organization (FAO) assigned two Technical Advisors, Alfred Huber and A. Koroleff, to advise the Government of India on the possibilities of transporting pulpwood from the high mountain areas and to assist in the organisation and establishment of a branch for the extraction, conversion, and transport of timber at the Forest Research Institute. To introduce indigenous softwoods in the paper industry, the Technical Advisors saw that it was necessary to introduce modern, efficient, and partly mechanised logging and transport operations to overcome the great difficulties of extraction from the high-altitude forests and to tap remote virgin stands. The Advisors surmised that with such improvements, it would have been possible to supply a newsprint mill of at least 50 tons daily capacity on a sustained basis. The mill site proposed was on the Beas River or preferably, Yamuna River, but the comparative inaccessibility and difficult terrain rendered the exploitation of the primeval Indian forests adjoining these rivers an unviable proposition (Huber 1953; Koroleff 1956).

The Forest Research Institute dealt mainly with bamboo, but its silvicultural rules overlooked logging (i.e. timber harvesting). According to the standard forest management rules of the forest-based industries of the 1950s, timber harvesting consisted of felling, branching, and crosscutting the logs in sections of required lengths, and transporting these materials from forest to mill. But in India, the average per capita wood output was only one-eighth of the world's average. Three-quarters of all wood was used for fuel, and considerable amounts of wood were wasted, even in fuelwood logging, mainly due to challenging terrain, undeveloped means of transport, untrained labour, and crude logging operations, which were carried out manually with axes instead of being cut by saws, and without any system of mechanised cutting (Huber 1953; Koroleff 1956).

The increased price of imported wood pulp revived interest in pulping trials for a wide variety of deciduous trees native to much of India such as Indian charcoal tree (*Trema orientalis*), which was found suitable for paper and pulp production, producing paper with good tensile strength and folding endurance. Salai or the Indian olibanum tree (*Boswellia serrata*) came into use in the National Newsprint and Paper Mills, Ltd. which was registered with the Registrar of Companies, Bombay in 1947. The mill, which was the first in India to produce newsprint, started production in 1955–56 (Podder 1979, 177, 196). Among the exotic species tested, pulping trials were made with the paper mulberry (*Broussonetia papyrifera*) and Australian wattles belonging to the genus *Acacia* (e.g. black wattle, *Acacia decurrens*). It was, however, the short-fibred *Eucalyptus globulus*, which was found to be the most suitable when blended with the long-fibred bamboo, especially for the manufacture of writing and printing paper (100 Years of Indian Forestry 1961, II, 186–187).

A way out of the problem of sourcing wood pulp seemed to be augmenting India's forest resources by reafforestation of depleted bamboo forests and by creating large-scale industrial plantations of the fast-growing *E. globulus*. The idea of creating eucalyptus plantations to feed the mills in India was raised under the auspices of the FAO with the creation of the UN Expanded Programmes of Technical Assistance on 21 January 1952. The FAO saw forest-based industries as a means to improve the living standards of the people. Its main argument was that the extraction and sale of forest-based products would improve the balance of payments, an improvement which was imperative for countries such as India that could not produce enough food to feed themselves (Huber 1953; Koroleff 1956).

Cropping exotic hardwoods in farm forests was not a novel idea in India, where acacias and eucalypts had been introduced for fuelwood and construction timber already in 1858 (100 Years of Indian Forestry 1961, I, 74), but this was the first time the same species were tried for papermaking purposes in India. The introduction of untried exotics for pulp manufacture had widespread negative effects on the already depleted bamboo forests, which virtually died out in many areas, with severe economic consequences for many communities in rural India, where bamboo constituted 'the common man's timber' for house construction and numerous other purposes, as well as having considerable nutritional value. Besides unforeseen impacts upon the forest ecosystem, the creation of large-scale industrial eucalyptus plantations for pulpwood has also had negative social effects. In some States, plantations deprived villagers of their traditional grazing rights for their cattle and

102 *Bamboo for papermaking*

their rights to collect faggots of firewood from nearby forests (Savur 2003, I, 22–28).

Conclusions

The British paper trade history has been defined since the mid-1850s by a quest for a new raw material to replace rags. Increasing demand for paper combined with the scarcity in the supply of rags induced British papermakers to look for new raw materials in the shape of tropical and semi-tropical grasses. The increased dependence on wood pulp, the likelihood of a pulp famine, and the consequent increase in price for imported wood pulp were the means for drawing attention to the possibility of making commercial volumes of good quality bamboo pulp. Although theoretically known since the mid-1870s, bamboo began being treated only after the First World War, when the Government of India offered financial incentives and concessions for the exploitation of forest areas to induce the creation of a pulp and paper industry based on utilising bamboo as the raw material. However, it took nearly 50 years for the bamboo pulping process to enter a period of commercially viable production. The bamboo pulp and paper industry developed in an economically viable manner only after tariff protection had become effective in 1925. Bamboo came into prominence as the main raw material of the Indian pulp and paper industry by the 1930s, when the quantity of sabai grass at an economically viable cost was becoming very restricted (for details, see Chap. 6). The final choice rested with bamboo, which was a cheaper and more readily available raw material than sabai. The first mills utilising bamboo existed mostly in and around Calcutta, while the raw material came mainly from eastern parts of Bengal. The number of mills using bamboo as a papermaking raw material rose to ten by 1939. This was due to research and development work as well as a favourable tariff policy and patronages regarding railway freights, which permitted transporting bamboo from wide areas at an economically viable freight cost.

The bamboo pulping technology was developed under British auspices, but was later adopted by Indian paper producers in response to the rising costs of imported wood pulp. In India, coniferous species were limited to the Himalayas, making the exploitation of softwood resources economically unviable. In their absence, papermakers in India adopted technologies and organisational solutions that distinguish them from the other British Empire and Commonwealth countries. The developments in India took place within national, colonial, and organisational frameworks, and reflected the availability of technology, knowledge, investments, and raw materials, on the one hand, and the demand characteristics, on the other. As the foregoing discussion has established, the use of bamboo as a primary raw material for making paper presented many problems, and India has remained the only country in the world, where bamboo has been used as a primary raw material for this purpose.

Notes

1 *The Indian Forester*, a pioneer in forestry journalism, started as the outcome of a resolution of the forestry conference held at Allahabad in January 1874.
2 A testimony of bamboo's suitability as a papermaking material comes in an issue of the *Journal of the Society of Arts* (27 May 1881) as it is printed on bamboo paper made by Thomas Routledge, and it has remained virtually intact, and without the tarnishing that often occurs with papers printed on acidic wood pulps.
3 During the First World War, Raitt continued his investigations at the Research Laboratories of the Imperial Institute, South Kensington.
4 According to Podder (1979), it was James C. Lowe, who designed the apparatus for node crushing (59).
5 Pearson was later nominated as Director of the Forest Products Research Laboratory, Department of Scientific and Industrial Research, Princes Risborough, Buckinghamshire. Established in 1923 and overseen by the Department of Scientific and Industrial Research (itself created in 1915), the Forest Products Research Board was mainly interested in the economic value of tropical forests in the British Empire.

References

100 Years of Indian Forestry 1861–1961 (1961) Vols. I–II. Forest Research Institute, Dehra Dun.

Bagchi, A. K. (1972) *Private Investment in India 1900–1939*. Cambridge University Press, Cambridge.

Bamboo Paper Company Limited (BPC). CLC/B/022, MS 28961, Memorandum and Letters of Association; MS 28963, Indenture; MS 28964/1–500 Letter Book; MS 28964/2/1–241, Letter Book; MS 28965/1–503, Letter Book. London Metropolitan Archives.

Bamboo Pulp for Paper Making. India (17 July 1916) *AY4/2202, Bamboo Pulp from India*. Tropical Products Institute and Predecessors. The National Archives, Kew.

Barton, G. A. (2002) *Empire Forestry and the Origins of Environmentalism*. Cambridge Studies in Historical Geography 34. Cambridge University Press, Cambridge.

Bernard, C. (19 January 1881) *MR/136/67, India*. Economic Products. Bamboo. The Library, Art & Archives Royal Botanic Gardens, Kew.

Brandis, S. D. (1899) 'Biological Notes on Indian Bamboos'. *The Indian Forester* 25, 1, 1–25.

Clapperton, R. H. & Henderson, W. (1947) *Modern Paper-Making*. 3rd ed. Basil Blackwell, Oxford.

Demand Forecast for Bamboo Sulphate Pulp (1965) National Council for Applied Economic Research, New Delhi.

Gamble, J. S. (1881) *A Manual of Indian Timbers: An Account of the Structure, Growth, Distribution, and Qualities of Indian Woods*. Office of the Superintendent of Government Printing, Calcutta.

Hole, R. S. (1911) *On some Indian Forest Grasses and Their Oecology*. The Indian Forest Memoirs, Vol. I, Part I. Superintendent of Government Printing, Calcutta.

Huber, A. (1953) *Report to the Government of India on High Mountain Timber Extraction*. Report No. 141. FAO, Rome.

Indian Tariff Board (ITB). (1924) *Enquiry Regarding the Grant of Protection to the Paper and Pulp Industries. Evidence Tendered by Applicants for Protection*. The Government of India, Calcutta.

104 *Bamboo for papermaking*

Indian Tariff Board (ITB). (1931) *Report of the Indian Tariff Board on the Grant of Protection to the Paper and Pulp Industries.* The Government of India, Calcutta.

Jardine, J. L. & Nelson, T. A. (16 March 1916) 'Improved Process for the Production of an Acid Magnesium Sulphite Solution and the Application of Same for the Extraction of Cellulose from Fibrous Vegetable Materials'. GB191502509A, Espacenet. The Online Patent Search, European Patent Office. https://worldwide.espacenet.com/. Accessed 29 July 2020.

Jones, S. (1992) *Merchants of the Raj. British Managing Agency Houses in Calcutta in Yesterday and Today.* Macmillan, Basingstoke and London.

Journal of the Society of Arts (JSA) (27 May 1881), 29, 1488, 584–585.

King, G. (1877) 'Calcutta Botanical Gardens'. *Journal of the Society of Arts*, XXV, 1302, 1027.

Koroleff, A. (1956) *Report to the Government of India on Efficiency Promotion and Research in Timber Harvesting.* Report No. 490. FAO, Rome.

Marsden, F. (1922) *Paper and Paper Pulp Production in the Madras Presidency.* Bulletins of Indian Industries & Labour 24. Superintendent Government Printing, Calcutta.

Milne, S. (27 July 1911) 'Improved Method of and Means for Treating Bamboo Preparatory to Making it into Pulp'. GB191020560A, Espacenet. The Online Patent Search, European Patent Office. https://worldwide.espacenet.com/. Accessed 26 July 2020.

Müller, L. (2014) *White Magic. The Age of Paper.* Transl. from the German by Jessica Spengler, Polity, Malden, MA.

Oosthoek, K. J. (2018) 'Origins and Development of State Forestry in the United Kingdom'. In K. J. Oosthoek & R. Hölzl, eds, *Managing Northern Europe's Forests. Histories from the Age of Improvement to the Age of Ecology.* The Environment History: International Perspectives 12. Berghahn, New York and Oxford, 130–165.

Paper Production of Bamboo from India (18 April 1952) *AY4/2288, Paper Production of Bamboo from India.* Tropical Products Institute and Predecessors. The National Archives, Kew.

Pearson, R. S. (1912) 'Note on the Utilization of Bamboo for the Manufacture of Paper-Pulp'. *Indian Forest Records*, IV, V, 1–121.

Podder, V. (1979) *Paper Industry in India. A Study.* Oxford & IBH Publishing Co., New Delhi, Bombay and Calcutta.

Progress Report of the Imperial Forest Research Institute 1906–1907 (1908) Superintendent of Government Printing, Calcutta.

Progress Report of the Forest Research Institute 1910–1911 (1911) Superintendent of Government Printing, Calcutta.

Progress Report of Forest Research Work in India for the Year 1922–23 (1924) Government of India Press, Simla.

Progress Report of Forest Research Work in India for the Year 1923–4 (1925) Government of India, Calcutta.

Raitt, W. (1912) 'Report on the Investigation of Bamboo as Material for Production of Paper-Pulp', *Indian Forest Records*, III, III, 1–37.

Raitt, W. (20 January 1922) *Report on the Tavoy River Pulping Concession. AY4/2223, Bamboo Pulp from India: Suitability for Paper.* Tropical Products Institute and Predecessors. The National Archives, Kew.

Raitt, W. (1928) 'Bamboo Hope'. In *Progress Report of Forest Research Work in India. For the Year 1926–7.* Government of India, Calcutta, 155–165.

Raitt, W. (1929) 'The Burma Paper Pulp Survey'. *The Indian Forest Records*, XIV, 1, 1–48.

Report of the Proceedings of the Forest Conference Held at Simla, October 1875 (1876) D. Brandis & A. Smythies, eds. The Superintendent of Government Printing, Calcutta.

Routledge, T. (1875) *Bamboo, Considered as a Paper-Making Material. Remarks Upon Its Cultivation and Treatment.* E. & F.N. Spon, London and New York.

Routledge, T. (1879) *Bamboo and Its Treatment: Cultivation and Cropping.* Privately printed in Claxheugh, Sunderland. MR/136/23–46, India. Economic Products. Bamboo. The Library, Art & Archives Royal Botanic Gardens, Kew.

Routledge, T. (11 October 1880) *MR/136/65, India.* Economic Products. Bamboo. The Library, Art & Archives Royal Botanic Gardens, Kew.

Savur, M. (2003) *And the Bamboo Flowers in the Indian Forests. What Did the Pulp and Paper Industry Do?* Vols. I–II. Manohar, Delhi.

Sindall, R. W. (1906) *Report on the Manufacture of Paper and Pulp in Burma.* Office of Superintendent, Government Printing, Burma, Rangoon.

Sindall, R. W. (1909) *Bamboo for Papermaking.* Marchant Singer & Co., London.

Watt, S. G. (1908) *The Commercial Products of India. Being an Abridgment of "The Dictionary of the Economic Products of India".* John Murray, London.

Wilkins, M. (1988) 'The Free-Standing Company, 1870–1914: An Important Type of British Foreign Direct Investment'. *Economic History Review*, 41, 2, 259–282.

6 The paper trade and the British Empire

The backdrop of the research and development work of Empire-grown raw materials comprised at least four separate yet interlinked phenomena: (1) the growth of the paper industry, (2) the insufficient supply of domestic raw materials, (3) the increasing prices of esparto, and (4) the difficulty in obtaining esparto and wood pulp during the First World War. To facilitate British manufacturers' independence from foreign raw material imports, it was clearly necessary to develop the resources of the British Empire, and, in particular, British India, where the Government, through the India Office, expended considerable sums of money with the view of developing the fibre resources. In 1880, a memorandum on raw materials suitable for the manufacture of paper, drawn up by L. Liotard of the Agricultural Department, directed attention to hemp, flax, jute, abacá (*Musa textilis*), and rhea fibres, for which development the Government offered a premium of £25,000 (Routledge 11 October 1880). From the papermakers' standpoint, problem was that raw textile plant fibres required a large amount of hand manipulation (i.e. to be cultivated, cut, dried, and steeped or retted) (Liotard 1880, 2), and, at the time, no suitable machinery had been devised for the purpose. Like Routledge before him (Routledge 1875), Liotard concluded that none of these fibres competed seriously with esparto, which did not need to be prepared for the market.

The Indian and Colonial Exhibition of 1886 was the first systematic attempt to showcase the various fibres collected from the different parts of the Empire, and processes developed for their treatment by the experts of the time (Colonial and Indian Exhibition 1886, 118–130). Subsequently, two reports on that exhibition were issued – one dealing with the bamboo being investigated by Routledge under the auspices of the Royal Society of Arts (Report of the Royal Commission 1887) and another dealing with other Indian fibres being studied by Liotard under the auspices of the Indian Government (Royle 1887). At the time of the Exhibition, among the British papermakers interested in the potential of colonial fibres was Edward Lloyd, the founder of the firm Edward Lloyd and Sons, who was at that time also looking out for new sources of supply for the manufacture of 'news', but his choice devolved to wood pulp from Norway (Phillips 1915, 634: see also Chap. 4). Although little came from these early attempts to secure at least a proportion of raw material supplies from colonial sources, the methods employed by Routledge and other experts of the time formed the basis of the research methods used by British chemists in subsequent years.

Research and development under the auspices of the Imperial Institute

The Imperial Institute, established by Royal Charter in 1888 to promote the commercial and industrial interest of the British Empire, functioned as the main centre for information and investigation concerning the paper trade and its promotion in the Empire. In 1893, the Institute moved to new premises in South Kensington which housed the Scientific and Technical Department that conducted most of the research work and issued the reports on the raw material sample consignments received from the various corners of the Empire. In all, the Imperial Institute compiled nearly 200 reports, which varied in length from a few pages to hundreds. Extracts of some of these reports were published in the official *Bulletin of the Imperial Institute* ('Experiments with New Materials' 1912). Taken as a whole, the reports bear witness to the staggering amount of research done on Empire-grown fibres that were of more or less use in papermaking.

At the beginning of 1903, the Imperial Institute was placed under the management of the Board of Trade. In the same year, Professor Wyndham Rowland Dunstan (1861–1949) was nominated as a Director of the Institute, a position that he held for more than 20 years (Henry 1959). Under Dunstan's directorship, the procedures regarding research work on Empire-grown fibres were placed on a more professional footing. In the early years, however, firms specialising in the pulp and paper trades, like Messrs. C. F. Cross & E. J. Bevan as well as Messrs. Clayton Beadle & Henry P. Stevens, also performed a considerable amount of research (Beadle 1904, 7–18; Cross & Bevan 1907).

In 1907, control of the Imperial Institute was transferred to the Colonial Office, but this organisational change proved unviable for the commercial and industrial needs of the post-First World War era. In 1923, a Committee of Inquiry was set up under the Chairmanship of Lord Harlech to examine the work of the Institute, and the Committee's report was followed by the Imperial Institute Act of 1925 which gave control of the Institute to the Department of Overseas Trade. In the following year, the Plant and Animal Products Department was formed, with its own laboratory and intelligence section, to carry out investigations into raw material sample consignments. Initially, large proportion of the samples investigated were derived from grasses, reeds, sedges, and rushes but interest in subtropical and tropical hardwood species was secondary, mainly because of the supremacy of coniferous softwoods in British papermaking. However, over the years, the Imperial Institute managed to amass a considerable amount of information which helped towards the assessment of the papermaking properties of various hardwoods,

108   *The paper trade and the British Empire*

including eucalypts. The Institute managed to establish, for instance, that, on average, the ultimate fibres of tropical hardwoods are only about half of the length of the conifers and for this reason they could not be expected to yield unprocessed pulps of more than a moderate strength. It was also determined that many hardwoods contain a relatively high proportion of resins, a feature which increased the quantity of chemicals necessary for pulping (Coomber 1952, 51–53).

The research procedure was never rigid, and it varied considerably according to the sample consignment in question. The overall pattern was similar in each case, however. It aimed at determining the optimum cooking conditions by the soda or the sulphite process, and it was followed by an assessment of the strength of the pulps and their response to beating. Bleaching trials were also carried out on most samples, and yields of cellulose were determined on pulps, which had already yielded a relatively high figure in preliminary laboratory investigations. Once it was determined in the laboratory conditions that the sample consignment exhibited satisfactory quality for papermaking, consideration was given to the many other factors related to the industry. These varied from industrial-scale service tests at designated paper mills to determine the technical workability of the materials to raw material prospecting expeditions to evaluate whether the stands were sufficient to furnish ample supplies over a long period at a reasonable cost. The availability of water and chemicals and of power resources and transport facilities were also subjects of investigations as the difficulty of coordinating these requirements often hampered the development of the paper industry in unindustrialised regions of the world. A separate branch of the Department was designated to collect and disseminate information on the arrangement of the paper trade and industry in the Empire. This branch functioned mainly on an educational basis and aimed to illustrate the potentialities of imperial raw materials for the prospective investors (Coomber 1952, 52).

Beginning of 1938, the evaluation of the sample consignments was carried out on standard sheets prepared and tested according to the official methods described in the Second Report of the Pulp Evolution Committee of the British Paper Makers' Association. A laboratory test of the material included examination of fibre characteristics. It was followed by a single soda boil under the normal cooking conditions of esparto pulp mills (i.e. 1% of NaOH for 1 hour at 100°C) to determine the yield of cellulose as well as the quantities of ash and resin (including waxes and fats) and their alkali solubility. The laboratory test usually gave enough evidence to be able to decide whether it was worthwhile to proceed with a comprehensive examination of the sample (Coomber 1952, 52–53).

The post-war era brought many organisational changes to the Imperial Institute. The Department of Overseas Trade was abolished in 1946, and the Imperial Institute was placed under the responsibility of the Secretary for Overseas Trade, where it remained until April 1949, when the scientific and technical work of the institute was handed back to the Colonial Office.

The paper trade and the British Empire   109

Following these institutional changes, the Plant and Animal Products Department was abolished, and its responsibilities were handed to the Colonial Products Advisory Bureau (Plant and Animal), which functioned as a part of the Colonial Office from 1949 to 1953. The name was changed to the Colonial Products Laboratory in 1953, which was in use until 1957 when the Imperial Institute's responsibilities were taken over by the Tropical Products Institute. It aimed to foster research and development work in research institutions, universities, and elsewhere on all kinds of potentially economically useful products of the British Empire. Among these products, timber was one of the most important (Coomber 1952).

Sources of supply in India and Burma

For nearly a generation before the introduction of bamboo to the paper industry, the leading Indian papermaking fibre had been sabai grass, the similarity of which in appearance and quality to esparto led British papermakers in India to utilise it for papermaking purposes in that country. When carefully collected, free from weeds and foreign matter, sabai was one of the best raw materials known for the production of finest printing and medium-quality writing papers. Because no portions of the leaf or flower culm differ materially in composition from other portions, with even the nodes not suffering any serious resistance to the action of the digestion liquors, sabai could easily be reduced to a standard pulp and the paper made from it was scarcely distinguishable from esparto. Before 1914, however, the sabai trade experienced a serious fall-off in quantity and quality, because, like esparto, sabai was suffering from the effects of over-cropping.

Technology transfer and the development of the pulp and paper industry in India up to c.1930

The transfer of mechanical papermaking technology from Britain to India started at the Serampore Paper Mill, on the River Hooghly, Bengal, where the first Fourdrinier was installed in 1832 under the supervision of J. Randall, an English paper engineer. The mill, which became known for the high quality of its cartridge papers as well as its printing papers, was closed down in the aftermath of the Sepoy Mutiny. In 1861, Messrs. Borneo & Co. bought the plant and equipment and set them up at Bally (Howrah). The mill was subsequently registered in 1867 as a joint-stock company called the Royal Paper Mill. In the 1880s and the 1890s, the success of the soda process using esparto encouraged a spate of new London and Calcutta funded mill developments in Bengal. Two new mills – the Titaghur Paper Mills Co., Ltd. at Titagarh in 1882 and the Imperial Paper Mill at Kankinara in 1893 – were set up on the River Hooghly, 14 and 25 miles, respectively, from Calcutta because of its proximity to the consumer market and transport facilities. The Titaghur Paper Mills Co. acquired the latter in 1903, and it was subsequently operated

110 *The paper trade and the British Empire*

as the Titaghur Paper Mill No. 2. The Bengal Paper Mills Co. Ltd. chose a different business strategy. In 1890, it constructed a mill in the interior at Raniganj because of the better supply of raw materials from adjoining Bihar and Orissa (Odisha) as well as coal for energy from the Raniganj Coalfield (Ray 2018, 157, 162–166, 170, 172; see also Tiwari 1937, 283–298).

The types of raw materials used by the mills were conditioned by their local availability and low price as well as cost of treatment. Raw jute fibres were available in abundance due to the large number of jute mills in Bengal, and various refuse materials such as recycled paper, worn-out gunny bags, jute textile waste, hessian cuttings, sails, ropes, and old garments were sourced from Calcutta (Ray 2018, 162–166). The papermakers in Bengal tended to prefer refuse materials to raw jute fibres even though they were cheap and availability was normally plentiful. The reason for this preference was the costs of preparatory manipulation needed to separate the ultimate fibres from extraneous matter in the raw fibres. Although suitable as a raw material for caustic soda treatment, jute yields a relatively low percentage of cellulose, bearing in mind the extra costs incurred by the necessary preparatory manipulation in the processes of cultivating, drying, heckling, and steeping (Routledge 1875, 6). Therefore, as Ray (2018, 157) has noted, in those mills in Bengal where raw jute was the primary raw material, profitability remained low. It was slightly higher when refuse materials were used along with raw textile plant fibres.

In India, the problem of knowing what the most suitable raw material was arose out of insufficient knowledge of the properties of plants. The breakthrough discovery was that by employing the soda process for indigenous Indian grasses with fibre characteristics similar to esparto, such as sunn hemp (*Crotalaria juncea*), babui (*Utricularia babui*), munj (*Saccharum bengalense*), sabai (*Eulaliopsis binata*, also known as *Ischaemum angustifolium*), hairy cottongrass (*Eriophorum comosum*), wild sugarcane (*Saccharum spontaneum*), cogongrass (*Imperata cylindrica*), and elephant grass or Indian reed-mace (*Typha elephantina*), high-quality printing and writing papers could be manufactured. Sabai grass, otherwise known as baib or barber or bhabhar grass, growing abundantly in the wild in the drier parts of Northern India, became prominent in the 1880s and remained the stable raw material of the mills in Bengal until about 1930, but after that, the supply of the grass was on the wane. It was expensive to carry grasses over long distances because of their high bulk-to-weight ratio and their combustible nature (Demand Forecast 1965, 11).

Sabai grass is a perennial plant belonging to the family *Poaceae*, to which bamboo also belongs. In terms of quality, sabai gives strong and durable paper, which is eminently suited to the manufacture of high-class book and printing paper. Its thin long leaves yield easy bleaching pulp in good volumes (40%) when cooked with caustic soda. Owing to its fibre characteristics, sabai paper is brittle however, and that is its main defect (Khandual & Sahu 2016). Other disadvantages of sabai as a papermaking material which prevented its more widespread use in the Indian paper industry after 1930 were

The paper trade and the British Empire   111

high extraction costs, a sharp rise in the cost of transport, and the unsteady nature of supply. Sabai grows in clumps similar to bamboo but in widely scattered patches, and in consequence, its extraction was a labour-intensive and costly process (Podder 1979, 51–52). Those high transport costs were another factor that hindered the supply of sabai at remunerative rates. Even in industrialised Bengal, where the East Indian Railway Company had opened a railway line between the Raniganj Coalfield and Calcutta in 1855, high railway freight charges combined with low-value plant fibres eroded the productivity of the mills (Ray 2018, 157, 166, 170; see also Tiwari 1937, 293–299). By 1914, the known sources of sabai were tapped in Bihar and Orissa owing to the perpetual cutting of the grass, and the Titaghur Paper Mills and the Bengal Paper Mills were forced to transport sabai over long distances from Nepal, Punjab, United Provinces, and Central Provinces to their mills in Bengal, thereby increasing transport costs even further (Bagchi 1972, 395–396, 398).

In view of these disadvantages in its raw material supply, how does one account for the relative success of the early stages of the paper industry in Bengal? Ray (2018) argues that the most forceful explanations related to favourable government policies, which sanctioned lower railway freight charges for plant fibres after 1891, and, on the other, the purchase policies of British imperial stores, which after 1876 endorsed the purchase of local printing paper as opposed to imported paper. These patronages continued through 1914–15 (Ray 2018, 172, 175, 177; see also Tiwari 1937, 283–299). Irrespective of these artificial advantages, the amount of imported paper remained high. From 1899 to 1915, it varied from one-third to almost three-quarters of the total paper consumption, and a significant amount of even the remaining portion of paper made in India was manufactured from imported wood pulp. In 1913–14 (the financial year ending 31 March 1914), the total consumption of paper in India may be estimated between 85,000 and 90,000 tons, of which only about 29,000 was manufactured in the country itself (Ray 2018, 178). From 1899 to 1910, British imports represented between 35% and 67.4% of the annual total paper and board imports into India, with the rest arriving from European paper mills on the Continent, particularly from Germany, Austria-Hungary, Sweden, and Norway (Table 6.1).

Despite their relative early success, the Indian mills were by no means immune to the complexities of the global pulp and paper industry. In their nascent stage, the mills were surrounded by a staggering abundance of various fibrous materials suitable for the manufacture of pulp and they enjoyed preferential treatment by the Government, but the high extraction and transport costs of sabai eroded profitability. The rapid expansion of the wood pulp industry in Scandinavia, Central Europe, and North America is another factor that hindered the progress of the paper industry in Bengal. Favoured by seemingly inexhaustible supplies of cheap coniferous wood as the primary raw material, hydroelectric power for energy, and efficient means of river and lake transport, mills in these regions could not only meet their own raw

112 *The paper trade and the British Empire*

Table 6.1 Paper and Board Imports into India 1899–1910 (Tons and %)

Year	Printing	Other papers	Board	Total
1899–1900	4,854.1	4,353.3	763.9	9,971.3
1900–01	5,472.0	3,325.0	1,005.8	9,802.8
1901–02	5,981.5	4,747.1	1,012.0	11,740.6
1902–03	6,464.8	4,737.2	1,321.7	12,523.7
1903–04	5,576.0	4,821.5	1,491.3	11,888.8
1904–05	7,883.3	11,226.3	1,567.8	20,677.4
1905–06	7,715.1	15,879.6	1,916.7	25,511.4
1906–07	11,032.0	16,055.1	1,866.3	28,953.4
1907–08	14,392.3	18,136.5	2,223.4	34,752.2
1908–09	12,014.3	19,930.8	2,406.0	34,351.1
1909–10	12,924.5	22,354.2	3,101.5	38,380.2
Total 1899–1910	94,309.9	125,566.6	18,676.4	238,552.9
% from total	39.5	52.7	7.8	100.0

Source: TN 1899–1910. The figures are calculated from imperial hundredweights (cwt). One imperial cwt equals 112 lb avoirdupois (about 50.8 kg).

demand for pulp and paper but periodically exceeded it, thereby leading to the sale of the excess at 'dump prices' in the world markets.

The savannah grasses were another group of grasses that were the subject of considerable study by the cellulose experts. The savannah grasses, common to much of thinly forested areas in Central and Northern India, are of a very different group of grasses from sabai, being much larger and coarser, more strongly lignified, and having harder and larger nodes. With a view of determining their papermaking value, the following five grasses from the Goalpara division of Assam were tested as to their suitability for papermaking: *Saccharum spontaneum, S. arundinaceum, S. munja, S. marenga*, and *Phragmites karka*. Each of them produced strong, long-fibred pulps, having some of the qualities which at that time could be obtained only by the use of linen and cotton rags. The savannah grasses possess fibres of a long, slender type, with tapering points, up to 4.7 mm in length. The consumption of chemicals for digestion and bleaching was found to be within economic limits, but the percentages of pulp yields were low, varying from 22% to 26.5%. In admixture with wood pulp, however, the savannah grasses were regarded as first-class raw materials, possessing the features desirable for the manufacture of high-grade writing papers (Phillips 1915, 624).

The grass districts were located in inland, upland, and comparatively dry country, with long railway leading to seaports, coalfields, and paper mills in Bengal, so there were similar transport problems frequently associated with the sabai trade. As for the cost of cutting and collecting, it was estimated to be more than for bamboo, as the latter's greater size and weight of individual culms permitted a larger quantity to be collected per labourer per day. So generally, and especially in the absence of water transport, the cost of harvesting the savannah grasses exceeded that of bamboo. In 1915, William Raitt

The paper trade and the British Empire   113

provisionally estimated that the cost per ton of unbleached savannah grass pulp at the factory in Calcutta would work out at between Rs.100 and Rs.119 per ton, which was roughly the same as for bamboo (Rs.118.6). By way of comparison, unbleached sabai pulp could not be produced at Calcutta paper mills for less than Rs.155, and in some instances Rs.170 per ton. The cost of savannah grasses was also less than the cost of imported chemical wood pulp, which stood at about Rs.150 per ton c.i.f. Calcutta before the war (Pearson 1912, 39; Phillips 1915, 625). Pulping trials with savannah grasses continued at the Forest Research Institute until 1934 when they were terminated as inconclusive. Although thoroughly suitable for papermaking, the savannah grasses could not be used at a viable economic rate, unless they were available at very low prices, a possibility denied by their remote location (Forest Research in India 1934, I, 61).

Bamboo as an Empire-grown raw material

After the First World War, there was an increasing amount of interest in the possibility of bamboo pulp being exported to Britain. The strongest advocate of bamboo as an Empire-grown raw material was William Raitt, the Government of India's cellulose expert, who during the war had continued his investigations at the Research Laboratories of the Imperial Institute. In 1928, Raitt explained his rationale in an address 'The Bamboo Hope', delivered before the London Division of the Technical Section of the Paper Makers' Association:

'The last 100 years has seen the industry proceed from rag to straw, from straw to textile wastes, from these to esparto, each in turn hailed as salvation, each in turn failing to provide for expansion, and now the latest saviour, wood, threatens to travel the same road. [...] future expansion can only be provided by the boundless areas of tropics and sub tropics stocked with species producing annual crops – not 60-year ones – so the mills have supplies in *perpetuo* at their back doors [...]' (Raitt, 1928, 157).

The setting for Raitt's bamboo hopes was the successful development work at the Forest Research Institute, Dehra Dun, where the chemists managed to solve the trouble with the dark brown colour which stained the soda pulp and had thus far slowed down the progress of the bamboo pulp industry. The chief revelation was that the culprit was not the cellulose, nor its encrusting lignin as is the case with wood, but the starch and pectous constituents of bamboo. These, combined with soda, produced a dark brown, almost black solution, which the pulp absorbed, as it is gelatinous in character. The trouble resolved itself in the discovery of the fractional system of digestion with the sulphate of soda process. Fractional sulphate, besides its much lower cost, produced easy bleaching pulp and was the reason for the large drop in steaming time and pressure, and, further, there was no need any more to select bamboo according to its age since stems of all ages could be harvested and utilised in an indiscriminate mixture (Raitt 1928, 160).

114 *The paper trade and the British Empire*

Based on these developments, Raitt believed it was possible to deliver unbleached bamboo pulp c.i.f. British ports at a cost of £11 10s per ton. The corresponding figure for Scandinavian chemical wood pulp for 1927 was reported at £13 15s per ton (Raitt 1928, 162). In the 1920s and 1930s, several London-based bamboo pulp schemes in the Burmese regions of Tavoy, Mergui, Arakan, and Bassein were launched with a view to exporting bamboo pulp to Britain, but none of them ever materialised before the outbreak of the Second World War (Progress Report 1928, 96; Forest Research in India, II, 1935, 107).

The business failure of the Bamboo Pulp Mills Limited, which held a monopoly from the Burma Government on the Tavoy River Bamboo Pulping Concession, offers an illustrative example of some of the problems encountered by the London-based companies engaged in the overseas raw material business in the interwar period. The Concession covered the bamboo jungles in the Heinze and Kaleinaung reserves of the Tavoy River System in South Burma, including its tributaries, and the right to fuelwood sufficient for the manufacture of 40,000 tons of bamboo pulp per annum. The bamboo was of the *B. vulgaris*, locally known as *Dinochloa maclellandii* or Wanwe (Banik 2016, 9), a thin-walled variety, which was one advantage, another being that it grows to a great size, up to 50 feet in length, suitable for rafting. In their report on *B. vulgaris*, Messrs. Sindall & Bacon, Chemical Engineers and Consulting Chemists in London, revealed that the plant gave a yield of 42% of unbleached pulp in laboratory conditions. For the manufacture of unbleached bamboo pulp, only lime and alkali were needed, and the concessionary rights provided enough fuelwood for energy to keep the cost of treatment low (Raitt 20 January 1922).

In his report, Raitt, who explored the Tavoy River and the bamboo fuel areas on its banks to a distance of 120 miles from the sea in September 1919, stated that 'I know of no area [where the requirements of the bamboo pulp industry] can more economically meet it than the Tavoy River Concession'. Raitt's glowing report and estimates of the profits waiting to be won were useful tools for the promoters of the Bamboo Pulp Mills Limited to court investments from London but also from colonial sources. The board consisted of 'the best known and respected people in the paper trade', including Captain Arthur McRae, late Manager of the Orange Grove Paper Mill, Trinidad, whose mill had utilised a mixture of bagasse, bamboo, and para grass (*Brachiaria mutica*) as in their fibre furnish until it was forced to close down because of the war (Raitt 20 January 1922).

From the prospectus and the expert report, the impression was created of a centralised, highly efficient, and organised bamboo industry, in complete charge of itself. This was useful for convincing investors to invest in the colonial raw material business, but it often bore little resemblance to the actual state of affairs at the concession where there were desperate shortages of both technical expertise and capital – the two most important resources for establishing a new pulp and paper industry in unindustrialised region of the world.

The paper trade and the British Empire   115

Ultimately, the company's capital needs – £250,000 – proved to be too heavy to be met by ordinary shareholders for mustering both the capital and expertise essential in opening up a new bamboo region in Burma (Raitt 20 January 1922). The business failure of Bamboo Pulp Mills Limited highlights the fact that in unindustrialised regions of the world, the raw material question was as much economic and financial as technical.

The raw material shortage created by the Second World War and its aftermath brought the possibility of using bamboo pulp in the British paper mills back on the agenda. On 18 April 1952, the Ministry of Materials, a short-lived ministerial office in the British Government, made enquiries to the Colonial Office on the economic and technical problems of producing paper from bamboo. In a confidential memorandum drafted by the Trade Commissioner in Calcutta, the present state of the bamboo pulp industry in India was assessed with a view of assisting British colonies to develop a local bamboo pulp and paper industry. The memorandum highlighted the fact that the use of bamboo for pulp production was not as simple as often imagined in Whitehall. The problems related to the harvesting process, the transport of the stems from the forests to the mills, and the regeneration of clumps had created serious problems for the papermakers in India. It was not possible to clear any one catchment area completely if there was to be proper regeneration. For these reasons, it seemed doubtful whether any system of mechanised cutting could ever be introduced. The fact that the removal of bamboo from the forests was impossible for about four months of the year necessitated the storing of much larger quantities than would have been necessary if harvesting could have been carried on throughout the whole year. Therefore, to obtain regular supplies, considerable capital outlays would need to be spent for the building of roads for the transport of the bamboo, unless the supplies of bamboo were situated near a navigable river. On the other hand, if the bamboo was floated down the rivers, the paper mill required a large frontage on the river for receiving the bamboo, and that was an extra cost factor. For the foregoing reasons, it was estimated that any immediate large-scale expansion in the use of bamboo would have to be delayed in India until considerable capital was spent on improving the means of transport from the forests to the mills. These problems were similar to those created by the cutting of hardwoods in tropical forests (Manufacture of Paper from Bamboo 18 April 1952).

Based on the memorandum, it was concluded that bamboo pulp might possibly be used in countries similar to India where ample supplies of bamboo were available. Even then, the size of the industry would be limited by the amount and accessibility of raw materials, chemicals, fuel, power, water, labour, and capital in the particular country. Therefore, it did not appear that continuous bamboo pulp shipment to Britain was likely to be economically viable. One surprising feature of the bamboo pulp question was that the only person paying no apparent attention to it was the British papermaker, yet of all the papermaking communities of the world the Britain's was the most adversely affected by the raw material shortage. In the late 1940s, there

116 *The paper trade and the British Empire*

were even attempts to use British-grown bamboo in papermaking in place of esparto and straw, but the propositions put forward by the British Bamboo Groves Ltd. of Lanivet, Bodmin, Cornwall, were met with a total lack of interest (Paper Division of the Raw Materials Department, Board of Trade to British Bamboo Groves Ltd. 16 March 1949). The only company interested in the scheme was Celotex Limited, which did investigate the use of bamboo in board manufacturing (Celotex Limited to British Bamboo Groves Ltd. 11 and 12 April 1949), but this is a rare example of any commercial interest in the use bamboo pulp for paper manufacturing in Britain.

British-grown fibres as sources of pulp

During the First World War, the difficulty in obtaining esparto and wood pulp forced the British mills to switch to straw and waste paper instead. The wartime pulp famine revived the interest in the possibility of using grasses native to the British Isles as a source of paper. During the war, considerable attention was devoted to *Molinia cærulea*, also known as Purple Heat Grass, growing on the moors of the Pennine uplands (Jeffries 1916). Another grass investigated by the Imperial Institute was marram (or beach) grass (*Ammophila arenaria*). This highly invasive plant grew by the sea, salt marshes, shingle, and sand dunes of the British Isles, as well as on the Continent, in North Africa and in temperate regions of North America and Australia, where it was introduced for stabilising drifting sand dunes and to prevent coast erosion. Messrs. Beadle and Stevens examined a consignment marram grass from the Norfolk Sandhills in 1916. The grass was boiled under pressure in a digester, without passing through crushing rollers, and then bleached, the result being that the yield of unbleached fibres on the original green weight of the stem was 17.7%, and on the dry weight 31.4%, with the yield of bleached fibres being 13.1% and 25%, respectively. In their report, the chemists stated that the fibre was soft and pliable and it produced a pulp with a low tear strength. It also suggested that if marram grass was to be deemed of sufficient importance as a papermaking material, its cultivation could be extended over considerable tracts of sandy country bordering the coast in various parts of the British Isles (Marram Grass and Spartina Townsendii for Paper Making 2 May 1918).

The trials with marram were still in progress when the Institute's attention was diverted to rice grass (*Spartina townsendii*) which grew in abundance near Poole Harbour at Bournemouth in Dorset. The plant first appeared in Southampton in the 1860s or 1870s, and it was believed to be a hybrid from the indigenous *Spartina stricta* and an American species *Spartina alterniflora*. Before the outbreak of the war, the extermination of this highly invasive plant by means of gas poisoning – as had been applied against the prickly pear (Opuntia) which had overrun large areas of grazing ground in Queensland, Australia – was investigated. During the war, however, the plan for the eradication of the grass was abandoned, and interest was directed into the plant's papermaking qualities (Oliver 1916, 3–4).

The paper trade and the British Empire   117

The Imperial institute's investigations fell into three parts: (1) the harvesting, cutting, drying, baling, and transporting of the material; (2) the supply and organisation of labour; and (3) the conversion into pulp and paper. In their report on a sample of *Spartina townsendii*, Messrs. Beadle & Stevens stated that the material, which they had treated similarly to esparto, proved to be very promising. The pulp had a very fair colour without bleaching, and the yield was high. The technical and economic viability of the proposal was also evaluated in comparison with esparto, which in 1916 was available at, on average, £3 10s c.i.f. at the principal British ports. Perfection of the process of manufacture and modification of the machinery took place over the next two years at the works of Messrs. Thomas & Green, Limited, Soho Mills, Wooburn Green, Buckinghamshire (Oliver 1916, 5–8). Harvesting of *Spartina* appeared to have been discontinued after the war owing to the absence of a system of mechanised cutting.

Interest in British-grown grasses and reeds continued throughout the wartime emergency, but the proposals for their use in papermaking during normal times proved unviable for technical and commercial reasons. However, towards the end of 1932, interest in British-grown grasses and reeds revived, partly because of the protective import duties the Government placed on some paper grades (for further details, see Chap. 4). Particular attention was paid to common reeds (*Phragmites communis*, formerly known as *Arundo Phragmites*), which occurred along the margins of rivers, especially in the tidal zone, in temperate regions in all parts of the world. Already in 1908, a mill had been erected at Braila at the mouth of the Danube in Rumania for making half-stuff from *Phragmites* by the sulphate process, but owing to shortcomings of the pulp, the mill was later converted into a chemical wood pulp mill (Imperial Institute to Messrs. John M. Watson and Co. 28 September 1929).

Sample consignments of *Phragmites* from various parts of the Empire, including Northern Rhodesia, were investigated at the Imperial Institute on a number of occasions up to the 1950s (Northern Rhodesia: Sedges and Rushes for Trials 20 August 1953). In Britain, large quantities of *Phragmites* thrived in Norfolk and other parts of East Anglia, such as the Ely marshes and other localities, including parts of Huntingdonshire. The interest in its use for papermaking purposes included the Imperial Institute, the Rural Industries Bureau, the Ministry of Agriculture and Fisheries, and the Norfolk Reeds Investigation Committee, which consisted of representatives of the Norfolk reed growers as well as the Paper Makers' Association. The purpose of the Committee was to search for fresh outlets for the reeds of East Anglia, where harvesting, cutting, and stacking for thatching purposes had been an important local industry until the use of industrial roofing materials had superseded the use of reeds (Norfolk Reeds for Paper-making 21 June 1932).

The pulping and beating trials of *Phragmites* took place in the laboratories of the Imperial Institute, and the service tests at the Glory Paper Mills of Messrs. Wiggins, Teape & Co. Ltd., Wooburn Green, Buckinghamshire, as well as at St. Anne's Board Mill Company Limited, Bristol. The trials

118   *The paper trade and the British Empire*

revealed that the Norfolk reeds resembled straw in their papermaking qualities, and though not suitable for fine white papers, they could be used in the manufacture of board. At the time of the Import Duties Advisory Committee negotiations in 1932, the negotiations commenced between the Norfolk Reeds Investigation Committee and Messrs. C.W. Glover and Partners who were considering erecting three strawboard mills, one at Littleport, near Ely, Cambridgeshire, another near Abingdon, and a third at Musselburgh, near Inveresk in Scotland. The factories were the first of their kind in Britain and were equipped with machinery to enable strawboards to be manufactured at 20% less cost than in the Dutch factories (Morning Post, 24 November 1932; Norfolk Reeds for Paper-making 21 June 1932; English Reeds 23 June 1932; Norfolk Reeds Investigation Committee: First Meeting 5 October 1932).

Another side of the very complex raw material problem was that the Norfolk reeds had to compete with cheap Belgian and Dutch straw pulp, which was used in Britain for the manufacture of boxboards and building boards like 'Essex Board', which was manufactured at the Thames Board Mills, Ltd., Purfleet, Essex. Besides cheap imported straw pulp, there was already a domestic raw material on the market which did not require pulping at all, *viz.* wood waste fibre in the form of waste woody papers. Wood waste fibre was used as a raw material in making insulating boards like 'Insulwood', which had been made since 1898 at the works of the Patent Impermeable Millboard Company Ltd., Sunbury Common, Middlesex. Another related problem concerned the higher harvesting, crushing, baling, and pulping costs of the bulkier Norfolk reeds, £2 per ton, compared to esparto, which produced better pulp with lower requirements of alkali and coal. Another great drawback for the use of Norfolk reeds for making paper was the expense involved in handling the raw material. Collection was difficult, owing to the swampy nature of the ground in which the plant grows, while the volume of material which would have to be handled was greatly in excess of that of the conifers usually employed for papermaking. In 1931, one estimate gave the amount of reeds by volume required to make a given quantity of pulp as 40 times as large as the amount of wood required to make an equivalent quantity of sulphite pulp (Norfolk Reeds for Paper-making 21 June 1932; English Reeds 23 June 1932; Norfolk Reeds Investigation Committee: First Meeting 5 October 1932).

Papyrus fibre from the Sudan as a source for pulp

Papyrus (*Cyperus papyrus*) is a tall, smooth-stemmed reed of triangular form, ten to 15 feet high, terminating in a tuft of leaves. The plant grew extensively in the marches of the Upper Nile, where the ancient Egyptians sourced it for the preparation of papyrus, their favoured writing medium. This 'Nile paper' was made by stripping off the interior cellular tissue of the inner bark of the stem and bleaching it in the sun. These strips were spread evenly and regularly on a slab and covered transversely by further strips. The whole was moistened and pressed together, glazed, and sized to give the papyrus a surface suitable for writing. The English word for paper is in point of fact derived from 'papyrus', which in turn is a word found in Greek and probably of Egyptian origin. Although it stood to reason during the Renaissance that European paper was a direct descendant of papyrus, what is today called paper is not a ready-made product of nature like papyrus. Paper is a sheet artificially felted from many minute fibres in which the original form of the raw material can no longer be recognised, and which does not bear much resemblance in its outward appearance to the papyrus of the ancients. In the preparation of papyrus, the individual fibres received no special treatment, whereas paper is an aqueous deposit of churned vegetable fibres, which has been obtained by mechanically or chemically separating plant fibres from each other (Beadle 1904; Cormack 1933, 4; Müller 2014, 7–8).

Despite the fact that papyrus bears little resemblance to paper, at the beginning of the twentieth century, considerable attention was paid to the papyrus fibre as a possible source for paper. The idea of making paper from papyrus had two irresistible attractions for the late nineteenth century rulers of British Africa – the modern application of an ancient process at a remote and romantic region of the Empire and the prospect of profits. Samples of papyrus from the Sudan and the East Africa Protectorate were experimented with at the Imperial Institute, where it was found that the manufacture of good paper from this material was possible (Phillips 1915, 630). On 4 September 1911, the commercial possibilities of papyrus became the subject of further investigation in connection with the flotation of a London-based company under the name of the Sudd Fuel (Suddite) Company Limited to make fuel briquettes and pulp in the vicinity of an enormous wasteland of swamp south of Malakal. Here, 600 miles beyond Khartoum stretching to the horizon were thousands of square miles of papyrus, other reeds, and aquatic plants, collectively known as the Sudd, and the British rulers of the region wondered why they could not make paper from it, like the ancient Egyptians had done with papyrus (Report of Directors 30 September 1914). After all, the Dynastic Egyptians had succeeded in creating a thriving papyrus business which had not died until papyrus was gradually ousted by the superior Arab paper over a period from the ninth century to the eleventh (Collins 2005, 242; Bloom 2017, 52–53).

The vast, poor, and populous regions of the Southern Sudan of the early twentieth century had barely come under the authority of the Sudan Government, which at the time had devoted no thought to the economic development of the country. Individual district commissioners would do their best with meagre resources to encourage productivity beyond subsistence, and occasionally to generate enough cash for taxes, which were more a symbol of submission to the Government than a payment for services. Although private entrepreneurs had been interested in the region to the south of Malakal before the papyrus pulp scheme, nothing had ever come of their interest. The natural obstacles, including the tyranny of distance, long and difficult

120 *The paper trade and the British Empire*

communications and transport to Port Sudan and the lack of familiarity with the languages and customs of the local Shilluk workforce, were some of the obvious reasons for interest being translated into commercial activity. Any scheme for the region's development would require a very significant amount of capital with significant risk of it never being returned, let alone at a profit (Collins 2005, 241–242).

The Sudan Government was not particularly welcoming for the development scheme. After bandying the subject about for years at tea parties in Khartoum, in 1913, a group of company promoters managed to purchase for £118,500 from the Sudan Government a ten-year concession over the principal Sudd of the Upper Nile. The concessionaires planned to harvest the Sudd from a strip five kilometres either side of the Bahr al-Jabal for a distance of 150 kilometres south of Lake No, on whose banks a factory was erected to process briquettes and pulp. With the regard to papyrus pulp, it was stated in the Prospectus that '[…] it would be possible to place on the London market, at a cost of three guineas per ton (including transport, canal dues etc.), unbleached papyrus pulp, the sale price of which has been estimated by experts at £6 10s, leaving roughly a net profit of about £1 a ton' (Report of Directors 30 September 1914; Phillips 1915, 630).

At the end of 1913, a Manchester firm shipped pulping machinery and a site was selected for the factory at Lake No. But there was delay in sending out an engineer for erecting the machinery, and then, 'too elderly a man' was despatched; and when the employee became ill immediately he arrived in the Sudan, developing 'an internal malady that entirely incapacitated him', another *monteur*, one Mr. Duke, had to be despatched. On 10 January 1915, when the manufacture of pulp had actually commenced, Grosbie Roles, the Chairman of the Company, wrote to Professor Dunstan, the Director of the Imperial Institute: 'Our first consignment is bulk of paper pulp from the reeds; & is now on its way. This will do well, I think; & if we can be successful [this] fibre will be the thing' (Roles to Professor Dunstan 10 January 1915).

In the harvesting of the Sudd, which contained a legion of different reed varieties, including many ill-suited for papermaking purposes, the main concern was the correct selection of the stems in situ: which was the correct plant for paper fibre and at what point of maturity it should be cut? But before these vexed questions had time to trouble the company's promoters, the ongoing worldwide war prohibited further development work at Lake No. Once operations stopped, the Shilluk labourers abandoned the pile of rusting machinery and the company's resident engineer Mr. Duke – destitute, half-naked, and starving – by Lake No (Report of Directors 30 September 1914).

In 1915, the company went into receivership, but interest in the project did not die. The commercial use of papyrus grass was the perennial question at the Imperial Institute, which examined samples of the material from the Sudan, Uganda, Nigeria, and Northern Rhodesia as well as from the Huleh Valley in Palestine over the next four decades. Papyrus had possibilities as an important Empire-grown fibre for papermaking purposes, but even if found to be chemically and otherwise suitable for such purpose, the economics of scale would again operate. The factor limiting the commercial exploitation of the papyrus fibre was that air-dried material could not compete with esparto on the British market. The lower cost and higher technical value of wood pulp from Scandinavia was another hindrance for the development (Commercial Utilisation of Papyrus 11 August 1944; Use of Papyrus for Papermaking 24 December 1946).

Empire-grown timber resources

After the Second World War, British papermakers turned their attention back to the Empire. By opening up of new forest areas and building up new production capacity in the British Dominions and the Colonies, papermakers tried to secure at least a proportion of their business by building production capacity in the Empire and obtaining supplies on a permanent basis. There were many factors in favour of locating a pulp mill in the tropical and subtropical regions of the Empire near the sources of timber. The close scheduling of logging and processing operations meant less deterioration of the pulpwood which, along with lower labour costs, was included among important advantages, the most obvious being the reduction of volume and weight in shipping (Hess 1952, 8). Moreover, a better local political situation could be established because in some British Empire and Commonwealth countries rich in forest resources (e.g. Canada), there was a strong feeling against the export of pulpwood resources without preliminary processing treatment in the country of origin (Kuhlberg 2012, 106). However, in all but a few dominions, British investments in manufacturing enterprises were encouraged and protected and, if it was possible to include one or more carefully selected firms of the country as stockholders or subcontractors, the position of the British company could be very strong.

In Australia, where the first paper mills had been established as far back as 1818, the value of some indigenous grasses similar to esparto had been discussed since the publication of a report on the Intercolonial Exhibition of Australasia in Melbourne in 1866–67 (Intercolonial Exhibition of Australasia 1867). However, the country's tariff policy primarily served the British imperial system, which guaranteed that British paper products could enter Australian markets duty-free. For that reason, the constantly increasing demand for paper was chiefly met through imports from the UK and to some extent from Canada. For several years before the outbreak of the First World War, the idea that it should be possible to establish the nucleus of a pulp and paper industry in the Commonwealth was debated in the Australian Federal Parliament. In 1913, a pulp mill for the production of sulphate pulp from two of Australia's native conifers, *Araucaria cunninghamii* and *Araucaria bidwillii*, was opened up at Yarraman Creek, 120 miles north-west of Brisbane, Queensland. The mill, which was the first of its kind in Australia, was ceremonially

122   *The paper trade and the British Empire*

opened by the Governor of Queensland, Sir William MacGregor, who described it as the first step towards creating a national pulp and a paper industry in Australia (Phillips 1915, 626–627; Dadswell 2018, 218).

After the war, the Government was anxious to encourage the establishment of a pulp and paper industry in the Commonwealth. In the quest that followed for a suitable indigenous raw material, attention was turned to Tasmania, the smallest of the States of the Australian Commonwealth, famous for its great variety of forest trees. Two of them, the blue gum tree (*Eucalyptus globulus*) and the stringybark (*Eucalyptus obliqua*), were of special interest for the purpose of papermaking. Although the first specimens of eucalyptus paper had already been made during the war and scientific experiments to ascertain the suitability of eucalyptus for the manufacture of pulp and paper had begun in 1920 (Phillips 1915, 627; Dadswell 2018), it was not until 1928–30 that The Tasmanian Paper Pty Ltd. established in service tests that newsprint could be produced from mixtures of eucalypt groundwood and sulphite pulp. Commercial production of eucalypt pulp commenced at a mill of the Associated Pulp and Paper Mills Ltd. in Burnie, Tasmania, in 1938–39. And in early in 1941, Australian Newsprint Mill Ltd. began operations at its mill in Boyer, near New Norfolk in Tasmania. The company was the first to make newsprint containing a high percentage of eucalypt mechanical pulp in its fibre furnish. The pulp was obtained mainly from virgin stands of *E. regnans*, with smaller quantities from *E. gigantea* and *E. obliqua*. There were many reasons for the long delay between the beginning of scientific experiments and the first commercial use of eucalypts as raw material for making paper in Australia. Being hardwoods, eucalypts have short fibres (with an average fibre length of approximately 1 mm), and it was natural that the first experiments confined their use only for those types of papers where short-fibred pulps were already being employed, namely fine writing and printing papers. The next experiments were mainly devoted to the sulphite and mechanical processes, with the object of making newsprint, and it was only many years later that experiments were started, which finally proved that eucalypt kraft pulp could be used as a major part of the fibre furnish in the manufacture of wrapping papers and in the liners of boards (Jeffreys 1965, 241).

One of the most promising sources of pulpwood was from plantations of exotic pine species of South Africa, Australia, and New Zealand, each of which demonstrated the practicability of obtaining very rapid growth and high volume yields from planted exotic pines (Hess 1952, 3). The first scheme to enter into the commercial production stage was in the Union of South Africa, where South African Pulp and Paper Industries Ltd. sponsored a scheme at Springs near Johannesburg for the construction of a mill making pulp and paper from wheat straw and planted *Pinus patula* in 1937 (MGC 10 September 1937). Similarly, in Australia, the Government had created forestry plantations of *Pinus radiata* (also known as *Pinus insignis*) in the south-east of South Australia with a view to supplying logs as sawnwood and thinnings for pulpwood. Private plantations of the same species were established along the

South Australian-Victorian border, and together, the Government and the private plantations comprised a total of 70,000 acres of wood with a possibility to be extended up to 150,000 acres. In regard to the proposal for making paper from *Pinus radiata*, in 1937, Messrs. Bertrams Ltd., the paper mill engineers, millwrights, and ironfounders of St. Katharine's Works at Sciennes, Edinburgh, conducted service tests with the material and found it to make excellent paper in every respect (Species of Wood Used in Various Processes in Making Paper Pulp 20 March 1937).

Another example of exotic pine plantations can be found in New Zealand, where the Albert E. Reed & Co., the major post-war paper manufacturer in Britain and the biggest consumer of wood pulp in Europe, together with the Commonwealth Development Finance Corporation and the Norwegian Sande Træsliperi, opened up negotiations with the Tasman Pulp & Paper Company with a view to erecting a pulp mill in New Zealand. The New Zealand Government and the Fletcher Construction Company had formed the Tasman Pulp & Paper Company in 1952 to erect an integrated mill on the basis of a rated capacity of 36,800 tons of sulphate pulp and 75,000 tons of newsprint per annum. The raw material was harvested from industrial forest plantations at Kaingaroa in the central North Island, which the New Zealand Forest Service had established with great difficulty from 1925 to 1935, from the barren volcanic pumice lands that supported prodigious growth of timber, especially *Pinus radiata*. The pulp and newsprint were mostly aimed at Australian markets, which due to the country's larger population provided a ready export market (Sykes 1981, 372; Roche 2018).

By an agreement between the parties in October 1954, Reed Paper Group invested £1.5 million and the Commonwealth Development Corporation £3 million, divided in £0.5 million in ordinary shares and £2.5 million by means of debentures in the Tasman Pulp & Paper Company. The New Zealand Government, represented by Prime Minister, Sidney Holland, and the New Zealand Forestry Service, represented by Alexander Entrican, as well as Sir James Fletcher, on behalf of the Fletcher Construction Company, were guarantors of the remaining stock capital. The Reed Paper Group and the Anglo-Canadian Pulp and Paper Company, the two biggest newsprint exporters to Australian markets, agreed to switch some of their tonnage to other markets in order to facilitate Tasman's access to the Australian market. The mill, which is located near Onepu, on the Tarawera River, went into production in July 1955. After this, the New Zealand forestry industry grew very rapidly, and within a few years, its exports ranked second only to the country's primary products of butter, cheese, meat, and wool (Roche 2018). The story of The Tasman Pulp & Paper Company is a rare example of a successful post-war British capital export scheme in the field of papermaking. Simultaneously, in 1952, Reed had negotiated with Anglo-Canadian about another kraft scheme, which involved the possibility of participating through the acquisition of the Dryden Paper Company, Dryden, Ontario, at a cost of £1 million, but this scheme floundered due to the Canadians' unease at the

124 *The paper trade and the British Empire*

prospect of increasing British production capacity behind a possible future tariff wall (Sykes 1981, 371–374, 395; see also Kuhlberg 2018).

Conclusions

To compensate for their lack of domestic raw material resources, the British papermakers had numerous strategies for expansion to the tropical and sub-tropical parts of the Empire, especially after the Second World War. Deterrents against the establishment of a pulp mill in tropical regions of the world were equally imposing. In the metropolitan context, there was always the reluctance to make larger than necessary investments in operations in the Empire. There was usually a long period of time between the flotation of a company and commencing production, a period in which there could be dramatic changes in world demand for pulp and paper, and political instability or shortages of labour could seriously affect the success of the venture. Technical hazards also affected operations which might have shown promising during pulping trials and service tests but would later prove not to be commercially viable at greater volumes. Lack of familiarity with the language and customs of the local workforce was in many cases a real obstacle. Superintendence, which comprised technical men and supervisors, required a larger salary and other compensations for working in tropical countries. There also was insufficient knowledge of the properties of the raw materials intended to be utilised, of the processing methods best adapted to each species, and of the methods of forest management. Fear of political upheaval or entanglement resulting in unreasonable costs, or even expropriation, was undoubtedly the single factor, especially after the Second World War, which mostly accounted for the delay in the development of subtropical and tropical resources. Tariff advantages partially offset these deterrents, leading to some success. But for the survival of the British-owned paper industry, the Empire sources of supply proved too little too late.

References

Annual Statement of the Sea-Borne Trade and Navigation of British India with the British Empire and Foreign Countries (TN) (1899–1910) Office of the Superintendent of Government Printing, Calcutta.

Bagchi, A. K. (1972) *Private Investment in India 1900–1939.* Cambridge University Press, Cambridge.

Banik, R. L. (2016) *Silviculture of South Asian Priority Bamboos.* Tropical Forestry 12. Springer, Singapore.

Beadle, C. (1904) *Chapters on Papermaking.* Vol. I. Comprising a Series of Lectures Delivered on Behalf of the Battersea Polytechnic Institute in 1902. H. H. Grattan, London.

Bloom, J. M. (2017) 'Papermaking: The Historical Diffusion of an Ancient Technique'. In J. Heike, P. Meusburger & M. Heffernan, eds, *Mobilities of Knowledge.* Knowledge and Space 10. Springer, Cham, 51–66.

Celotex Limited to British Bamboo Groves Ltd. (11 and 12 April 1949) *AY4/2287, Bamboos for Paper-making: Production and Processing.* Tropical Products Institute and Predecessors. The National Archives, Kew.

Collins, R. O. (2005) *Civil Wars and Revolution in the Sudan.* Tsehai Publishers and Distributors, Hollywood, CA.

Colonial and Indian Exhibition, 1886. Empire of India: Special Catalogue of Exhibits by the Government of India and Private Exhibitors (1886) William Clowes & Sons, London.

Commercial Utilisation of Papyrus (11 August 1944) *AY4/2267.* The National Archives, Kew.

Coomber, H. E. (1952) 'Pulping Studies with Colonial Tropical Hardwoods as Papermaking Materials'. In *Tropical Woods and Agricultural Residues as Sources of Pulp.* Papers Presented at the Fifth Meeting of the FAO Technical Committee on Wood Chemistry, Appleton, WI. September 1951. FAO Forestry and Forest Product Studies. FAO, Rome, 51–62.

Cormack, A. A. (1933) *Our Ancient and Honourable Craft. Being an Account of the Rise and Development of Paper-making in Scotland, and at Culter, Aberdeenshire, in Particular.* Reprinted from *The Paper Market.* Loxley Bros, London.

Cross, C. F. & Bevan, E. J. (1907) *A Text-Book of Paper-Making.* 3rd ed. E. & F. N. Spon, London; Spon & Chamberlain, New York.

Dadswell, G. (2018) 'Making Paper in Australia: Developing the Technology to Create a National Industry, 1818–1928'. In T. Särkkä, M. Gutiérrez-Poch & M. Kuhlberg, eds, *Technological Transformation in the Global Pulp and Paper Industry 1800–2018: Comparative Perspectives.* World Forests 23. Springer, Dordrecht, 217–236.

Demand Forecast for Bamboo Sulphate Pulp (1965) National Council for Applied Economic Research, New Delhi.

English Reeds (Phragmites): Conference on Use for Paper Making: Formation of Norfolk Reeds Investigation Committee (23 June 1932) *AY4/2260.* Tropical Products Institute and Predecessors. The National Archives, Kew.

'Experiments with New Materials for the Manufacture of Paper' (1912) *Bulletin of the Imperial Institute,* X, 372–379.

Forest Research in India, 1933–34. Part I. (1934) Forest Research Institute, Dehra Dun.

Forest Research in India, 1934–35. Part II. Provincial Reports. (1935) Forest Research Institute, Dehra Dun.

Henry, T. A. (1959) 'Wyndham Rowland Dunstan 1861–1949'. *Obituary Notices of Fellows of the Royal Society,* 7, 19, 63–81.

Hess, R. W. (1952) 'Pulpwood from Tropical Forests'. In *Tropical Woods and Agricultural Residues as Sources of Pulp.* Papers Presented at the Fifth Meeting of the FAO Technical Committee on Wood Chemistry, Appleton, WI. September 1951. FAO Forestry and Forest Product Studies. FAO, Rome, 1–9.

Imperial Institute to Messrs. John M. Watson and Co. (28 September 1929) *AY4/2258, Reeds and Guilford Grass in Western Australia: Paper Making Properties.* Tropical Products Institute and Predecessors. The National Archives, Kew.

Intercolonial Exhibition of Australasia, Melbourne 1866–67 (1867) *Official Record Containing Introduction Catalogues, Reports and Awards of the Jurors and Essays and Statistics on the Social and Economic Resources of the Australasian Colonies.* Blundell & Co., Printers, Melbourne.

Jeffreys, R. B. (1965) 'Pulp and Paper Making from Eucalyptus in Australia'. In *Pulp and Paper Prospects in Latin America.* Report on the Latin American Meeting of the

126 *The paper trade and the British Empire*

Experts of the Pulp and Paper Industry. Second part: Working papers submitted to the Meeting. FAO, United Nations, 240–248.

Jeffries, T. A. (1916) 'The Vegetative Anatomy of Molinia cærulea, The Purple Heat Grass'. *New Phytologist*, XV, 3 & 4, 49–71.

Khandual, A. & Sahu, S. (2016) 'Sabai Grass: Possibility of Becoming a Potential Textile'. In: S. S. Muthu & M. Gardetti, eds, *Sustainable Fibres for Fashion Industry*. Vol. 2. Environmental Footprints and Eco-Design of Products and Processes 6. Springer, Singapore, 45–60.

Kuhlberg, M. (2012) 'An Accomplished History, An Uncertain Future: Canada's Pulp and Paper Industry Since the Early 1800s'. In J.-A. Lamberg, J. Ojala, M. Peltoniemi & T. Särkkä, eds, *The Evolution of Global Paper Industry: 1800–2050: A Comparative Analysis*. World Forests 17. Springer, Dordrecht, 101–134.

Kuhlberg, M. (2018) 'Natural Potential, Artificial Restraint: The Dryden Paper Company and the Fetters on Adopting Technological Innovation in a Canadian Pulp and Paper Sector, 1900–1950'. In T. Särkkä, M. Gutiérrez-Poch & M. Kuhlberg, eds, *Technological Transformation in the Global Pulp and Paper Industry 1800–2018: Comparative Perspectives*. World Forests 23. Springer, Dordrecht, 133–160.

Liotard, L. (1880) *Memorandum on Materials in India Suitable for the Manufacture of Paper.* Home, Revenue and Agricultural Press, Calcutta.

Manufacture of Paper from Bamboo (18 April 1952) *AY4/2288, Paper Production from Bamboo in India.* Tropical Products Institute and Predecessors. The National Archives, Kew.

Marram Grass and Spartina Townsendii for Paper Making (2 May 1918) *AY4/2208.* Tropical Products Institute and Predecessors. The National Archives, Kew.

Morning Post (24 November 1932).

Müller, L. (2014) *White Magic. The Age of Paper.* Transl. from the German by Jessica Spengler. Polity, Malden, MA.

Norfolk Reeds Investigation Committee: First Meeting (5 October 1932) *AY4/2292.* Tropical Products Institute and Predecessors. The National Archives, Kew.

Norfolk Reeds for Paper-Making (21 June 1932) *AY4/2259.* Tropical Products Institute and Predecessors. The National Archives, Kew.

Northern Rhodesia: Sedges and Rushes for Trials (20 August 1953) *AY4/2375.* Tropical Products Institute and Predecessors. The National Archives, Kew.

Oliver, F. W. (1916) *Memorandum on the Utilisation of Spartina Townsendii as a Source of Paper.* W. S. Hallett, Poole.

Paper Division of the Raw Materials Department, Board of Trade to British Bamboo Groves Ltd. (16 March 1949) *AY4/2287, Bamboos for Paper-Making: Production and Processing.* Tropical Products Institute and Predecessors. The National Archives, Kew.

Pearson, R. S. (1912) 'Note on the Utilization of Bamboo for the Manufacture of Paper-Pulp'. *Indian Forest Records*, IV, V, 1–121.

Phillips, S. C. (1915) 'The Empire's Resources in Paper-Making Materials'. *Journal of the Royal Society of Arts*, XLIII, 3261, 613–636.

Podder, V. (1979) *Paper Industry in India. A Study.* Oxford & IBH Publishing Co., New Delhi, Bombay and Calcutta.

Progress Report of Forest Research Work in India for the Year 1926–7 (1928) Government of India, Calcutta.

Raitt, W. (20 January 1922) *Report on the Tavoy River Pulping Concession. AY4/2223, Bamboo Pulp from India: Suitability for Paper.* Tropical Products Institute and Predecessors. The National Archives, Kew.

The paper trade and the British Empire   127

Raitt, W. (1928) 'Bamboo Hope'. In *Progress Report of Forest Research Work in India. For the Year 1926–7*. Government of India, Calcutta, 155–165.

Ray, I. (2018) *The Development of Modern Industries in Bengal: Reindustrialisation, 1858–1960*. Routledge Explorations in Economic History 81. Routledge, London and New York.

Report of Directors. Sudd Fuel (Suddite), Limited (30 September 1914) *AY4/2200, Papyrus Fibre. "Sudd" Fibre. Sudan*. Tropical Products Institute and Predecessors. The National Archives, Kew.

Report of the Royal Commission for the Colonial and Indian Exhibition (1887) William Clowes & Sons, London.

Roche, M. (2018) 'Technology Transfer and Local Innovation: Pulp and Paper Manufacturing in New Zealand, c.1860 to c.1960'. In T. Särkkä, M. Gutiérrez-Poch & M. Kuhlberg, eds, *Technological Transformation in the Global Pulp and Paper Industry 1800–2018: Comparative Perspectives*. World Forests 23. Springer, Dordrecht, 189–216.

Roles to Professor Dunstan (10 January 1915) *AY4/2200, Papyrus fibre. "Sudd" fibre. Sudan*. Tropical Products Institute and Predecessors. The National Archives, Kew.

Routledge, T. (1875) *Bamboo, Considered as a Paper-making Material. Remarks Upon Its Cultivation and Treatment*. E. & F.N. Spon, London and New York.

Routledge, T. (11 October 1880) *MR/136/65, India. Economic Products. Bamboo.* The Library, Art & Archives Royal Botanic Gardens, Kew.

Royle, J. R. (1887) *Report on the Indian Section of the Colonial and Indian Exhibition 1886*. William Clowes & Sons, London.

Species of Wood Used in Various Processes in Making Paper Pulp (20 March 1937) *AY4/2303, Pinus Radiata Wood in South Australia: Paper Pulp Production*. Tropical Products Institute and Predecessors. The National Archives, Kew.

Sykes, P. (1981) *Albert E. Reed and the Creation of a Paper Business 1860–1960*. X.525/5617, unpublished manuscript. The British Library, London.

The Manchester Guardian Commercial (MGC) (10 September 1937).

Tiwari, R. D. (1937) *Railway Rates in Relation to Trade & Industry in India*. Longmans, Green and Co., Ltd., Calcutta.

Use of Papyrus for Paper-making (24 December 1946) *AY4/2268*. Tropical Products Institute and Predecessors. The National Archives, Kew.

7 A retrospective view of the British paper industry

This chapter focuses on the history of the British paper industry and the environment in which it has operated from the birth of mechanised papermaking in the first years of the nineteenth century to the changing market dynamics and consumer behaviour of the last years of the twentieth century. The chapter shows how the nature, the scale, and the distribution of papermaking changed in Britain over a period of about 200 years. Britain was the first country in the world to enter into the field of the paper manufacturing industry. It is a matter of particular significance to analyse with hindsight the consequences of coming first in a line of business. With this case method, it is hoped to provide information which will add to our understanding of British paper manufacturing history, and possibly extend or clarify our understanding of the history of the paper manufacturing industry as a whole. Tables 7.1–7.5 and Figure 7.1 provide the particulars of the Census of Production returns quoted below.

The birth of mechanised papermaking

The history of the British paper industry, for the purposes of this chapter, begins in the early years of the nineteenth century. Before that period, paper was produced by fairly simple manual work, which fell into three distinct processes: the preparation of the pulp, the manufacture of a wet sheet of paper, and the drying and finishing off of the paper. The first effects of the Industrial Revolution were felt particularly in the cotton, wool, and iron trades but also indirectly in the paper industry. The growth of the industry as a whole increased the demand for papers of all kinds, both for the domestic and for export trade (Hills 1988). The industrial production of paper based on steam power got off to a slow start compared to the textile and iron industries. The reason for this comparative slowness in experimenting with steam power in papermaking lay in the smallness of eighteenth-century vat mills (they usually had from 6 to 17 employees) and their remoteness from coal supplies, railroads, and canals (Spicer 1907; Coleman 1958).

Paper mills were typically established on good waterpower sites, which might first have made steam power unattractive to the paper manufacturers.

The business history of Bridge Hall Mills, near Bury in Lancashire, reveals that paper mills based on waterpower continued to be developed, regardless of the improvements in steam engine technology that were being made (Tillmanns 1978). However, before long manufacturers realised that transfer from waterpower to coal brought certain advantages. Falls of water required constant repair and were liable to cause heavy floods or to fail altogether in the driest seasons. With steam, the manufacture could be carried on regularly throughout the year, which made steam engines attractive to manufacturers willing to take risks in building new factories. One of the early examples of this business pattern was Springfield Mill, which was erected by William Balston in Maidstone in 1805. This pioneering mill was based on steam power, and it utilised spring water in papermaking (Balston 1954).

How, then, was the mechanised production of paper made a workable economic enterprise in Britain? Such a development would have been impossible without improvements in papermaking technology. The story of the introduction of the first paper machine in Britain is connected to Henry Fourdrinier (1766–1854) and his brother Sealy Fourdrinier (1773–1847), who in 1801 together with John Gamble bought the patent rights on a machine for making paper from a Parisian, Nicolas-Louis Robert, of Didot's paper mill at Essonnes. This true mother of invention, which was subsequently simply known as the 'Fourdrinier', produced a continuous roll of paper instead of producing one sheet of paper at a time. In 1802, the Fourdrinier brothers came in contact with a British engineer called Bryan Donkin, whom they helped to set up in an engineering workshop at Bermondsey on the South Bank of the River Thames. For the next five years, Donkin worked on the machine financed by the Fourdrinier brothers, who invested in the experiments the large sums they obtained from the wholesale stationery business in the City (Clapperton 1967, 284; McConnell 2004). Experiments with the new technology made at Frogmore Mill on the River Gade, near Hemel Hempstead in Hertfordshire and the adjoining Two Waters Mill, where the first Fourdriniers were installed in 1803 and 1804, started the slow emergence of the paper machine.

Although the original idea of the paper machine technique was not Donkin's, the development work on the machine was due to him, and his work was rewarded by being exhibited at the Great Exhibition of 1851 in Hyde Park, London (Coleman 1958; Clapperton 1967; Lloyd-Jones 2004). It is perhaps enough to state here that by this time, the Fourdrinier was already a fairly complex and costly machine. What is important to emphasise is the stimulus given by this initial mechanisation to the whole the process of paper manufacture. At the heart of the early British industrial success lay an evolutionary change of technology, mechanical alterations and improvements in the preparation of stock and the production of paper itself. Paper mills, paper machine manufacturers, and papermakers themselves were often important players in transmitting new technology through the industry. Improvements in technology allowed papermakers to concentrate on the quality of the final

130 *The British paper industry*

product and to organise the industry to be better able to meet the growing demand for paper of various kinds (Magee 1997a, 1997b).

The Fourdrinier machine experiment was made at the expense of craftsmen, who often opposed the introduction of machinery, and, indeed, financiers, who, like the Fourdrinier brothers, eventually went bankrupt (Shears 1967). It was not until the 1830s that mechanisation became truly widespread in the industry in Britain, owing to capital costs that were too heavy for many manufacturers. Ultimately, the mechanisation of the industry was financed by using the well-tried methods of partnership, mortgage, and loan on bond. Through this network of loans and leases, mortgages, purchases, and partnerships, the world of papermaking came into being (Coleman 1958).

The transition from mercantile to industrial capitalism was made by concentrating production, providing a regular flow of raw materials, keeping account of the flow of funds, and controlling a workforce. These were new tasks for many businessmen. By the Great Exhibition of 1851, Britain had become the 'Workshop of the World', but the effects of industrial mechanisation were still confined to a narrow range of industries, and particular regions, and agriculture and domestic manufacturing employment remained extremely important. Nevertheless, a steady transition from mercantile to industrial capitalism was already pervading British business life (Wilson 1995).

Who, then, were the entrepreneurs who built up the paper industry in the first decades of mechanisation? The pattern was not uniform throughout. New industrialists came in alongside the old established families. To the growth of an industrialist class, the lower middle class made an important contribution. Nepotism was the traditional route into management. Managers were brought into the firm because of their family or religious connections and learnt their jobs through practical training (Pollard 1965; Wilson 1995). The important English papermakers during these early decades of mechanisation included John Dickinson, who had several mills in Hertfordshire. James Wrigley and Son, John and Thomas Bonsor Crompton as well as Charles and Henry Hilton manufactured in Lancashire. In Kent, there were William Jaynson and William Balston and, in Surrey, Sir William and James Magnay. Furthermore, there were papermakers working on a considerable scale in Oxfordshire, Berkshire, Buckinghamshire, and Hampshire (Shorter 1971).

In Wales in 1821, William Hill installed a Fourdrinier machine in his Abbey Mills, situated in the small village of Greenfield, near the town of Holywell, Flintshire. Greenfield was an advantageous site for making paper by mechanical means. There was a constant supply of fresh water issuing from St. Winifred's Well, coal for raising steam available at the nearby Englefield colliery, and, at Flint, there was Muspratt's chemical works, which supplied bleaching powder and processing chemicals. In about 1865, Abbey Mills adopted esparto grass as a raw material for making stationery papers for its customers in the City, which was the principal market for stationery (Chater 1977, 26–27).

The British paper industry   131

In Scotland, the paper mills were grouped on the Water of Leith, Edinburgh. In 1763, there were three vat mills producing 6,400 reams per annum, but less than three decades later, in 1790, there were already 12 mills that were producing over 100,000 reams making Edinburghshire (Midlothian) the largest producing county of the time in Britain. In Scotland, too, at the beginning of the nineteenth century, increasing population and the general adoption of the steam-powered printing press increased the demand for paper in a way previously unforeseen. To meet the increased demand, the dawn of the age of the machine emerged in 1812 at Edinburgh. By that time, paper mills could be found as far east as Eyemouth, as far west as Glasgow, and as far north as Aberdeen, where the first mill, Culter Paper Mill, beneath the Gorge of Culter Burn, the north bank of the River Dee, was established in 1750.[1] By 1835, there were already four mills running in Aberdeenshire, all equipped with the Fourdriniers (Cormack 1933, 16, 22, 33–4; Galloway 1968, 10–11; Thomson 1974).

Economic determinants of the early paper industry

A number of economic determinants of the British paper industry flowed directly from technical needs. These include (1) the location of the mills, (2) raw materials, (3) capital, and (4) skilled labour. Prior to the introduction of the steam engine, the location of paper mills was conditioned by water supply, which was needed both as a source of power and for the paper manufacturing process. Water had to be clear, lacking in silt, and unpolluted, or specks would show up in the paper. In addition, water with a high iron content produces paper with a reddish or brownish cast. To produce very white paper, the presence of calcium or magnesium carbonate in the water helped, as could the addition of lime, which is calcium, to the pulp (Kurlansky 2017, 72).

The fast growth of the paper industry could not have been achieved in Britain without the existing abundant waterpower resources. The paper mills based on waterpower had to be situated along rivers where a fall in level could be exploited by building dams, channels, and waterwheels. Thickly veined with swiftly running rivers and brooks, the British Isles offered ideal surroundings for making paper. At first, the industry grew up in river valleys in the north (Lancashire and Yorkshire), the south-east (Buckinghamshire and Kent), and Scotland (based around Edinburgh market), where both fast-running streams and clean water were available (Coleman 1958; Spicer 1907; Shorter 1971; Magee 1997b).

After the introduction of the steam engine to the paper mills, coal replaced water as a power supply, and the most successful paper mills tended to be located near coalmines. However, the distribution of paper mills was conditioned by existing water sources as large amounts of clean and fresh water were needed for the production process. In principle, with steam, power manufacturing could be carried on regularly throughout the year if all the other

132   *The British paper industry*

production requirements – *viz.* raw materials, skilled labour, and capital – could be met. The older mills were built to satisfy the local demand for paper, but improvements in technology made it possible to produce greater quantities for wider markets. This development forced manufacturers to consider the best locations for their mills for the rail and canal transport of both raw materials and finished products. During the early period of the mechanised paper industry, a number of the older mills were shut down due to their remote location from the coalmines and the means of transport – the canals, railways, and ports. The network of railways to the towns linked the newer mills. The general tendency of change was towards the towns and towards the coal deposits (Spicer 1907; Coleman 1958; Shorter 1971), which therefore had emerged as one of the defining factors of mechanised papermaking.

The second important economic determinant of papermaking was the raw materials for making paper. Traditionally, the most important raw materials in British papermaking were cotton, linen, and hemp rags. Since rags were not typically available in abundance, the availability of rags in turn conditioned the location of the paper mills. Hence, the early paper mills tended to spring up at a relatively short distance from the major conurbations, especially London, which was the greatest market for paper and the centre of rag supplies. The expansion of overseas trade highlighted the importance of proximity to accessible docks so that the raw materials and finished goods did not have to be transhipped far from ocean-going vessels (Spicer 1907; Coleman 1958; Shorter 1971).

The more economical methods of manufacture and larger output to meet larger demand led to the quest for new raw materials. It was the introduction of esparto grass for papermaking that first offered a solution to the raw material shortage in Britain. Since the first and fundamental utilisation of esparto grass in the paper industry by Thomas Routledge, who took out a patent in 1856, esparto was used in British mills for papermaking. Esparto mills were numerous especially in Scotland, where established manufacturers, like Tullis Russell, adopted esparto on the inception of the trade in the early 1860s (Ketelbey 1967, 107–110). Esparto also brought new mills in the papermaking business, such as The Guard Bridge Paper Company, on the mouth of the River Eden, Guard Bridge, Fife, founded in 1873. The following four fundamentals of mechanical papermaking largely defined success and failure in the esparto business: access to transport, coal, chemicals, and markets. The Guard Bridge Paper Company was among the successful ones because it had rail access for its supplies of bulky raw materials: coal for power from the Fife Coalfield, and deliveries of esparto through Tayport. The railway also provided an easy link with Edinburgh and an outlet to London, the main market for writing and printing paper (Weatherill 1974, 3–4).[2]

Despite the expansion of the esparto trade, the demand for raw materials was in no way satisfactorily met. Many modern processes for the isolation of cellulose from wood were tried out in an elementary way by several British papermakers. Matthias Koops, a papermaker from Bermondsey, made the first and most important attempt in Britain as early as 1800, but it proved fruitless (Koops 1801). Nevertheless, by the early 1870s, international break-throughs in the production of chemical wood pulp made the raw material available for the British manufacturers. Wood pulp began its steady rise to prominence in Britain at first at the expense of esparto but then later at the expense of both esparto and rags.

Among other reasons for the success of esparto was the ability of the British chemical and mining industries to produce processing chemicals and miner-als. The discovery of bleaching and colouring as well as the introduction of wood pulp further increased the demand for minerals and chemicals. The processing chemicals needed comprised the basic materials such as salt and limestone. Common salt, though not a processing chemical itself, was the main raw material for the production of caustic soda and chlorine, both pro-duced industrially − as a rule by electrolysis of common salt. Since both salt and limestone were relatively low-cost items, the main factor in the delivered cost of these materials was transport. Salt and limestone were required in large quantities, but the main sources of supply typically not being located near the mill site added to transport costs. The second group of important chemicals included salt cake (sodium sulphate), soda ash, and sulphur. Salt cake was available either from natural deposits or as an industrially produced chemical in hydrochloric acid plants. Soda ash was produced from salt, lime-stone, and coke. Rock sulphur was found from natural deposits either in elementary form or as pyrites and other sulphide ores. And kaolin, which was obtained from Cornwall, was an important clay mineral that had come to be used in British papermaking at the turn of the eighteenth and nineteenth centuries. It was added in very small quantities to the pulp in order to give body and weight to the finished sheet. So long as the main raw material used was rags, a small amount of kaolin was needed. However, the introduction of esparto and wood pulp increased the consumption of China clay (Spicer 1907; Coleman 1958).

Thirdly, since papermaking is a mill industry, it requires a substantial amount of capital. The poorly developed state of capital markets made it preferable to rely on internal sources for investment requirements. This led to the creation of the 'web of credit' by which is meant the combination of merchants, industrialists, banks, and acceptance houses (merchant bankers) to invest in the paper industry (Wilson 1995). By the late nineteenth century, Britain had risen to the world's largest creditor nation and the City of London was the centre of the capital market. Crucial to the City's domination were its financial institutions, which had been developed over a number of dec-ades: the Bank of England, the joint-stock banks, the Stock Exchange, and the commodity markets (Kynaston 2012; McRae & Cairncross 2017). The main attraction of the City was that the metropolitan business community could offer a bundle of competitively priced financial, marketing, and con-sulting services. The Bank Charter Act and the Joint Stock Banking Act of 1844 had laid the foundations for the banking system, with the functioning

134 *The British paper industry*

of the international gold standard at its heart. The legislative foundation of the gold standard was the Coinage Act of 1816, promulgated in the aftermath of the Napoleonic Wars. The increased adoption of the single gold standard occurred in the aftermath of the Great Depression of the 1870s (Green 1982, 21–22; Ally 1994, 1–6). The City was recognised uncontestably as the centre of the world's money market, attracting funds from all around the world and then reinvesting them in different parts of it. Well into the twentieth century, however, the City of London was dominated by 'gentlemanly capitalism', where industrial interests were shunned as socially inferior to the more lucrative and prestigious business of exporting capital (Cain and Hopkins 1994).

Finally, the presence of specialised labour in the productive process was another factor that defined the paper industry. Papermaking techniques did not allow the setting up of a vat mill on the basis of semi-skilled or unskilled labour. A major theme regarding skilled labour during the early period of the mechanised paper industry was the hostility of skilled workers and their organisations to changes that altered the existing customs and arrangements regarding employment in the paper industry. A strong craft tradition existed in handmade paper manufacture. The spread of the paper machine brought to the manufacturers a ready-made answer to the problem of labour relations since it allowed them to be free from the power of skilled and organised labour. This persuaded the manufacturers to mechanise the industry even further (Spicer 1907; Coleman 1958; Shorter 1971).

Measuring technology transfer

As a result of technology transfer, the scale of the British paper industry changed as well. Mechanisation affected the size, number, and output capacity of the paper mills. The general impression of what statistics offer is that the paper industry grew steadily during the early period of mechanised papermaking. The extent to which the production increased cannot be measured with precision; it varied from mill to mill and according to the grades of paper, and it changed over the years. From 1805 to 1860, the total output of machine-made paper in Britain increased from 557 to 95,971 tons. At the same time, in handmade paper manufacture, the total output decreased from 16,502 to 3,839 tons. Handmade paper thus constituted only about 4% of total production in 1860. In 1824, machine-made production exceeded for the first time production from the vats making paper by hand. The number of machines outnumbered vats for the first time in 1848. In 1860, there were 340 machines compared to 130 vats running in Britain. It is also noteworthy that small mills were disappearing and that papermaking was being concentrated into larger hands and into fewer districts. In 1851, Lancashire had the two largest mills in Britain, Bridge Hall and Farnworth. The leading counties in terms of the total number of mills were Lancashire and Kent. The total number of mills in England and Wales in 1860 was 306 (Lewis 1969; Shorter 1971).

The British paper industry   135

In Scotland, the change towards larger mills and the elimination of vats in favour of machines were also well underway by 1860 (Thomson 1974). The Edinburgh District continued to dominate in the Scottish paper industry. In 1851, it had 18 out of 48 working mills (Shorter 1971). The absence of old mills in the most remote areas, excellent port facilities, rapid industrialisation in both the linen and chemical industries, and the rapid growth of towns are some reasons for the rapid development of the early Scottish paper industry (Coleman 1958). The Irish paper industry did not have a similarly positive outlook because of the lack of capital, a comparatively low standard of living, the lack of accessible coal resources in Ireland itself, the unstable political situation, and the general decline in the population from 1840 onwards (Shorter 1971).

In the first part of the nineteenth century, Britain was the world's largest and lowest-cost producer of paper. The reasons behind the increased production included improvements in technology and the constant supply of rags, the raw material of the day for paper. Furthermore, the manufacturers in Britain were operating with significant advantages on their side, including a supply of cheap and readily accessible coal, available craftsmanship, a relatively orderly society, and an efficient transport system (Mokyr 1990). However, what was more important was an increased effective demand for paper caused by the growing population. The census of 1801 showed that the population of the British Isles was 15 million in 1801. In 1861, it was nearly 29 million, almost double the figure for 1801 (Census records for England and Wales; Scotland; Ireland 1861).

The biggest customer of the paper industry was the printing industry, which was undergoing technical and organisational changes, enabling the printing presses to become capable of producing a much higher output during the latter part of the nineteenth century. In 1850, the fastest press was capable of producing 8,000 unperfected sheets per hour, whereas in 1901, a rotary press could produce 52,000 larger, perfected sheets per hour (Alford 1963, 3). New patterns of social intercourse, increased literacy, and heightened social consciousness are all included among the important reasons for the increased demand for paper. The number of literate people was rising rapidly after the introduction of national education in England and Wales under the Education Act of 1870. Hundreds of millions of letters went through the post office every year. Penny and halfpenny newspapers, journals, magazines, reviews, and cheap editions of books came within the reach of the very poorest. In indirect ways, the mechanisation of industry gave people and institutions more reasons to need paper. The early growth of mass communication through new forms of cheap publications was made possible by mechanical printing and papermaking. Without the paper machine or improvements in mechanical printing, it would have been impossible to bring many of these cheap publications into existence (Coleman 1958).

The technological transformation of raw materials and the more scientific use of both chemicals and minerals, together with the adoption of factory

136   *The British paper industry*

methods of production and the improvement of machinery, meant increased production (Spicer 1907; Magee 1997b). Increased production also meant enlarged diversity of output. The *Phillips' Paper Trade Directory of the World* (1910) listed some 40 different products, ranging from cigarette paper to carpet felt, and from cheque paper to strawboard, which were manufactured by the British paper mills. Lower costs of raw materials, chemicals, wages, and fixed charges together with increased production led to a drop of 60% in the average price of paper between 1861 and 1902 (Spicer 1907).

This combination of increased output and lower costs brought new businessmen and capital to the industry. More than 150 new firms were launched solely between 1870 and 1900 (Bartlett 1980). The number of mills dropped, however, because production concentrated in larger establishments. Between 1860 and 1900, the number of mills operating in England and Wales decreased from 306 to 211, while the number of machines grew from 300 to 418 (Shorter 1971). The typical paper mill of the time was a single-machine mill employing between 20 and 70 workers. The development towards larger mills intensified in the latter part of the nineteenth century. For instance, Newbattle Mills near Dalkeith in Scotland is said to have employed some 300 people in 1870 when it operated with three machines (Robert Craig & Sons, Ltd. 1920).

Organisation of labour

Unions of workmen had been in existence in Britain since 1789, but the first serious craft organisation to represent the interests of the craftsmen of the vat mills was the Original Society of Papermakers, which was founded in 1800. The progress of trade unions in the machine industry was very modest until the latter decades of the nineteenth century, and an increasing number of machine workers found themselves without adequate representation. Into this vacuum stepped in 1853 the Union of Machine Workers, also calling themselves the United Brotherhood of Paper Makers. From 1869 to 1894, there existed two societies for the craftsmen of the machine mills, the United Brotherhood and the Modern Society of Paper Makers. In 1894, they reunited in the Amalgamated Society of Papermakers, but it continued to represent beatermen, machinemen, and finishers only. The skilled union did not open its membership to unskilled or semi-skilled workers, even though the general union was weak and unstable. Instead, it was eager to merge its identity with that of the old craft union of vat mill workers. The National Union of Paper Mill Workers was founded in 1890 for unskilled mill workers but did not have a long existence as an independent union. In 1914, it amalgamated with the National Society of Printers' Warehousemen and Cutters (Spicer 1907; Coleman 1958; Bundock 1959; Harris 1994). Divisions between vat and machine mill workers, on the one hand, and within machine production between skilled and unskilled workers, on the other, made the organisation of labour in the paper industry severely divided at a time when efforts to shorten

The British paper industry   137

the working week were under negotiation (Magee 1997a, 1997b). Low wages and irregular employment characterised unskilled employment in particular, widening the gap between skilled and unskilled workers (Pollard 1963).

During the First World War, the trade unions within each industry had been forced to collaborate closely, and this encouraged a movement towards the amalgamation of the small societies into larger bodies. Ultimately, the Trade Union (Amalgamation) Act of 1917 made amalgamation easier and helped to create large national unions (Pollard 1963). The National Union of Printing, Bookbinding, Machine Ruling and Paper Workers (from 1928 onwards known as the N.U. of Printing, Bookbinding & Paper Workers) was founded in 1921 to represent workers in paper and allied trades. At its height in the late 1950s, the union had over 160,000 members (Bundock 1959). Following mergers with several small unions, it joined with the National Society of Operative Printers and Assistants to form The Society of Graphical and Allied Trades (SOGAT) in 1966 (Gennard and Bain 1995).

What were the relationships between employers and employees like? The family-based management structure dominated the industry in the nineteenth century. Paternalism best describes the employment relationship in the industry. With the advance of limited liability ownership, personal employer paternalism diminished (Harris 1994). After the Second World War, the strongly personal nature of the British paper business scene was replaced by a type of corporate paternalism, which saw company welfare schemes as an integral part of modern industrial management. Broadly speaking, histories of trade unionism indicate that the stability of relationship was dependent on employers delivering a valuable set of welfare benefits (Pollard 1963; Harris 1994). Although there is some evidence of worker's resistance from the late nineteenth century, all in all peaceful industrial relations prevailed in the industry. During the First World War and the interwar period, national trade unions were both strong enough and militant enough to challenge employers, both in narrow skirmishes and on a broad front, like that of the 1926 General Strike (Richardson 2006). The Trade Disputes and Trade Unions Act of 1927, which made general strikes illegal, illustrated that employers were still able to gain considerable victories over organised labour. It was not until the Trade Disputes and Trade Unions Act of 1946 that the 1927 Act was repealed (Pollard 1963).

How many people worked in the industry? It is difficult to find an adequate answer to this simple but important question. The most satisfactory estimates are largely based on the occupation tables of the Census of Population returns, which are available from 1831 onwards. In 1861, total employment in paper manufacture in Britain was 17,669, of whom 13,248 worked in mills in England and Wales and 4,421 in Scotland. Fifty years later, in 1911, the total employment had increased to 34,954, of whom 24,844 worked in England and Wales and 10,113 in Scotland (Shorter 1971). It should be noted, however, that these figures do not show the total employment which paper manufacture provided. According to one estimate made by Coleman (1958),

138   *The British paper industry*

total employment provided by paper mills in 1861 was twice that given by the census figures. This would bring employment in the Britain in 1861 to 35,000. Furthermore, the census figures do not take any account of a range of occupations also dependent on the paper industry. In 1861, these together added another 17,000 for England and Wales.

In what conditions did they work? During the early period of papermaking, the most unattractive and unhealthy places were the rooms where the rags were sorted and cut. The work of the papermakers themselves in the vat mills was heavy and tiring. Moreover, extremely disagreeable odours emanated from the retting of rags, and it was noisy too because of the constantly running stampers. Yet both these workers and their successors in the machine mills were generally regarded as a healthy and long-lived section of the artisan class. The prevalence of accidents, however, was a common feature during the early period of mechanisation (Coleman 1958). The first important improvement in the state of labour in paper mills was the passing of the Act for the Extension of the Factory Acts in 1867, which restricted the employment of children and women in manufacturing work. The subsequent Acts, generally, meant better working conditions (Spicer 1907; Paper and Paper Board Manufacture and Coating 1947; Shorter 1971).

What did they earn? There are two major problems in estimating wages paid. Firstly, the data available for the nineteenth century is inadequate. It has been estimated by Coleman (1958) that English papermakers' wages increased by 38% between 1803 and 1865. Secondly, under the Census of Production Act of 1906, the Board of Trade was prohibited from enquiring into the amount of wages paid in connection with a Census of Production. Voluntary enquiries on this subject were, however, conducted by the Ministry of Labour in respect of both 1930 and 1924. Comparison of wages paid to other industrial groups reveals that average annual earnings per operative in the paper trade in 1930 were between £121 and £140. With that salary, the paper trade workers belonged to the same relatively well-paid category of workers such as, for instance, workers in iron and steel foundries. They earned more than workers in the textile trades (not exceeding £100 or between £101 and £120 p.a.) but less than workers in the printing and publishing sectors (over £160 p.a.) (CP 1924, 1930).

The growth of the paper industry

A dramatic increase in paper and board production (204.2%) took place between the census of production years 1907 (850,000) and 1951 (2,586,500) (Table 7.1). The growth is predominantly reflected in the labour productivity (Figure 7.1), while the number (Table 7.2), size by employment (Table 7.3), and distribution (Table 7.4) of the mills remained relatively constant. The number of mills decreased rapidly, to 306 in 1924 and 267 in 1935. In 1938, paper was produced by 192 companies in 228 paper mills, widely distributed throughout the country, but predominantly located in Kent, Hertfordshire,

The British paper industry   139

Table 7.1 Total Output of Paper and Board 1907–1951 (Tons and %)

	Tons	% Share from total
1907	850,000	6.9
1912	1,018,200	8.3
1924	1,268,300	10.3
1935	2,250,300	18.3
1937	2,546,100	20.7
1948	1,772,200	14.4
1951	2,586,500	21.1
Total	12,291,600	100.0

Source: CP 1907, 1912, 1924, 1930, 1935, 1948, 1951. The manufacturers of paper were required to state the total weight of paper and board made by them in the year, whether sold or added to stock or used by them in their works for further manufacture. Similar information was not required in 1907, but an estimate of the total make in that year was made by the Census Office on the basis of the information furnished in the returns. The figures for 1948 concern Great Britain only.

Table 7.2 Number of Establishments 1924–1951

	N
1924	306
1930	272
1935	267
1948	275
1951	282

Source: CP 1924, 1930, 1935, 1948, 1951. The table lists firms engaged in the manufacture of paper and board and coating paper (in 1948 Great Britain only).

Buckinghamshire, Lancashire, and the West Country, and, in Scotland, in Edinburgh, Glasgow, and the north-eastern region. In addition to the small esparto pulping units, there were three chemical wood pulp mills. Those directly employed in the production side of the industry numbered 67,000 (TN 1882–1964; Sykes 1981, 274–276, 280). After the war, the number of mills started to rise again, reaching 282 in 1951. From analysis of the size of the mills by employment figures in the Census of Production returns for the years 1935, 1948, and 1951, we can determine that in each of these years, the largest concentration of mills (over 50) had between 50 and 99 and 100 and 199 employees. There were five mills which employed over 1,000 persons in 1935, three in 1948, and four in 1951. After the war, the size of the mills increased. In 1948 and 1951, there were four mills in both years that had over 1,500 employees (Table 7.3).

From 1907 onwards, we can base our estimates on the total number of persons employed in the industry on the information provided by the Census of Production returns. The Censuses of 1907 and 1924 extended to all firms,

140　*The British paper industry*

Table 7.3 Size of Establishments by Employment 1935–1951

Average number employed	1935	1948	1951
11–24	16	20	18
25–49	42	30	36
50–99	53	61	58
100–199	54	53	51
200–299	43	43	38
300–399	19	20	27
400–499	13	12	16
500–749	18	23	19
750–999	4	6	11
1,000–1,499	5	3	4
1,500 over	–	4	4
Total	267	275	282

Source: CP 1935, 1948, 1951. The table lists firms engaged in the manufacture of paper and board and coating paper (in 1948 Great Britain only).

Table 7.4 Distribution of Mills and Employment by Standard Region 1948 and 1951

Region	Establishments		Persons employed		Average number employed per establishment	
	1948 (GB)	1951 (UK)	1948 (GB)	1951 (UK)	1948 (GB)	1951 (UK)
Northern	11	11	2,054	2,290	187	208
East and West Ridings of Yorkshire	16	16	2,342	2,764	146	178
North Midlands	11	14	834	1,090	76	79
Eastern	10	9	4,406	4,857	441	540
London and South Eastern	56	61	15,331	18,584	274	305
Southern	15	14	3,641	4,181	243	299
South Western	25	25	6,259	6,774	250	271
Midlands	10	10	1,914	2,150	192	215
North Western (including Northern Ireland in 1951)	67	66	13,274	13,833	198	210
England (and Northern Ireland in 1951)	221	226	50,055	56,523	226	250
Wales	4	6	1,518	2,081	380	347
Scotland	50	50	14,567	15,086	291	302
UK	275	282	66,140	73,690	241	261

Source: CP 1948, 1951.

however small, but in 1912, firms employing not more than five persons were required to state only the average number of persons employed by them in the year. The exemption of small firms in 1912 resulted in the exclusion of an important proportion of some of the paper trade and, both for that reason and because the First World War interrupted the task of dealing with incorrect returns, the information available for that is not sufficiently complete to warrant its use for detailed comparisons. The Censuses of 1907 and 1912 covered Great Britain and the whole of Ireland, but that of 1924 applied only to Great Britain and Northern Ireland. However, the exclusion of The Irish Free State in 1924 does not seriously affect the comparability of the figures. The 1948 and 1951 figures concern firms employing on average more than ten persons. The number of persons employed increased from 1907 (40,955) to 1951 (73,690) by 80% (Table 7.5).

Peak employment in the paper trade was reached in 1959, at 100,000 persons. Compared with the numbers employed in other branches of trade, it can be determined from the Census of Production returns that the relative importance of the paper, printing, and stationery trades in 1924 was 4.7% and in 1930 5.3% of all trades. They came 32nd in order of importance in the larger

Table 7.5 Number of Persons Employed in the Paper Trade 1907–1951

	Number of persons employed (thousands)
1907	41
1912	42.1
1924	51.4
1930	53.8
1935	59.9
1948	66.1
1951	73.7

Source: CP 1907, 1912, 1924, 1935, 1948, 1951. The table includes operative (wage earners), administrative, technical, and clerical staff (salaried persons) (in 1948 Great Britain only).

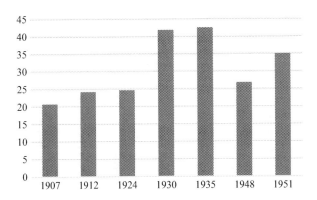

Figure 7.1 Labour Productivity (tons per employee) in the Census of Production Years 1907, 1912, 1924, 1935, 1948, and 1951.
Source: CP 1907, 1912, 1924, 1935, 1948, 1951.

142 *The British paper industry*

industries in the UK in 1924 and 34th in 1930. It should be noted, however, that in 1924, for instance, the share of employment provided by firms engaged in the manufacture of paper, board, and coating paper was only 14.7% (51,390) of the total employment figure of the paper, printing, and stationery trades (359,922) (CP 1924, 1930; Deane & Cole 1969).

The distribution of mills and workers is provided in the Census of Production returns for 1948 and 1951. The analysis by Standard Region reveals that the British paper industry was distributed in the south-east (based around London) and the north-west of England as well as in Scotland. In 1948, the south-eastern region had 56 mills and 15,331 workers, the north-western region had 67 mills and 13,274 workers, and in Scotland, there were 50 mills and 14,567 workers. In 1951, the number of mills in the south-eastern region had increased to 61 and the number of persons employed to 18,584. In the north-western region and Scotland, there were few changes in 1951 compared to 1948 (Table 7.4).

The increase in production capacity was partly due to the development of wider and in particular faster machines and partly to the changes in the fibre furnish and in the papermaking methods. In 1861, some 18,000 employees working in the industry produced 96,000 tons of paper (5.3 tons per employee). In 1907, the corresponding figures were 41,000 producing 850,000 tons of paper (20.7 tons per employee), and in 1951, 73,700 producing 2,586,500 tons of paper (35.1 tons per employee) (Figure 7.1; Tables 7.1 and 7.5) With these figures, labour productivity in Britain was higher than in the Netherlands (Bouwens 2012, 196–197) but behind output realised in Finland (Ahvenainen 1974; Järvinen et al. 2012, 43–45).

Newsprint manufacturing was largely responsible for leading the industry with ever wider, faster, and more efficient machines, thus realising lower labour, overhead, and capital costs per ton of finished product. The fast technology transfer in the newsprint industry was a logical development because newsprint was one of the cheapest paper grades made and because it was required in large quantities. By the early 1920s, British-owned mills independent from newspaper groups had become rarities, and the British paper industry was on the whole dominated by newspaper owners. Vertical integration towards the market provided better results than linking newsprint production to the supply of raw materials. Established papermakers like Albert E. Reed, along with newcomers like Eric Bowater, built large newsprint empires by the end of the 1930s (For further, see Reader 1981; Sykes 1981). In Scotland, large producers included Inveresk Paper Company and Tullis Russell (For further, see Ketelbey 1967). In 1928, the total production capacity of newsprint mills in Britain had exceeded 650,000 tons, from which amount only about 100,000 tons was produced by small, independent mills (Scanticon 13 April 1931; Ahvenainen 1976).

After the slump of the 1930s, living standards started to rise and there were plenty of potential customers. Between 1930 and 1937, *Daily Mail* was ousted from first place among the dailies both by *Daily Express* and *Daily Herald*.

The British paper industry   143

By 1937, each of these three papers reported circulation figures above two million. Among the Sunday papers, *News of the World* and *The People* reached over three million readers. The British acquired a reputation as the keenest newspaper readers in the world (Reader 1981). In 1935, British production of newsprint stood at 857,300 ton, which furnished 38.1% of the total production of paper and board (2,250,300 ton) in that year. Newsprint imports were 366,000 tons and exports 70,400 tons. Therefore, 1,152,900 tons of newsprint was available for use in the UK in 1935 (CP 1935). With that figure, more newsprint was being consumed per head of the population in Britain than in any other country of the world (Clapperton & Henderson 1947).

The Second World War changed the situation, and in 1950, the consumption of newsprint in Britain was 46% less than it had been in 1939. For most of the 1950s, the papermakers enjoyed sellers' markets as standards of living were rising. Since global demand for paper was increasing, great hopes were placed on the development of machine-glazed kraft papers. New products of all kinds and new versions of old ones were flooding into the shops, like tissues, paper towels, toilet paper, and other products of that kind. The marketing opportunities also looked attractive for women's magazines like *Woman*, *Woman's Own* and *Woman's Realm*, as well as for the *Radio Times* and *TV Times* that list radio and television programmes (Reader 1981).

The strong market situation benefited most of all the packaging, wrapping paper, and board sectors of the paper industry which had growth potential especially by improving the waste paper recovery rate and using of waste paper in the packing and wrapping papers and boards. The foundation of the cardboard box industry had been laid in the USA in 1879, when the Scottish-born Robert Gair patented the machine process for making folding boxes. But it was not until the second quarter of the twentieth century that the full potential of folding boxes was realised in Britain, where Cropper & Co. was the first licensee of Gair's invention. The benefits of folding cardboard boxes over other typical packaging materials of the time – wood, metal, glass, and later plastics – included producing and delivering boxes in flat, setting up and filling the boxes in the factories where the products were made and advertising them on the printed exteriors, and, therefore, generating the impulse to purchase the product. These benefits together with eye-pleasing appearance and natural feel of the packaging material made the folding cardboard box a panacea for many difficulties of the modern packaging industry, including the methods of transporting, retailing, and presenting that goes with it (Sykes 1981, 364–366, 388, 391; Cropper 2004).

The outlook of newsprint production was depressed, however. The days when manufacturers could confidently commission wider and faster paper machines in their quest for ever larger production capacity were past. The old business formula, which had relied on an unlimited extension of markets parallel with the extension of productive capacity, had survived through the 1930s in spite of the formidable raw material problem which the industry had had to overcome. Increases in production capacity had enabled the British

144   *The British paper industry*

papermakers to hold their ground against their competitors in Scandinavia and North America, where paper mills were standing adjunct to pulp mills with integrated operations. But after the war, the main competitors were installing new paper machines which were before long even wider and faster than those in the British mills. By the mid-1950s, the widest and fastest newsprint machines were in North America and Scandinavia in integrated mills with advanced process control (Kuhlberg 2012; Toivanen 2012; Nykänen 2018). With their natural advantages, inherent in integrated pulp and paper operations, the competitors were questioning the viability of the production of bulk grades of paper in the UK. It was no longer feasible simply to add new machines to paper mills in Britain since the costs outweighed the advantages.

The surge of rationalisation and reorganisation

In 1956, when some 200 British paper mills were running at its full capacity, exceeding 3.3 million tons of paper and board, problems started to mount. The Restrictive Trade Practices Act of 1956 deemed agreements between companies on pricing or production to be contrary to the public interest, and brought to a sudden end the system of bilateral trade agreements, which had been the fabric of the industrial structure since the early 1930s. The Act imposed new guidelines on the conduct of business and generated a new outlook by management, and consequently business after 1956 was different from what had gone before (HC Deb 26 November 1956; Sykes 1981; TN 1882–1964).

The ending of family control and the creation of a British corporate economy were among the other significant post-war business trends (Wilson 1995). The Government started to openly encourage the creation of large business conglomerates which would be more capable of competing with the Scandinavian pulp and paper giants such as Stora of Sweden and United Paper Mills of Finland. In the 1960s, pressure on profit margins forced the closure of some 35 mills all over Britain. There was no single reason for the closures; they were due to intensified competition, changes in equipment and in the organisation of the industry as well as factors arising from the overall market situation (Shorter 1971). The abolition of tariff barrier between the EFTA members and the advantages of vast forests, integrated pulp and paper production and cheap hydroelectric electricity enjoyed by Scandinavian producers were some of the reasons for the quickly deteriorating market situation in Britain after 1960 (Jensen-Eriksen 2008), but not all of them. In an attempt to maintain its competitiveness against Scandinavian producers, the British paper industry had been forced to operate on low-profit margins since the interwar years and this had prevented major investments in new plants and machinery suitable for reprocessing greater proportions of waste paper or recovering larger amounts of processing chemicals. The need to modernise the industry had been delayed by the continuation of protection for the first 15 post-war years, and this proved overwhelming for the survival of the British-owned paper industry.

British participation in the European Economic Community in 1973 once again worsened the prospects for the British paper industry. The domestic markets were under European competition, and there was little hope of expanding export trade in the Commonwealth countries. The only place British paper industry could hope for any real expansion was the booming economies in Western Europe, now operating in the same Common Market system, but the Continent was a foreign territory to them. British firms were accustomed to establishing themselves as manufacturers in the British Empire and Commonwealth countries, but on the Continent, there were foreign languages and laws to contend with as well as altogether different conceptions of doing business.

There were several different strategies with which British papermakers tried to overcome their adverse market situation. The substitution of imported wood pulp by waste paper became a necessity for the survival of that part of the industry which concentrated on bulk grades of paper. Producers of high-quality writing and printing and specialised paper grades, like Tullis Russell, concentrated on niche markets (Ketelbey 1967). International expansion strategy was chosen by large newsprint manufacturers such as Reed and Bowater, who invested in new plants in North America while cutting back their domestic production. They also diversified into new commodity grades and new kraft paper products, leading to several large acquisitions and mergers (Reader 1981; Sykes 1981). By the end of the 1970s, most of these strategies had failed with the exception of specialisation.

By the 1980s, British business culture had changed dramatically, and the paper firms developing a strong international dimension led the way in breaking the old mould. The period of rationalisation and reorganisation lasted until the late 1980s. Only 71 national and multinational companies remained in 1991, with 109 mills in operation between them. Only 40% of the total production capacity was British-owned. The industry was still concentrated in the south-east and the north-west of England, and Scotland. The industry was much more capital-intensive than previously. Therefore, there was a steady decline in the numbers of persons employed along with the number of mills. In 1991, an average mill had some 300 employees (Gennard and Bain 1995).

In the 1990s, a remarkable modernisation took place in the British paper industry. Investments in recycling technology created new business opportunities for British companies. Investment in 1995 in a new paper machine for the first time in more than 30 years at Reed's Aylesford Paper Mills, near Maidstone in Kent, is a prominent example. Modernisation of the industry meant changes in ownership structure as well, and new projects were more likely to be undertaken by Scandinavian than British-owned companies. The surviving companies targeted their products at sectors of the market where a British-based producer could compete against imports. In 1997, only

146   *The British paper industry*

few British-owned companies remained, including PBP Industries, API Industries, and Inveresk Paper Company, concentrating on bulk grades based on waste paper and high-value-added grades. The total number of foreign-owned and British-owned companies was 62, the total production capacity being 6.5 million tons. The most important raw materials were waste paper (59% of total pulp equivalent), imported wood pulp (29%), and British manufactured wood pulp (11%). The industry owned by multinationals was much more export oriented than previously. In 1997, it exported 22% (1.438 million tons) of its total output (Owen 2000).

Conclusions

This chapter has provided insights into developments in the British paper industry and evaluated its particular problems from a retrospective view. What can we learn from it? Britain was the first country in the world to enter into the field of mechanical papermaking. The first Fourdrinier papermaking machines were introduced in the early 1800s, but it was not until the 1830s that mechanisation became truly widespread in the paper industry in Britain. After a relatively slow start in the mechanisation process, the industry developed with some rapidity, and by 1860, the world of mechanised papermaking had been born in Britain. The changes brought on by technology transfer were the dominant features from 1860 to 1914. The principles of papermaking changed very little; the changes came through modification of traditional methods and raw materials, rather than of complete mechanisation. The machines themselves were modified to improve the quantities and qualities produced and at the same time to obtain finer control over their working. The influence of technical changes can be perhaps best seen by the way in which labour productivity improved over time.

Britain continued to lead the field in the papermaking industry until the latter decades of the nineteenth century, after which the momentum of being the first nation successfully to mechanise the production of paper was gradually lost to some of its major competitors in North America and Scandinavia. In hindsight, it is not difficult to demonstrate the weakness in the British paper industry structure compared to its major competitors. The difficulty in obtaining esparto and wood pulp during the First World War forced mills to switch to wheat, oat straw, and waste paper instead, revealing Britain's vulnerability in terms of the supply of raw materials, and this problem recurred during and immediately after the Second World War when there was a very severe shortage of all fibrous materials in general and of wood pulp in particular (Shorter 1971). As it turned out, after the First World War, the British papermakers lost their technological edge over the major overseas competitors. In other words, Britain started to pay the price for being the pioneer in the mechanised papermaking business.

While the impetus of early mechanisation was gradually lost in Britain, North American and Continental producers became major players in the field of papermaking at the close of the nineteenth century when the utilisation of wood as a raw material for making paper revolutionised the whole paper industry. A remarkable expansion of the industry was witnessed in Canada and the Nordic countries (Reich 1927; Järvinen et al. 2012; Kuhlberg 2012). Endowed with hydroelectric energy resources, raw material, and networks of lakes and rivers, they became major importers to the British markets that operated under the free trade principle. The increased foreign competition led to the introduction of protective tariffs.

The details of the period from 1914 to 1960 show much greater complexity compared to the development of the simple pattern of growth of the pre-1914 era. The whole period was one beset with national and international difficulties, which had repercussions on the paper industry. The progress of the trade was more gradual, and there were setbacks because of the world wars and their aftermaths. These bore on the industry in a number of ways. During and after the Second World War, there was a loss of orders from the customers (i.e. the printers) and deliveries of raw materials, chemicals, labour, and energy were disrupted. Raw material, labour, and energy shortages and the drop in the proportion exported lowered production and closed paper machines with the effect that the mills produced under capacity for much of the period. The contraction of the export market was not accompanied by increases in demand for fine-grade printing and writing papers from the domestic market. Esparto paper mills were more adversely affected than the rest of the trade because buyers were not prepared to pay high enough prices (Sykes 1981).

Unfavourable conditions alone do not fully account for the problems. There was also a lack of understanding of exactly why the paper trade was in difficulties. The absence of a long-term view of the development of the industry was accompanied by a lack of confidence in the business environment which delayed investments. After the Second World War, a high demand for paper was accompanied by a high price for raw materials or a difficulty in even getting raw materials. This situation led to severe competition in the domestic paper market, where a loss of market share could not be compensated for with an increase in the export business. The high price of papers and excess capacity in the paper trade were caused by unwise expansion overseas by some companies. There was also tension between management and the workforce, as discussed more fully in an earlier section of this chapter (Sykes 1981).

There were also problems on the productivity side, which further contributed in the 1950s to the reluctance to invest in more efficient new machinery and process control. There is no evidence of cost-consciousness, and there were no rigorous checks on the efficiency of production or the use of Empire-sourced raw materials. In much of the British paper industry, there were too few scientifically or technically trained and experienced people in top management. This situation had its roots in the nature of the highly personalised Victorian society and education system. Nonetheless, considerable improvements were undertaken in both production capacity and performance. At the

148 *The British paper industry*

end of the research period, labour productivity was higher than at any other time as a cumulative effect of the various improvements (Figure 7.1; Weatherill 1974, 88–90; Sykes 1981).

In the 1960s, the British paper industry oriented itself towards the changing world, and it became attached to the global market system. As a consequence, the continuing problem of low productivity was alleviated. This was due to the cutting back of domestic production, caused by several large acquisitions and mergers. For instance, in 1950, at the Guard Bridge Paper Company, productivity per employee was 20.7 tons, which was lower than for most of the 1930s. On the other hand, the changes accompanying modernisation in the 1960s were equally dramatic. In 1960, productivity per employee was 25.5 tons, while 10 years later, it was already 56 tons (Weatherill 1974, 29, 84–87, 94).

The English-speaking world dominated the geographical horizons of the British paper industry up to the 1960s. The bulk of exports went to the British Empire and Commonwealth countries, while Canadian and Nordic firms were major importers. The inherent weakness of the British paper industry had been masked in the 1930s by the low cost of pulp and in the 1940s and the early 1950s by the excess of demand over supply. In Britain, the paper industry prospered because the price of pulp in Canada and the Nordic countries was falling faster than the price of newsprint in Britain, and because British newspaper owners were able and willing to pay somewhat higher prices for British-made newsprint than for imports, in order to keep British industry healthy (Reader 1981). After the Second World War, the negative consequences of being the first in the papermaking business were revealed. British entry into EFTA in 1960 gradually dismantled the protective tariffs and subjected the British paper industry and its domestic markets to a flood of Scandinavian competition. At the same time, new competitors, notably the Japanese, breached traditional British export markets, such as Australasia. Finally, British entry into the EEC in 1973 oriented the British paper industry towards Europe.

Notes

1 Culter Mills Paper Co, Ltd, Peterculter, Aberdeenshire, remained in the papermaking business 230 years until it was closed and demolished in about 1980.
2 Guard Bridge Paper Co, Ltd, Guard Bridge, Fife, was in the papermaking business from 1873 to 1984.

References

Accounts Relating to Trade and Navigation of the United Kingdom (TN) (1882–1964).

Ahvenainen, J. (1974) 'The Competitive Position of the Finnish Paper Industry in the Inter-War Years'. *Scandinavian Economic History Review*, 22, 1, 1–21.

Ahvenainen, J. (1976) *The History of Star Paper, 1875–1960.* Studia Historica Jyväskyläensia, 13. University of Jyväskylä, Jyväskylä.

Alford, B. E. W. (1963) 'Business Enterprise and the Growth of the Commercial Letterpress Printing Industry, 1850–1914'. *Business History*, 7, 1, 1–14.

Ally, R. (1994) *Gold & Empire. The Bank of England and South African's Gold Producers 1886–1926*. Witwatersrand University Press, Johannesburg.

Balston, T. (1954) *William Balston. Paper Maker 1759–1849*. Methuen, London.

Bartlett, J. N. (1980) 'Alexander Pirie & Sons of Aberdeen and the Expansion of the British Paper Industry, c. 1860–1914'. *Business History*, 22, 1, 18–34.

Bouwens, B. (2012) 'The Paper and Board Industry in the Netherlands, 1800–2000'. In J.-A. Lamberg, J. Ojala, M. Peltoniemi & T. Särkkä, eds, *The Evolution of Global Paper Industry: 1800–2050: A Comparative Analysis*. World Forests 17. Springer, Dordrecht, 191–209.

Bundock, C. J. (1959) *The Story of the National Union of Printing, Bookbinding and Paper Workers*. Oxford University Press, Oxford.

Cain, P. J. & Hopkins, A. G. (1994) *British Imperialism: Innovation and Expansion, 1688–1914*. Longman, London and New York.

Chater, M. (1977) *Family Business. A History of Grosvenor Chater 1690–1977*. Grosvenor Chater, St. Albans.

Clapperton, R. H. (1967) *The Paper-Making Machine: Its Invention, Evolution and Development*, Pergamon, Oxford.

Clapperton, R. H. & Henderson, W. (1947) *Modern Paper-Making*. 3rd ed. Basil Blackwell, Oxford.

Coleman, D. C. (1958) *The British Paper Industry, 1495–1860*. Clarendon, Oxford.

Cormack, A. A. (1933) *Our Ancient and Honourable Craft. Being an Account of the Rise and Development of Paper-making in Scotland, and at Culter, Aberdeenshire, in Particular*. Reprinted from *The Paper Market*. Loxley Bros, London.

Cropper, M. (2004) *The Leaves We Write On: James Cropper: A History in Paper-Making*. Ellergreen Press, London.

Deane, P. & Cole, W. A. (1969) *The British Economic Growth 1688–1959*. 2nd ed. Cambridge University Press, Cambridge.

Final Report on the Census of Production of the United Kingdom (CP) (1907, 1912, 1924, 1930, 1935, 1948, 1951)

Galloway, J. (1968) *Galloways of Balerno*. Newman Neame, London.

Gennard, J. & Bain, P. (1995) *SOGAT. A History of the Society of Graphical and Allied Trades*. Routledge, London.

Green, T. (1982) *The New World of Gold: The Inside Story of the Mines, The Markets, The Politics, The Investors*. Weidenfeld & Nicolson, London.

Harris, J. (1994) *Private Lives, Public Spirit: Britain 1870–1914*. Penguin Books, London.

Hills, R. L. (1988) *Papermaking in Britain 1488–1988. A Short History*. Athlone Press, London and Atlantic Highlands.

House of Commons Debates (HC Deb). (26 November 1956) vol 561 cc34–164. Available at https://api.parliament.uk/historic-hansard/index.html. Accessed 27 July 2020.

Jensen-Eriksen, N. (2008) 'A Stab in the Back? The British Government, the Paper Industry and the Nordic Threat, 1956–72'. *Contemporary British History*, 22, 1, 1–21.

Järvinen, J., Ojala, J., Melander, A. & Lamberg, J.-A. (2012) 'The Evolution of Pulp and Paper Industries in Finland, Sweden and Norway 1800–2005'. In J.-A. Lamberg, J. Ojala, M. Peltoniemi & T. Särkkä, eds, *The Evolution of Global Paper*

150 *The British paper industry*

Industry: 1800–2050: A Comparative Analysis. World Forests 17. Springer, Dordrecht, 19–48.

Ketelbey, C. D. M. (1967) *The History of R. Tullis & Company and Tullis Russell & Co. Ltd. 1809–1959.* Tullis Russell, Markinch, Five.

Koops, M. (1801) *Historical Account of the Substances which Have Been Used to Describe Events, and to Convey Ideas, from the Earliest Date to the Invention of Paper.* Jaques and Co., London.

Kuhlberg, M. (2012) 'An Accomplished History, An Uncertain Future: Canada's Pulp and Paper Industry since the Early 1800s'. In J.-A. Lamberg, J. Ojala, M. Peltoniemi & T. Särkkä, eds, *The Evolution of Global Paper Industry: 1800–2050: A Comparative Analysis.* World Forests 17. Springer, Dordrecht, 101–134.

Kurlansky, M. (2017) *Paper. Paging Through History.* W.W. Norton & Company, New York and London.

Kynaston, D. (2012) *City of London. The History.* Vintage Books, London.

Lewis, P. (1969) *A Numerical Approach to the Location of Industry. Exemplified by the Distribution of the Papermaking Industry in England and Wales from 1860 to 1965.* University of Hull Publications, Hull.

Lloyd-Jones, R. (2004) 'Donkin, Bryan (1768–1855)'. In H. C. G. Matthew & B. Harrison, eds, *Oxford Dictionary of National Biography.* Oxford University Press, Oxford. Available at https://doi.org/10.1093/ref:odnb/7810. Accessed 9 October 2020.

Magee, G. B. (1997a) 'Technological Divergence in a Continuous Flow Production Industry: American and British Paper Making in the late Victorian and Edwardian era'. *Business History,* 39, 1, 21–46.

Magee, G. B. (1997b) *Productivity and Performance in the Paper Industry. Labour, Capital, and Technology in Britain and America, 1860–1914,* Cambridge Studies in Modern Economic History 4. Cambridge University Press, Cambridge.

McConnell, A. (2004) 'Fourdrinier, Henry (1766–1854)'. In H. C. G. Matthew & B. Harrison, eds, *Oxford Dictionary of National Biography.* Oxford University Press, Oxford. Available at https://doi.org/10.1093/ref:odnb/9997. Accessed 9 October 2020.

McRae, H. & Cairncross, F. (2017[1985]) *Capital City: London as a Financial Centre.* Routledge, London.

Mokyr, J. (1990) *The Lever of Riches. Technological Creativity and Economic Progress.* Oxford University Press, Oxford.

Nykänen, P. (2018) 'Research and Development in the Finnish Wood Processing and Paper Industry, c. 1850–1990'. In T. Särkkä, M. Gutiérrez-Poch & M. Kuhlberg, eds, *Technological Transformation in the Global Pulp and Paper Industry 1800–2018: Comparative Perspectives.* World Forests 23. Springer, Dordrecht, 35–64.

Owen, G. (2000) *From Empire to Europe. The Decline and Revival of British Industry since the Second World War.* HarperCollins, London.

Paper and Paper Board Manufacture and Coating (1947) Industrial Information Series 28, Ministry of Labour and National Service. His Majesty's Stationery Office, London.

Phillips' Paper Trade Directory of the World 1909–1910 (1910) S.C. Phillips, London.

Pollard, S. (1963) *The Development of the British Economy 1914–1950.* Edward Arnold, London.

Pollard, S. (1965) *The Genesis of Modern Management. A Study of the Industrial Revolution in Britain.* Edward Arnold, London.

The British paper industry 151

Reader, W. J. (1981) *Bowater. A History*. Cambridge University Press, Cambridge.

Reich, N. (1927) *The Pulp and Paper Industry in Canada*, McGill University Economic Studies 7. St Martin's House, Toronto.

Richardson, M. (2006) 'Rapprochement and Retribution: The Divergent Experiences of Workers in Two Large Paper and Print Companies in the 1926 General Strike'. *Historical Studies in Industrial Relations*, 22, 27–51.

Robert Craig & Sons, Ltd. A Century of Papermaking, 1820–1920 (1920) R. & R. Clark, Edinburgh.

Scanticon (13 April 1931) *FP2691. Finska Paperskontoret (FP)*. Central Archives of United Paper Mills, Valkeakoski.

Shears, W. S. (1967) *William Nash of St. Pauls' Cray. Paper Makers*. Batchworth Press, London.

Shorter, A. H. (1971) *Paper Making in the British Isles. An Historical and Geographical Study*. David & Charles, Newton Abbot.

Spicer, A. D. (1907) *The Paper Trade. A Descriptive and Historical Survey of the Paper Trade from the Commencement of the Nineteenth Century*. Methuen, London.

Sykes, P. (1981) *Albert E. Reed and the Creation of a Paper Business 1860–1960*. X.525/5617, unpublished manuscript. The British Library, London.

Thomson, A. G. (1974) *The Paper Industry in Scotland, 1590–1861*. Scottish Academic Press; Chatto and Windus, Edinburgh and London.

Tillmanns, M. (1978) *Bridge Hall Mills. Three Centuries of Paper and Cellulose Film Manufacture*. Compton Press, London.

Toivanen, H. (2012) 'Waves of Technological Innovation: The Evolution of the US Pulp and Paper Industry, 1860–2000'. In J.-A. Lamberg, J. Ojala, M. Peltoniemi & T. Särkkä, eds, *The Evolution of Global Paper Industry 1800–2050: A Comparative Analysis*. World Forests 17. Springer, Dordrecht, 49–80.

Weatherill, L. (1974) *One Hundred Years of Papermaking. An Illustrated History of the Guard Bridge Paper Company Ltd. 1875–1975*. Guard Bridge Paper Company Ltd., Fife, Scotland.

Wilson, J. F. (1995) *British Business History, 1720–1994*. Manchester University Press, Manchester and New York.

8   Conclusions

The investigation has provided a discussion of some of the economic and technological considerations relevant to the establishment of new pulp and paper industry in the British Empire and Commonwealth countries and led to the following conclusions. The British paper industry was historically deficient in terms of the industry's traditional fibre resources, and it was initially forced to satisfy its domestic demand for pulp through imports. This shortcoming was an impediment to the growth of the industry. Since the mid-nineteenth century, industry and papermakers cooperated to overcome their fibre challenge by using various strategies. The most notable of these was the introduction of esparto grass to the British paper industry. Nonetheless, the demand for raw materials was in no way satisfactorily met. The First World War was both a short-term curse and a long-term blessing for many pulp and papermakers, and the conflict certainly highlights how necessity is truly the mother of invention. This investigation has underscored how the shortage of pulp in the UK was the impetus behind its producers searching for alternative supplies of raw materials, and how their quest led them to the British Empire and its enormous stock of fibrous raw materials. This was the precursor to a colonial policy that sought first to foster the development of the native pulp and paper industry in the dominions and colonies, and to later efforts by both local and British firms to develop the technology to process these fibrous resources into marketable paper products.

From 1861 to 1960, the main pulp and paper consumption centres were the industrialised regions of Western Europe and North America. Their raw material needs were fed by the nearby regions (Scandinavian countries and Canada) that had an ample supply of raw materials consisting mainly of coniferous forest and, to a lesser extent, of temperate hardwoods (Lamberg et al. 2012; Särkkä et al. 2018). They provided about 95% of all raw materials used for paper, most of the remainder being manufactured from tropical and subtropical hardwoods, certain grasses (e.g. esparto, sabai, bamboo), and agricultural residues (e.g. sugarcane bagasse and straws) (FAO 1954, 54). This concentration of manufacturing capacity placed the smaller paper consumption countries – distant from the main paper production centres – in a disadvantageous situation. Deliveries were expensive and liable to interruptions as the experience of the First World War so decidedly highlighted. Since the most important raw material for papermaking – vegetable fibrous materials – is almost ubiquitous, nearly every country was endeavouring to develop its own industrial capacity in the 1920s and 1930s based on locally available fibre, whether indigenous (e.g. eucalypts in the case of Australia and bamboo in the case of India) or exotic (e.g. *Pinus radiata* in the case of New Zealand). In many projects relying on non-traditional raw materials, progress was at first hampered by technical problems.

During and after the Second World War, new economic compulsions were making themselves felt in those regions of the world deficient in pulp and paper. It is not difficult to see why pulp and paper investment appeared attractive in the post-war years. Local markets were increasing in size and diversity; communications were improving; local fuel and power resources were developed. Country after country was turning its attention to the possibilities of manufacturing its own pulp and paper in order to avoid a rapidly worsening balance of payments or finding its development programmes held up for lack of paper. Proposals for the development of new pulp and paper capacity in Latin America, Africa, Asia, and Oceania multiplied rapidly during the period of soaring prices towards the end of the 1940s and the start of the 1950s.

Factors affecting the geographical distribution of the pulp and paper industry

Certain basic information was necessary before a firm decision to build a new mill could be taken. These included the availability of raw materials, chemicals, fuel and power, water, labour and capital, and careful consideration of the potential markets. These factors had important implications when investors came to consider the establishment of a new industry in a hitherto unindustrialised region of the world. The discussion of production factors has served to illustrate how very different the conditions of pulp and paper production in the British Colonies and Dominions were from those in the established traditional production centres in Western Europe and North America. As one would expect, the lessons and conclusions from Britain had very limited application in, say, India (Chap. 5).

In the projects discussed in the preceding chapters, quite a number of projects were based on virgin coniferous wood stands or industrial plantations from fast-growing coniferous species. It is not surprising that these projects were prominent in the initial stages, since the pulping of conifers presented fewer technological problems and involved lower production costs than the pulping of unconventional raw materials such as grasses, bamboos, and tropical hardwoods. The use of exotic conifers was not limited to those countries where natural resources were scant; even in those countries where there were adequate natural stands of perfectly suitable species for papermaking purposes, extraction costs in some cases weighted the balance in favour of

154   *Conclusions*

plantation-based developments. Herein lies the explanation of the fact that the world's virgin subtropical and tropical hardwoods were as yet hardly tapped for pulping in the 1950s (FAO 1954, 46).

The development of pulp and paper industries was often closely related to the present state of knowledge concerning the chemical composition of various raw materials and the techniques and costs of various pulping processes, as discussed in Chap. 2. With the development of suitable pulping methods for grasses, straws, bamboo, and eucalypts, the production of pulp and paper progressed rapidly in the regions outside the traditional production centres. The potential resources of raw materials for papermaking were virtually unlimited, as the basic raw material for paper is cellulose in the form of fibre, and cellulose is a major constituent of nearly every form of plant fibre. Plants do not yield their fibre with equal ease, however. Nor do all plant fibres give good pulp. Moreover, technical suitability did not itself guarantee commercial exploitability. For example, unless the raw material was suitably located, paper manufactured from even an ideal fibre tended to be prohibitively high in price by the time it reached the ultimate consumer. Bamboo, considered as a papermaking material in Chap. 5, is a case in point (FAO 1954, 54). What the paper mills required was a sufficient and constant supply of suitable raw materials that were within economic reach of one or more of the world's consumption centres, as discussed in Chaps. 4 and 7. This rationale largely explains the geographical distribution of the world's pulp and paper industry during the research period.

The fibrous material constituted only one of the items affecting the total cost of the finished paper product. Other factors could be of equal importance and ultimately determine the economic feasibility of a new project. These included the availability of chemicals, fuel and power, water, labour and capital, and careful consideration of the potential markets. Turning to these other factors and their impact on final costs, a few words should be said about the integration of pulp and paper mills. As a rule, pulp mills had to be located near their main supply of fibrous material, since the cost of transport of such bulky materials over long distances was usually prohibitive, especially in regard to newsprint manufacturing, as discussed in Chap. 4. Paper mills, on the other hand, as a result of such factors as transport facilities, markets, and the availability of rags, historically tended to locate near the major conurbations which rarely coincided with the areas of virgin fibre stands. The discussion of the history of the British paper industry in Chap. 7 showed the great importance of fibrous raw material costs, which were, on average, over half of the total costs at British mills. For finished paper, the relative importance of this cost item was much lower. It could range from 10% (in the case of newsprint) to 35%, depending on the category of paper produced (FAO 1954, 66).

As noted in Chaps. 5 and 6, however, in the mills erected in British India, fibrous raw material costs formed a smaller proportion of the total cost, partly because of favourable concessions and partly because the other cost items were usually more expensive than in the established production centres in Europe or North America. These other cost items included, for instance, chemicals, fuel and power, labour, and transport costs. The last mentioned cost factor was particularly heavy, because the manufacture of pulp and paper requires large quantities of basic vegetable fibres, chemicals, fuel, and equipment, all of which had to be brought to the factory by various means of transport. Therefore, to establish a pulp and paper industry in regions distant from these resources, it was a necessary prerequisite to build a railroad with a mill siding and a connection to a harbour for ocean-going vessels. Understandably, such requirements were out of the reach of companies on their own and depended on the assistance of local governments in order to be feasible, as the discussion on the progress of the alfa trade in North Africa in Chap. 3 revealed.

For the production of chemical pulp, large quantities of processing chemicals were needed for the pulping operation and for bleaching, sizing, loading, and finishing. A detailed discussion of various chemicals, their availability, market price, and freight rates is beyond the scope of the present investigation, but the observations provided in Chaps. 2, 3, 5, and 7 indicate some of the factors involved. Fuel and power costs represented an important fraction of the total production cost. In general, if reasonably cheap fuel and power were not available, the erection of a pulp or paper mill was not feasible. Many wood-grinding plants were initially cost-effective due to cheap energy. However, the development of hydroelectric power stations for the sole purpose of feeding a new pulp and paper unit could not generally be considered to be economically viable unless the mill had a large capacity, say, over 40,000 tons per annum, the amount which was considered the economic minimum at the Bishop's Falls Mill in Newfoundland in 1911 (Chap. 4).

New mills erected in areas where power was not readily available for purchase had therefore to produce their own electricity in thermal stations, which required access to cheap fuel (e.g. coal or fuelwood), as shown in the discussion of the making of bamboo pulp and paper at the Titaghur Paper Mills in Bengal (West Bengal) (Chap. 5). Still, larger quantities of power were required if the pulp was converted into paper. At Guard Bridge paper mill, Scotland, it took around four tons of coal to produce one ton of paper when steam engines were used in the 1880s and 1890s, and slightly less when electric motors came into use at the beginning of the 1900s (Chap. 7). Over time, energy efficiency in papermaking improved as well. In the early 1950s, fuel requirements for a completely independent integrated mill were estimated at about 1.6 tons of coal or oil or 4.3 tons of fuelwood for each ton of paper produced (FAO 1954, 67). In other words, a wood-fuelled factory consumed twice as much wood for producing steam and power as it did in the actual pulping process. This factor became important when setting up mills based on local fibrous raw materials, since fuelwood requirements increased as the area of harvesting expanded. There is a compensating advantage, however, as it is possible to use the unsuitable species or thinnings as fuelwood. Therefore, the production of energy, along with pulp production, plays a

156   *Conclusions*

crucial role in considering the economic viability of new projects, as the outlook of the global pulp and paper industry today highlights.

One of the main factors affecting the choice of site for a pulp and paper mill was the possibility of obtaining the large amounts of clean and fresh water needed for the production process. In the mid-1950s, consumption of water ranged anywhere from about 50 cubic metres per ton of mechanical pulp production to 600 cubic metres or more for the production of one ton of fine papers in an integrated mill. Given these numbers, it will be understood that the industry's demands on water for production were very heavy. The mills needed to be built in proximity to an ample supply of good water in order to avoid heavy installation and pumping costs (FAO 1954, 67), as the discussion on the geographical locations of British paper mills in Chap. 7 revealed. The environmental factors which determined the possibilities of successful investment in pulp and paper projects were also becoming steadily more imperative, though they were not a threat to the paper companies until the enforcement of later legislation, in the post-1960 era. The black processing water from a pulp and paper factory was usually heavily contaminated by processing chemicals as well as dissolved substances such as lignin, fibres, and other impurities. The disposal of these large quantities of effluents regularly could create serious problems for local river systems, especially if they were not tidal or rapidly running. A related problem was steam pollution as discussed in Chaps. 3 and 5.

The skilled labour required to operate a pulp and paper mill was not usually available in unindustrialised regions. When a new mill was set up, technicians and supervisory personnel were typically foreign until local labour was trained. Labour productivity in many unindustrialised regions investigated in this study was low, sometimes because of poor labour management, sometimes because of the tropical diseases of a hot climate, and more often because of malnutrition. The lower productivity of labour, however, did not necessarily involve higher total labour costs, since it was offset by wage rates lower than in the British paper industry. The number of workers required to produce one ton of pulp and paper varied considerably, however, according to the quality produced, the mill size, the raw material used, and other related factors. Labour did not include only operating and repair personnel but supervisory and office staff, as well as the labour required for harvesting, planting, and soil improvement work (FAO 1954, 68). The corresponding number of employees required for operating a mill erected in British India, using local labour for all unskilled work, could easily be twice as many as in Britain (Chaps. 5 and 7).

The pulp and paper question in unindustrialised regions of the world was as much economic and financial as technical. The most important resource in establishing a new pulp and paper industry was capital. This study has not discussed the means or possibilities of raising the necessary capital, but has simply given approximate indications of the amounts likely to be required. The economics of scale being considerable, the capital needs tended to be heavy. A general idea of the relative importance of the different costs which together make up the total cost of production – the mill cost – may be obtained from the figures provided in preceding chapters. These figures represent broad generalisations, and wide variations could occur within the same region depending on such factors as the mill site, the equipment, the pulping process, and managerial skills (i.e. the quality and experience of the local management employed). As a rule, however, a new pulp or paper mill represented a considerable investment even in the early 1900s.

Normally, several years elapsed between the time when a prospectus of a new company was issued and the time when production began. In a rising pulp and paper market, both the planning and construction stages were likely to be accelerated, but when the market outlook was uncertain, planning and construction work slowed down, and projects were often postponed or even cancelled. Only a few British Colonies and Dominions gathered definite and systematic information regarding raw material resources, production costs and markets, and the various colonial projects analysed in this investigation ranged in degrees of certainty from a firm intention to build a new mill, with contracts already placed, to what was little more than a gleam in the eye of a City investor. On numerous occasions reported in this study, colonial authorities, investors, and cellulose experts lent their authority and backing to mill projects whose viability in the long term was by no means assured. Ill-judged ventures were apt to have undesirable repercussions which went far beyond the particular project of concern, as they frequently discouraged future developments. The business failure of the Sudd Fuel (Suddite) Company Limited is a case in point (Chap. 6).

Before 1960, a new pulp and paper industry in regions outside the main paper consumption centres of the world had to rely primarily on the domestic market. Only in especially favourable circumstances could it rely on a supplementary market in neighbouring countries. But in order to operate economically, it should certainly not have to depend on selling on the international free market. The pulp mill of the Tasman Pulp & Paper Company in New Zealand is a case in point (Chap. 6). This was so because cost estimates for new mills outside the main producing centres tended to be precarious, especially if the mills were to operate using non-traditional fibres. Unless railroad facilities were adequate and fuel, labour, and maintenance inexpensive, a land haul of several hundred miles could be more expensive than a sea haul of several thousand miles (Chap. 5). Where to locate production remained the crucial question until about the 1960s when technological developments in seaborne transport and the subsequent dramatic reduction in the cost of shipping started to erode the importance of distance between raw material sources and markets (Ojala & Tenold 2018; Chap. 7).

However, even before 1960, a mill in a colony whose intended scale of operations fell below what was judged economically viable in Britain was not necessarily unviable in her colonies and dominions. The elements of uncertainty about costs under actual operating conditions were by no means strong

158 *Conclusions*

deterrents when a mill was planned to satisfy local demand only, especially in areas remote from the main exporting countries. Because markets in many colonies and dominions were small but rapidly expanding, it was possible in some instances for a small paper or board factory operating on sundry locally available fibres and imported pulp to operate successfully, as the discussion on the development of the bamboo pulp and paper industry in British India revealed (Chaps. 5 and 6). During the research period, paper requirements were rising rapidly, and the possibility of satisfying these requirements by increasing imports from the traditional exporting centres was limited by underdeveloped means of transport, global upheavals, and finally the inability to pay for an increasing scale of imports. It was therefore inevitable that the British Colonies and Dominions would progressively develop their own resources. In the initial stages, development was inevitably scattered; in some cases, it was experimental; frequently, it was on a small scale.

A detailed investigation preceded any decision to create a new pulp and paper mill, as reports issued by the Imperial Institute clearly illustrate. They covered not only the laboratory tests and the technical factors of production, but also the less obvious circumstances influencing production costs as well as the definite possibilities of marketing the products, as discussed in Chap. 6. In selecting the site for a mill from a variety of sites that satisfy certain basic conditions, the relative pulls of various factors related to the location had to be weighted up. The main considerations were the fibrous materials, chemicals, fuel and power, water, labour, capital, and markets. Choosing the ideal site for an integrated pulp and paper mill was a much more complex problem than locating a non-integrated pulp or paper mill. The problem was further complicated by the fact that the cost curves for pulp and paper are by no means the same and were strongly affected by trade policy measures such as Customs and Excise duties, tariffs, trade agreements, and price fixing, as noted in Chaps. 3–5 and 7.

The cost of production for pulp and paper diminished rapidly with an increase in the scale of operations. This was especially true for pulp establishments, since raw material costs tended to rise as the more accessible supplies became depleted, as the discussion on esparto and sabai grasses revealed (Chaps. 3 and 6). The economies of integration were most marked in the production of newsprint, since large quantities were manufactured with uniform specifications from only one or two kinds of pulp. Further savings arose from the fact that in the manufacture of pulp and paper in a combined operation a single power installation can serve both stages of manufacture (FAO 1954, 47; Chaps. 4 and 7). The benefits arising from integration were less marked in the production of fine papers, which were usually made in smaller quantities and often in great variety, to meet the special requirements of the customers, and by using many different types and grades of pulp. With fine esparto and sabai papers, therefore, market considerations, such as the need to ensure prompt delivery of special qualities in small quantities, often offset the advantages of integration (Chaps. 3 and 6).

General political factors also contributed to increased integration of pulp and papermaking. Because of the interruptions to the supply of raw materials during the First World War, papermakers became more interested in the continuity and security of their supplies. Therefore, the papermaker's interest in ensuring a secure and continuous supply of pulp of the right quality, free from sudden price fluctuations, led firms to seek to own or control the source of the supply of pulp. For this reason, papermakers tended to prefer to obtain their supplies from a source that was near rather than far away, since the greater the distance the more they could be subject to fluctuations in freight costs and in exchange rates, and to export and import regulations (Chaps. 4 and 7). This was one of the factors making for increased integration of pulp and papermaking worldwide (Ojala et al. 2012).

Another important factor contributing towards geographical and financial integration was the reduction of transport costs, which resulted from the fact that it was no longer necessary to dry, handle, and transport the pulp over long distances overseas. A different web of factors influenced the choice of site for a paper mill. Market considerations usually weighted most heavily. However, what has been said above relating to the papermakers' interest in continuity of supply and freedom from price fluctuations applied equally to the paper converter, newspaper publisher, cardboard box maker, or manufacturing stationer (Chap. 7).

The discussion on the factors affecting the geographical distribution of the pulp and paper industry can be concluded by stating that while the technology behind the mechanical papermaking process is both complex and multidisciplinary, the basic economic and technological principles of paper manufacture changed little during the 100-year research period. Therefore, it is axiomatic that the simple rationale 'history matters' has much to offer to the pulp and paper industry.

References

FAO. (1954) *Wood Pulp and Paper Resources and Prospects.* A survey prepared by the Food and Agriculture Organization in co-operation with the secretariats of the United Nations Educational, Scientific and Cultural Organization (UNESCO); the Economic Commission for Europe (ECE); and the Economic Commission for Latin America (ECLA). AO, New York.

Lamberg, J.-A., Ojala, J., Peltoniemi, M. & Särkkä, T. (2012) 'Research on Evolution and the Global History of Pulp and Paper Industry: An Introduction'. In J.-A. Lamberg, J. Ojala, M. Peltoniemi & T. Särkkä, eds, *The Evolution of Global Paper Industry 1800–2050: A Comparative Analysis* World Forests 17. Springer, Dordrecht, 1–18.

Ojala, J. & Tenold, S. (2018) 'Creating Global Markets: Seaborne Trade in Pulp and Paper Products Over the Last 400 Years'. In T. Särkkä, M. Gutiérrez-Poch & M. Kuhlberg, eds, *Technological Transformation in the Global Pulp and Paper Industry 1800–2018: Comparative Perspectives.* World Forests 23. Springer, Dordrecht, 261–278.

160 *Conclusions*

Ojala, J., Voutilainen, M. & Lamberg, J.-A. (2012) 'The Evolution of the Global Paper Industry: Concluding Remarks'. In J.-A. Lamberg, J. Ojala, M. Peltoniemi & T. Särkkä, eds, *The Evolution of Global Paper Industry 1800–2050: A Comparative Analysis.* World Forests 17. Springer, Dordrecht, 344–363.

Särkkä, T., Gutiérrez-Poch, M. & Kuhlberg, M. (2018) 'Technological Transformation in the Global Pulp and Paper Industry: Introduction'. In T. Särkkä, M. Gutiérrez-Poch & M. Kuhlberg, eds, *Technological Transformation in the Global Pulp and Paper Industry 1800–2018: Comparative Perspectives.* World Forests 23, Springer, Dordrecht, 1–10.

Index

Note: **Bold** page numbers refer to Tables. *Italic* page numbers refer to figures and Page numbers followed by "n" refers to endnotes.

abacá (*Musa textilis*) 106
Abbey Mills 130
Abnormal Importations (Customs Duties) Act 62
Acacia 101
agricultural residues 15, 27, **29–30**, 38, 152; *see also* bagasse; straw
Albert E. Reed & Company 55, 57–58, 66, 123, 142
alfa 4, 40, 41, 81, 155; *see also* esparto grass (*Stipa tenacissima*; *Lygeum spartum*)
Algeria 38, 40–42, 55, 69, 77
Amalgamated Society of Papermakers 136
Andhra Paper Mills 93
Andrew Yule & Co. 84, 99
Anglo-Canadian Pulp and Paper Company 123
Anglo-Newfoundland Development Co., Ltd. 157
API Industries 146
Arab paper 17, 119
aspen 23, 26, **29–30**, 56
Assam Pulp Mills Ltd. 99
Associated Pulp and Paper Mills Ltd. 122
Association of Makers of Esparto Papers 43
Australia 23, 29, 60, 63, 66, 99, 101, 116, 121–123, 153
Australian Newsprint Mill Ltd. 122
Aylesford Paper Mills 5, 145

babui (*Utricularia babui*) 110
bagasse 25–27, 29, **30**, 93, 114, 152; *see also* agricultural residues; straw
balsam fir (*Abies balsamea*) 55–57
Balston, William 129–130

bamboo: catchment area 74, 94–95, 115; chipping 97; cropping 76–77, 86, 94; cutting 75, 77, 80–82, 86, 94–95; crushing 74, 77, 80–81, 84, 86–87, 96–97, 103n4; cultivation 76–77, 86; felling 77, 94–95; flowering 74; harvesting 74, 76, 86, 93–96, 99–100, 112, 115; rafting 76, 95–96, 114; transplanting 73
Bamboo Paper Company 7, 83, *85*
Bamboo Paper Industry Protection Act 89, 91
Bamboo Pulp Mills Limited 114–115
Bamboo species: *B. arundinacea* 73–74, 80, 92; *B. polymorpha* 73–74, 78, 80; *B. vulgaris* 75, 114; *Bambusa balcooa* 76, 94; *Cephalostachyum pergracile* 80; *Dendrocalamus strictus* 92; *Melócanna bambusoides* 80
beating 18, 39, 46, 80, 97–98, 108, 117; *see also* Hollander
Belgium 38, **67**
Bengal Paper Mills Co. 79, 83, 88, 90, 110
Bevan, Edward John 27; *see also* Messrs. C. F. Cross & E. J. Bevan
Biochemical Oxygen Demand (BOD) 48
birch 23, **30**
Birla Group of Companies 93
Bishop's Falls 58, 155
Bisulphite **30**, 79, 81–82
black liquor 97
black spruce (*Picea mariana*) 57
bleaching 21, 23, 79, 96, 98, 108, 112, 117–118, 133, 155; chlorine 20, 37, 45; powder 39, 87, 130; pulp 39, 110, 113; *see also* hydrochloric acid; hydrogen chlorine gas

162   *Index*

blue gum tree *see* eucalypts
Board of Trade 64, 107, 116, 138
Bowater 2, 69, 142, 145
boxboards 118
Brandis, Dietrich 76
Brazil 24, 29
Bridge Hall Mills 129
British Bamboo Groves Ltd. 116
British Colonies and Dominions 60, 68, 153, 157–158
British industry: chemical 39, 135; cotton 37; linen 135; paper 2–5, 9–10, 37, 39, 42, 49, 58–59, 64, 68–69, 128–148, 152, 154; iron and steel 8; textile 8, 37, 77, 80
British Paper Makers' Association 7, 40, 59, 108
Burgess, Hugh 19, 39
Burma 76–78, 82, 94, 99, 109, 114–115

Caima Pulp Company 23
calcium 20, 27, **30**; bisulphite 81; hydrogen sulphite 20; hypochlorite 45, 98; or magnesium carbonate 131
Canada 5, 20, 26, 29, 49, 55–60, 63–64, 67, 69, 82, 99, 121, 147–148, 152
Canadian pulp and paper industry 28, 55
Canadian Pacific Sulphite Pulp Company Ltd. 57
carbonate of soda (washing soda) *see* soda ash
caustic soda 19, 27, **29–30**, 39, 43, 45, 48, 79–80, 82, 97–98, 110, 133
caustic soda–chlorine process *see* Pomilio process
cellulose 14, 19–20, 26, 36–37, 44, 46, 48, 56, 76, 79–81, 84, 87, 97, 108, 110, 113, 132, 154; chemistry 1, 8, 9, 15, 78; expert 19, 47, 57, 78, 80–81, 84, 112–113, 157; *see also* fibre
Celotex Limited 116
cetico (*Cecropia sp.*) 24
Ceylon 99
chemi-groundwood 21, **30**; *see also* pulping processes
Chile 27
China 5, 15–16
China clay *see* kaolin
chlorine 38, 45, 133
Cold War 66
Colonial Office 107–109, 115
Colonial Products Advisory Bureau (Plant and Animal) 109

Common Market 145
Common reeds (*Phragmites*) 117
common salt 133
Commonwealth Development Finance Corporation 123
conifers 25, **30**, 108, 118, 121, 153; fir (*Abies* spp.) 22; hemlock (*Tsuga canadensis*) 22; larch (*Larix spp.*) 22; pine (*Pinus* spp.) 22; spruce (*Picea* spp.) 22
Controller of Paper 60
cooking 16, 19–20, 38, 43, 45, 75, 80–82, 97, 98, 108; liquor 14, 21, 81, 98; *see also* digester; digesting; digestion
cotton: American 35; fabrics 3, 17; famine 38; fibre 3, 21, 80; freightage article 77; Indian 3, 35; industry 37; linters 35; merchants 40; manufacturing 59; mills 35; plant 17; rag 4, 17, 81, 112, 132; stalks 35; trade 128; waste 69
Crompton, John and Thomas Bonsor 130
Cross, Charles Frederick 27; *see also* Messrs. C. F. Cross & E. J. Bevan
Cropper & Co. 143
Culter Paper Mill 131
customs duties 5, 9, 36, 38, 59, 158; export 37, 42, 59; import 62, 66, 89, 91, 117

Dahl, Carl Ferdinand 20
Daily Chronicle Mills 54
deciduous wood **29–30**; *see also* hardwoods
defibration **29**
Dehra Dun 78, 82, 100, 113
delignification 14–15, 19, 27, **30**
demand for paper: Australia 121; Britain 4, 36–37, 42, 65, 69, 102, 128, 130–132, 135, 143, 147; China 5; global 143, 147; India 83
Demerara (British Guiana) 75
Denmark 67
Department of Overseas Trade 107
Dickinson, John 130
digester 16, 20, 45, 48, 79, 80, 82, 97, 116; *see also* cooking; digesting; digestion
digesting 19, 21, 36, 45, 75, 80; *see also* cooking; digester; digestion
digestion 20, 27, 29–30, 45, 81, 90, 97, 98, 109, 112–113; *see also* cooking; digester; digesting
Dominion Pulp Company Ltd. 57
Donkin, Bryan 39, 129
Dryden Paper Company 123

Index 163

Dunstan, Wyndham Rowland 47, 49,
107, 120
dye 46, 87, 98

East Africa Protectorate 119
East Asia 16–17
Eaton, Asahel Knowlton 20
École Française de Papeterie of
Grenoble 24
Economist 59
effluent 45, 48, 97–98, 156; *see also*
emission; pollution
Egypt 118–119
Ekman, Carl 20
Ekman Pulp and Paper Company 54
elephant grass *see* Indian reed-mace
(*Typha elephantina*)
emission 20; *see also* effluent; pollution
energy 5, 19, 37, 58, 75, 76, 110–111, 147,
155; coal 4, 42, 65, 75–76, 86, 90, 97,
110, 118, 128–133, 135, 155; fuelwood
114; hydroelectric 5, 27, 111, 147;
renewable 10; resources 1, 86; steam
128–129, 131, 155; waterpower 5, 27,
54–58, 69, 128, 131
Entrican, Alexander 123
environmental legislation 156; reasons
23–24; problems 98
Equatorial Africa 24
Esk Mills 81, 84
esparto grass (*Stipa tenacissima*; *Lygeum
spartum*): fibre characteristics 47–49,
108, 110, 121; harvesting 41–43;
papermaking 4, 35, 43–47, 79, 98,
108–109, 116, 130, 132–133, 139; price
4, 9, 25, 40, 42–43, 69, 106, 117–118,
121, 147, 158; Routledge's experiments
19, 38–39, 132; trade 25, 54–55, 58, 60,
64–65; transporting 25, 35, 39–43
eucalypts: *E. gigantea* 122; *E. regnans* 122;
Eucalyptus globulus 23, 101; *Eucalyptus
obliqua* 122; raw material 26, **29–30**;
plantations 23–24, 101
European Economic Community 145
European Free Trade Association (EFTA)
67; EFTA 2, 68, 144, 148
Eynsham Mill 38–39

fibre: ábaca 106; bagasse 26, 27; bamboo
6, 9, 16, 25, 73–74, 79–81, 87, 97–98,
153; cotton 3, 17, 21; delignification
14, 16, 26; esparto 25, 37, 44, 46–49;
eucalypts 122, 153; flax 3, 17, 22, 106;

hemp 17, 21–22, 106; jute 17, 21, 106,
110; papyrus 118–121; ramie 22; raw
35, 37, 39, 54; resources 3; recovered
21, 64; recycled 17, 35; rhea 17, 106;
sabai 25, 109–110; savannah grasses
112; sheet formation 17–18; straw 37,
43, 60; synthetic 27; wood 9, 18–19,
23, 26, 56, 100–101, 108; *see also*
cellulose
Finland 5, 20, 29, 61–67, 88–89, 99,
142, 144
Finnish Pulp and Paper Association 6–7,
61; Finnpap 63
First World War 3, 5, 9, 35, 42, 47,
53, 54, 58, 78, 81–83, 88, 91, 102,
106–107, 113, 116, 121, 137, 140, 146,
152–153, 159
flax 3, 17, 22, 106; *see also* linen
Fletcher, Sir James 123
Follum Træsliperi 55
Food and Agricultural Organization
(FAO) 100; FAO 14, 101
Ford Paper Mills 6, 39
forest: Australia 121–123; bamboo
24, 73–74, 76, 92, 94–97, 99–102, 113,
115; Boreal 22–23; British Isles 61,
68; Canada 55–57; coniferous 23, 58,
152; Finland 61–62, 65; management
22; New Zealand 123; Newfoundland
57–58; Norway 54–55, 65; industrial
plantation 21, 24; reafforestation 101;
secondary 21; Sweden 60, 65; tropical
24, 115; virgin 21, 24
Forest Botany 78
Forest Products Laboratories of
Canada 55
Forest Research Institute of India *see*
Dehra Dun
forestry: Australia 122; Britain 68; Canada
55, 57; Finland 62; India 76–79, 83,
103n1; New Zealand 123
Fort William 69
Fourdriner, Henry and Sealy 129–130
Fourdrinier *see* paper machine
France 24, 26, 43, **67**
French Indochina (Vietnam) 81
French West Africa 24
free trade 2, 4, 53, 59–60, 62, 67,
88–89, 147
Frogmore Mill 3, 19, 129

Gair, Robert 143
Gamble, John 129

164   *Index*

ganpi see Wikstroemia canescens
General Agreement on Tariffs and Trade
   (GATT) 66
Germany 60–61, 64, **67**, 88, 111
Glory Paper Mills 117
gold standard 2, 61–62, 134
Guard Bridge Paper Company
   132, 148
Grand Falls Mill 57
Great Depression: of the 1870s 134; of
   the 1930s 53
grinder 19, 58
grinding 5, 14, 19, 21, 26–27, **30**, 54–55,
   58, 155
groundwood 19, 21, 26–27, **29–30**, 122

hairy cottongrass (*Eriophorum
   comosum*) 110
hardwoods 22–24, 101, 107–108, 115,
   122, 152–154
Harmsworth, Alfred and Harold 57
hemp 15, 17, 21–22, 106, 110, 132
Hill, William 130
Hilton, Charles and Henry 130
H. M. Stationery Office 64
Hole, R. S. 78
Holland, Sidney 123
Hollander 18, 46, 98; *see also* beating
Hønefoss Træsliberi 55
hydrochloric acid 39, 133; *see also*
   bleaching
hydrogen chlorine gas 39; *see also*
   bleaching

Imperial Economic Conference 63, 91
Imperial Institute 6, 47–48, 103n3,
   107–109, 113, 116–117, 119–120,
   158; Plant and Animal Products
   Department 7, 107, 109; Tropical
   Products Institute 6, 109
Imperial Paper Mill 109
Imperial Preference 62–64, 66, 91
Import Duties Act 62–63
India Office 76, 106
India Paper Pulp Co. 84, 86–87, 89–91,
   93, 97
Indian charcoal tree (*Trema orientalis*) 101
The Indian Forester 76, 103n1
Indian olibanum tree (*Boswellia serrata*) 101
Indian Paper Makers' Association 89
Indian reed-mace (*Typha elephantina*) 110
Indian Tariff Board (ITB) 89; ITB 89–91
Indonesia 99
Industrial Revolution 2, 36, 128
Inveresk Paper Company 142, 146

Ireland 135, 141; Irish Free State 141;
   Irish Republic 66–**67**
Italy 26, 42

jack pine (*Pinus banksiana*) 56
James Brown & Co., Ltd. 84
James Wrigley and Son 130
Japan 16–17, 29
Japanese paper 16–17
Jardine, James Lockhart 81, 84, 89
Jaynson, William 130
jute 17, 21, 77, 80, 88, 96, 106, 110

Kankama Fibre Company 56
kaolin 46, 98, 133
Keller, F. G. 19
King, George 76
Koops, Matthias 36, 132
Korean War 53, 65
Kraft Paper Agreement 63
Kymin Oy 62

labour 43, *85*, 147, 153–158; costs 5, 40,
   62, 64, 80, 87–88, 90, 96–97, 121, 142,
   156; Indian 88, 100–101, 111–112,
   115; organisation 117, 136–138;
   productivity 138, *141*–142, 146, 148,
   156; shortage 82, 124, 147; skilled
   131–132, 134, 156
Latin America 25, 153
Libya 38, 41–42
lignin 14, 20, 37, 45, 76, 97, 113, 156
lime 15–16, 38–39, 45, 79, 114, 131, 133;
   process 15–16, **29**
linen 3–4, 17, 112, 132, 135; *see also* flax
Liotard, L. 106
lithographs 47–48; *see also* printing
Lloyd, Edward 54, 106
loading 46, 86, 155
London 7, 10, 36–37, 40, 42, 56–58, 69,
   78, 83, *85*, 87, 109, 113–114, 119–120,
   129, 132–134, **140**, 142; City of 7, 10,
   56, 88, 129–130, 133–134, 157
lye 16, 39

Magnay, Sir William and James 130
magnesia bisulphite 79, 81
magnesium carbonate 131
Malaya 99
mallows 16
marram (or beach) grass (*Ammophila
   arenaria*) 116
Messrs. Balmer Lawrie & Co. 83, 99
Messrs. Bertrams Ltd. 81, 123
Messrs. Borneo & Co. 109

Messrs. Clayton Beadle & Henry P. Stevens 107, 116–117
Messrs. C. F. Cross & E. J. Bevan 107
Messrs. C. W. Glover and Partners 118
Messrs. F. W. Heilgers & Co. 80, 83, 94, 96
Messrs. Ide & Christie 42
Messrs. James Bertram & Son 86
Messrs. Perry, Bury and Co. 40
Messrs. Sindall & Bacon 114
Messrs. Thomas & Green Ltd. 78, 117
Messrs. Wiggins, Teape & Co. 69, 117
Milne, Samuel 81
Morocco 38, 42, 69
munj (*Saccharum bengalense*) 110
Mysore Paper Mills 92–93

Naihati Mill 84, 86–88, 90, 97
National Newsprint and Paper Mills, Ltd. 93, 101
Neckinger Mill 37
Nelson, Thomas A. and Ian 81–82, 84, 89
Netherlands 37–38, **67**, 88, 142
New Zealand 24, 60, 63, 66, 99, 122–123, 153, 157
Newbattle Mills 136
Newfoundland 5, 54–55, 57–58, 60–61, 63, 69, 155
Nigeria 120
Nordic countries 61–62, 67, 69, 147
North Africa 4–5, 9, 17, 35, 38, 40–41, 116, 155
North America 2, 5, 22, 88, 111, 116, 144–146, 152–153, 155
North Atlantic Treaty Organization 66
North of Ireland Paper Mill Company 78
Northern Ireland **140**–141
Northern Rhodesia 117, 120
Northfleet Mill 54
Norway 5, 29, 54–55, 58, 61–64, 66–67, 81, 88–89, 99, 106, 111
Norway spruce (*Picea abies*) 23
Norwegian Papermakers' Association 63

Olive & Partington Limited 47
Orange Grove Paper Mill 114
Orient Paper Mills 92–93
Oriental paperbush or giant leaf paper plant (*Edgeworthia papyrifera*) 16
The Oriental Power and Pulp Company 56
Original Society of Papermakers 136

packaging materials 14, 22, 143
Palestine 120

paper grades: board 8, 14, 22, 27, **30**, 62, 68, 92, **112**, 116, 118, 122, 143; cultural paper 15, 92; industrial paper 14, 22, 92; newsprint 9, 14, 20, 22, 26–**30**, 37, 46, 53–55, 62–65, 68, 89, 92–93, 100–101, 122–123, 142–145, 148, 154, 158; printing and writing 6, 9, 14, 16, 20, 25–27, **30**, 35, 43, 47, 49, 53, 60, 62, 75, 89, 92, 101, 109–**112**, 122, 132, 145, 147; wrapping 14, 20–22, **30**, 62, 92, 122, 143
paper industry: capital-intensive 6, 73, 100, 145; mechanisation 4, 18, 36, 129–130, 134–135, 138, 146; path-dependent 6, 73
paper machine 18, 46, 98, 129–130, 135, 143–144
paper mulberry (*Broussonetia papyrifera*) 15–16
Papermakers Straw Trading Co. Ltd. 43
Papermaking: handmade 134, 18, 36; mechanical 3, 6, 15, 109, 132, 146, 159
papyrus (*Cyperus papyrus*) 17, 118–121
para grass (*Brachiaria mutica*) 114
paraná pine (*Araucaria angustifolia*) 24
parasolier (*Musanga cecropioides*) 24
Parkside Works 81, 84
Patent Impermeable Millboard Company Ltd. 118
Patent Office 84
Payen, Anselme 19
PBP Industries 146
Pearson, Sir Ralph Sneyd 82, 103n5
Pegu *see* Burma
Peter Dixon & Son Ltd. 61
Philippines 99
Phillips' Paper Trade Directory of the World 136
Picea morinda 100
Pinus insignis see Pinus radiata
Pinus patula 24, 26, 122
Pinus radiata 24, 26, 122–123, 153
pollution 20, 45, 98, 156; *see also* effluent; emission
Pomilio, Umberto 27
Pomilio process 27, 42, **30**
poplar (*Populus tremuloides*) 23, 26, **29**, 55–56
Portugal 23, 38, 67
potash 39
price-fixing 69
printing 74, 78, 81; houses 54; industry 49, 135; lithographic 78; mechanical 36; press 4, 17, 131; process 28; sector 138; technology 17, 47–48; trade 142; *see also* lithographs

166   *Index*

processing chemicals 20, 25, 27, 75, 86, 130, 133, 144, 155–156
publishing industry *see* printing industry
pulp: bleached 27, 37; chemical 14, 19, 23, 26, **30**, 58, 66, 79, 81, 155; famine 9, 37, 75, 78, 102, 116; mechanical 14, 19, 21, 23, 26–**30**, 54–56, 58, 61, 66, 69, 89, 93, 122, 156; unbleached 20, 26–28, 42
pulping processes: 5, 14–15, 18–19, 23, 29, 154–155, 157; chemical 15, 20, 26–27, 39; combined 21; *see also* grinding
pulpwood 23–24, 55, 57, 61, 64–65, 68–69, 100–101, 121–122
Punalur Paper Mills 93
Purple Heat Grass 116

rags *see* refuse materials
Raitt, William 79–80, 82, 103n3, 112–114
ramie 22
Raniganj Coalfield 86, 110–111, 113
rayon *see* viscose
refining 46
refuse materials: rags 4–5, 9, 15, 17–18, 21–22, 36, 37–39, 41, 45–46, 53–54, 58–59, 69–70, 81, 93, 102, 112–113, 132–133, 135, 138, 154; waste paper 21–22, 35–36, 43, 54, 60, 64, 68–69, 93, 116, 143–146
Régie Industrielle de la Cellulose Coloniale 24
resin 26, 97, 108
Restrictive Trade Practices Act 115
rhea 17, 106
rice grass (*Spartina townsendii*) 116–117
Robert, Nicolas-Louis 129
rock sulphur 87, 133
Rohtas Industries 92–93
Routledge, Thomas 7–8, 19, 38–39, 44, 49, 75–79, 103n2, 106–107, 132
Royal Botanic Gardens, Calcutta 76
Royal Botanic Gardens, Kew 7, 38, 75
Royal Commission on Paper 60
Royal Paper Mill 109
Royal Society of Arts 77, 106
rush 107
Russia 61

sabai (*Eulaliopsis binata*) 25, 89–90, 94–96, 102, 110–113, 152, 158
Safeguarding of Industries (Customs Duties) Act 62
St. Anne's Board Mill Company Limited 117

St. Katharine's Works 81, 123
salai *see* Indian olibanum tree (*Boswellia serrata*)
Sande Paper Mill 66
Sande Træsliperi 66, 123
savannah grasses: *Saccharum spontaneum, S. arundinaceum, S. munja, S. marenga, and Phragmites karka* 112–113
sawnwood 122, 57
Scandinavian: countries 5, 67, 152; mills 62–63, 68, 114, 145; sales organisations 7, 9, 66, 69, 152; timber 9; wood pulp 54, 60–61, 63, 89, 114
Scan-organisation 63; *see also* Scandinavian sales organisations
Scotland 43, *85*, 118, 131–132, 135–137, 139–**140**, 142, 155
Scots pine (*Pinus sylvestris L.*) 23
Second World War 2, 14, 21, 24–25, 27, 43, 53, 64, 92, 114–115, 121, 124, 137, 143, 146–148, 153
sedge 41, 107
Serampore Paper Mill 109
shipping 41–42, 60, 75, 83, 87–88, 121, 157; *see also* transport
silica 75–76, 97
silver fir (*Abies pindrow*) 100
Sindall, Robert Walter 78–79, 87; *see also* Messrs. Sindall & Bacon
Sindicato Cellulosa Pomilio 27; *see also* Pomilio process; Pomilio, Umberto
Sirpur Paper Mills 92–93
Sitka spruce (*Picea sitchensis*) 65
sizing 46, 97–98, 155
Snodland Paper Mill 54
Societé Franco Algérienne 40, 77
soda: ash 39, 133; mills 21; process 19, **29**, 39, 56, 79–82, 90, 108–110, 113; pulp 55, 78–79, 82, 113; recovery 45, 79
soda-chlorine process 27
soda-sulphur process 24, **30**
sodium hydroxide *see* caustic soda
sodium sulphate 20, 82, 98, 133
softwoods *see* conifers
Soho Mills 78
South Africa 23, 24, 27, 63, 66, 122
South African Pulp and Paper Industries Ltd. 122
Soviet Union 29, 64–66
Spain 4, 9, 25, 35, 38–39, 43, 55
Spartina alterniflora 116
Spartina stricta 116
Springfield Mill 129
Star Paper Mills 62

Sterling Area 62
Stock Exchange 56, 84, 133
Stora 144
strainers 45–46, 98
straw 5, 16, 18, 22, 25, 27, 29–**30**, 35–38, 43–44, 48–49, 54, 58, 61, 80, 93, 113, 116, 118, 122, 146, 152, 154; *see also* agricultural residues
stringybark *see Eucalyptus obliqua*
Sudan 118–120
Sudd 119–120
Sudd Fuel (Suddite) Company Limited 119, 157
sugarcane *see* bagasse
sulphate: process 20–21, 25–27, **30**, 45, 79, 81, 97, 117; pulps 23, 49, 55, 81–82, 99, 121, 123
sulphate of soda: method 91; process 113
sulphite: liquor 21; process 20, 27, **30**, 44, 79, 81–82, 84, 89, 91, 97, 108, 122; pulp 20, 23, 26, 28, 45, 49, 55–57, 61, 69, 88, 118, 122
sulphur dioxide 20, 79
sunn hemp (*Crotalaria juncea*) 110
Sweden 5, 20, 29, 54, 58, 60–67, 87–89, 99, 111, 144
Swedish Paper Mills Association 63
Switzerland 67

tariff 28, 59–60, 62, 67–69, 144, 147–148, 158; Australia 121; Canada 124; India 88–91, 96, 102
Tasman Pulp & Paper Company 123, 157
Tasmanian Paper Pty Ltd. 122
Tavoy River Bamboo Pulping Concession 82, 114
The Times 47, 54, 59
Thomas Nelson & Sons, Ltd. 84
Thunes Mekaniske Værksted 81
Tilghman, Benjamin Chew 20
timber 23–24, 109; British 68–69; Canada 55–57; Empire-grown 121; Finland 65; India 100–101; New Zealand 123
Titagarh Mill 80
Titaghur Paper Mills Co., Ltd. 80, 82–83, 90, 93–99, 109, 111, 155
Tonkin Pulp and Paper Co. 81
Toppila Mill 61
transport 1, 4–5, 57, 80, 97, 101, 108–109, 112, 115, 117, 120, 132, 135, 143, 157–158; costs 4–5, 24, 37, 40–42, 49, 86, 95–96, 111, 102, 133, 154–155; *see also* shipping

Trinidad 114
Tullis Russell 132, 142, 145
Tunisia 38, 41–42, 69
Tunisian Esparto Fibre Supply Co. Limited 40
Turn Lee Mills 47
Two Waters Mill 3, 129

Uganda 120
Union of Machine Workers 136
United Brotherhood of Paper Makers 136
United Nations (UN) 66; UN 101
United Paper Mills 7, 114
Uruguay 27
USA 19–20, 22, 24, 26, 29, 56, 65–**67**, 82, 99, 143

Valmet 5
Vietnam 81, 99
viscose 27, 93
Voelter, Heinrich 19
Voith, Johan Matthäus 19

Wales 130, 134–138, **140**
War Office 64
washi see Japanese paper
waste paper *see* refuse materials
water 16–19, 25, 28, 37, 44–46, 79–80, 98, 108, 115, 129–131, 153–154, 156, 158; washing 80
Watt, Charles 19, 39
wattle *see Acacia*
Western paper 17, 21
white mulberry tree (*Morus alba*) 16
white spruce (*Picea glauca*) 56
Wikstroemia canescens 16
wild sugarcane (*Saccharum spontaneum*) 110
wood: deciduous 16, 23, **29–30**, 101; pulp 4–5, 9, 19–20, 27, 29, 42–45, 48–49, 53–70, 82–83, 86, 88–93, 100–102, 106, 111–114, 116–117, 121, 123, 133, 139, 145–146
wood anatomy and technology *see* forestry
wood ash *see* lye
wood chemistry *see* cellulose chemistry
The World's Paper Trade Review 7
writing mediums: parchment 17; papyrus 17, 118–119; wooden tablets 15–16

Yoshi see Western paper

Printed in the United States
By Bookmasters